AF323648

EAST ASIA

Growth, Crisis and Recovery

EAST ASIA

Growth, Crisis and Recovery

(The Western Shuttle Model of Economic Takeoff)

David L. Western

Curtin Business School

World Scientific

Singapore • New Jersey • London • Hong Kong

Published by

World Scientific Publishing Co. Pte. Ltd.

P O Box 128, Farrer Road, Singapore 912805

USA office: Suite 1B, 1060 Main Street, River Edge, NJ 07661

UK office: 57 Shelton Street, Covent Garden, London WC2H 9HE

British Library Cataloguing-in-Publication Data
A catalogue record for this book is available from the British Library.

The views expressed by the author do not necessarily reflect those of the Curtin Business School.

ISBN 981-02-4405-3

Printed in Singapore by Uto-Print

FOREWORD

Once upon a time, finance and economics proper were fully integrated subjects. Sometimes perhaps during the heyday of monetarism—finance and "real" economics went their separate ways. That is too bad.

Finance severed its connection to the real economy and economic growth ascended without any concern whatsoever with financial institutions or, for that matter, even with money. A similar schism left a gap between international finance and international trade theory.

Divorce normally does some damage to one party or the other, whether the terms of settlement are expressed in barter or in financial assets. Surely, with the East Asian crisis of 1997, the cost of separation is abundantly clear. For a pleasant period the real growth in East Asia was considerable, even exuberant. Thereafter arose bubbles in real estate and in financial markets, characterized by the only colorful phrase ever uttered by Alan Greenspan, "irrational exuberance." In retrospect, most economists would agree that these were bubbles because of their bursting.

If finance had nothing to do with the rapid real growth of the Asian economies, the bursting of bubbles should have nothing to do with negative real growth. This suggestion is at best inconvenient since it falls so far short of what indeed happened. Growth of the Asian Tigers turned negative as the bubbles burst. In that process, the same foreign funds that had been flowing into emerging nations suddenly flowed out. We are reminded of, if nothing else, the fickleness of foreign financial capital.

In truth, rapid economic growth and the potential for financial crisis may be two sides of the same coin, especially when the coin is not of the realm. That is, the external hard currency that helped to finance rapid economic growth may provide too much of a good thing. Just as with American stock markets, finance can be overdone; finance can become self-fulfilling folly when it takes on a life of its own, a life separate from bedrock economics. When finance becomes the subject and the object, it is easy to lose the connection between money and real output. This, it appears, happened in East Asia.

What went wrong in economic analysis was mirrored in East Asian economic reality. Most economists got it wrong and the economies reflected a similar failure. In order to return to its former pattern of rapid real economic growth, the policy makers in East Asia will need a model of economic growth that incorporates these important financial components. All of which brings me to the present volume.

David Western tells a compelling and persuasive economic growth story of the Asian Tigers. The story holds together for both the rise and for the fall and for the possible rise again. I do not want to underestimate the soundness of the story or its readability. It comprises of the most convincing explanation for the rise and fall of these Asian economies to date. Policy makers ignore its lessons at their peril.

Although, as Western tells us, both internal and external forces account for the region's real growth, the "miracle" could not have happened in the absence of all the right moves by the East Asian entrepreneurs and policy makers. Internal nominal profits and external finance were dual necessities in the positive growth process. The decisions to grow through exportation depended upon relatively high production costs in the advanced economies and a careful selection of products that could be successfully produced and differentiated. The careful coordination of entrepreneurial actions and favorable public policies took advantage of a cost gap that generated super-normal profits. Though the profits were financial, the economic growth was real. This, a paradox in standard growth theory, becomes a logical necessity in the story that Western relates so well.

As ever, too much of an otherwise good thing can have adverse effects. The accumulation of super-normal profits can create a financial overhang, just as too much alcohol can lead to a hangover. With too much liquidity, in either case, unwise choices are made. Among the Asian Tigers various kinds of assets become inflated in price. Though the bubbles were different in individual country cases, bubbles nonetheless rose over East Asia. Although the big story for this part of the global economy was the financial collapse, Western's story is about the entire bubble-making and growth-generating machine. Importantly, it is one machine.

In my judgment, David Western correctly identifies the forces of real economic growth and of financial crises in East Asia. His major contribution is to demonstrate that the major forces for growth are the same as those for the financial crises. The trick in maintaining positive real economic growth is keeping these forces balanced.

E. Ray Canterbery

ACKNOWLEDGMENTS

This book has its origins around the Pacific Rim. In Australia, the Curtin Business School (CBS) has spread its wings throughout the Asia region and as a consequence developmental issues have assumed greater academic importance. Support for this academic enquiry into regional issues, often in tangible ways, has come from Dean Michael Wood and Professors Harry Bloch, Geoff Crockett and Ron Goddard. In fact Professor Bloch's criticisms were well received as were those of Professor Prema-Chandra Authorakala (ANU) on Chapter 4. In short, this book is a by-product of my teaching and research conducted within the CBS.

Across the Pacific, in the USA, my PhD at Florida State University (FSU) focussed on Asia's economic growth and crisis experience, which in turn provided a solid base for the production of this book. Professor Ray Canterbery's astute insight and understanding proved invaluable in solidifying and polishing ideas. Professor James Gapinski's fresh brush with the Asian experience and econometric modelling also stimulated much thought. Professors James Cobbe and Scott Flannigan contributed via their 'hands on' development experience and so added a practical dimension to many areas of this book. My Russian collegue, Alexander Ilyin was a genious with the math editor.

My students around the region in places such as Hong Kong, Singapore, Bangkok, Kuala Lumpur and Jakarta have provided criticisms and comments within teaching forums that have been received with thanks. Class interaction and debate have been fertile discussion arenas. In short, teaching and research have interacted synergystically.

The assembly of this book in terms of data collection, collation and presentation has been a joint effort. Graduate students, including Chachada Changvitaya (Thailand) and Sze Kiat Bong (Malaysia) were of great assistance in this way. Fiona Scott was responsible for the Shuttle Model graphic and Adrian Brustur for technical assistance. The office staff of Linda Morgan, Glynn Vivian and Liz Fox were ever-patient in providing manuscript advice and office support. Last, but not least, I acknowledge the support of my mother (Yvonne) and father (Henry Thomas) over the years not only in my education but life in general.

CONTENTS

INTRODUCTION

It is the purpose of this book to examine East Asia's outstanding economic growth performance and recent economic downturn in the light of most recent theory and available evidence. While the theoretical determinants of economic growth are many, the specific catalysts of East Asian growth are more difficult to isolate and identify. While both old and new growth theory are useful points of departure in explaining East Asia's economic 'miracle' there has been some neglect of the importance of trade and financial variables in explaining such rapid development. Existing growth theory concentrates on how a closed economy develops, with heavy reliance on a production theoretic framework. Technological progress is incorporated as the centerpiece of long-term growth. Such a centerpiece is not applicable to the East Asian growth experience, as the 'long run' has not yet arrived.

The major focus of this study is on the relevance of the deep fault line that exists in the world's economic landscape, an historical accident, whereby the first world with high incomes per head and sophisticated capital stocks 'coexist' with a developing world characterized by low per capita incomes and low levels of capital per worker; that is, coexistence in a world of unequal partners. This gulf in income, price and wage levels has been a curse for some developing nations and yet a blessing for others. Indeed, it has been some of the small 'open' economies of Asia that have sought to exploit these differentials with calculating precision, yielding lucrative profits in the process via exports to mature economy markets.

Such price and cost differentials may be regarded as a financial force of growth creating super-normal profits from exporting to mature economy markets. Such export profits have been driven by the wide divergence of world prices and domestic marginal costs. A second, but equally important financial force is the acquisition of 'hard currency' in terms of $US, German Marks, Swiss Francs, Japanese Yen and the like. These two financial forces are related to the power of allocative efficiency in international trade, selling or allocating resources to their highest value use; namely, to rich overseas markets.

Most East Asian nations have achieved rapid economic growth and so may provide lessons for other developing nations aspiring to join the 'membership growth club.' The traditional 'catalysts' of growth are nominated as being foreign capital flows, physical investment, high levels of education, human capital, entrepreneurial skill, productivity, high rates of saving, macroeconomic stability and respect for property rights to name a few. However, they lack potency in explaining East Asian super-growth. Instead they are dwarfed by the powerful and overwhelming driving force of vast differences in income and price levels making 'openness' to trade the major engine of growth. The astute nation states of East Asia seized first-mover advantage in capturing these vast trade opportunities, ahead of many other nations with similar 'potential'.

In essence, this inquiry focuses on a 'two gap' story. The first gap is that of vast differences in income levels, yielding capital-labour (K/L) ratios that are poles apart. That is, a very high K/L ratio for developed nations and a very low one for developing nations, with a rise from this low level causing a temporary spurt of 'growth' until the next steady state is reached. The transition phase of the Solow model may fit this capital gap story.

According to neoclassical growth theory, a convergence in incomes will take place as these K/L ratios also converge. This convergence occurs for a domestic reason, as the higher marginal productivity of capital generates further investment opportunities, increases rates of return and encourages saving. It also occurs for an international reason, as capital should flow from developed nations to the developing world in search of the super-normal rates of return. This is a production-theoretic approach that concentrates on real flows and is in essence a supply-side explanation of growth and income convergence.

The second gap is that of vast differences in price (cost) levels that expose profitable trade opportunities for the developing world into mature economy markets. This price gap is explained more by a financial shadow approach that focuses on wide profit margins being driven by large price differentials between Asia and mature economies. There is no central focus placed on increases in capital or technology as the catalysts of growth, as these may be more the concomitants of growth. This second price (cost) differential gap is a demand-side explanation and in many ways a shadow or mirror image of the first capital gap story.

In theory, the export growth rate of the developing nation will be large until price and cost levels converge with those of the developed world which in turn cause export growth rates to become more 'normal' - on a par with those of developed nations. In summary, this is a 'two gap' model, as there is a transition to both a domestic steady state and an international steady state as the marginal productivity of capital (caused by large differences in K/L ratios) leapfrogs through two stages. But it is also a 'twin gap' model, in that there is a trade - financial - rate of return shadow that mirrors the real production side of the economy. Hence, it is argued that the marginal productivity of capital (MPK) for a developing 'open' economy is far greater than the marginal productivity of capital for a developing 'closed' economy.

This study examines four hypotheses.

First:	- East Asia's rapid growth experience is both export-led and semi- exogenous
Second:	- East Asian manufactured exports to mature economies were, in part, driven by a semi-exogenous force of differences in price, cost and income levels with mature economies.
Thirdly:	- The marginal productivity of capital (MPK) is largely profit driven and is explained by manufactured exports to mature economy markets.
Fourth:	- The forces of economic growth and crisis were basically the same.

The layout of the study is as follows.

Chapter 1 sketches the outstanding features of East Asia's economic performance. Despite such high achievements, the financial crisis of 1997 sent shock waves through the region and caused many economists to re-think their view on the 'miracle'. Even though growth theory has reached a degree of consensus concerning the central driving forces or engine(s) of growth for the OECD experience it fails to fully explain the case of the developing Asia. This chapter, by seeking to explicitly identify the central characteristics of East Asia's growth performance, calls for a re-examination of growth and development theory. A new development model is created and expounded in Chapter 2.

In Chapter 2 the Western Shuttle Model (WSM) of economic take-off is unveiled. This model seeks to explain catch-up growth or super-growth in terms of the strong links with mature economies. The rocket is manufactured exports to mature economy markets while the two rocket boosters are wealth and price differentials. There are two rocket engines are super-profits and hard currency that propel export economies into outer space (prosperity). The fuels for the rocket boosters and engines are factor accumulation, allocative and technical efficiency. This is the transition phase of growth whereas the steady state is attained when the shuttle disconnects from the rocket. Along the flight path profitability dissolves into productivity propulsion.

Chapter 3 focuses on the relevance of growth theory, in its current state, in explaining Asia's rapid growth experience. While traditional growth theory, such as the Solow model, and more recently the Romer model, contains explanatory power for mature closed economies, it possesses less explanatory power in the context of developing open economies. This is not to deny that the accumulation of inputs or a high MPK cannot explain an increase in output per head (Solow model), or that positive externalities are not powerful, or 'public knowledge' not important (Romer model), but that the fit in the EA case is somewhat loose.

Other classes of growth theory such as Lucas's model of human capital are useful, but only in a general sense, as they do not explain why EA has devoted substantial resources to education and learning by doing. Gapinski (1997) fails to find support for human capital in an EA context. Nor do human capital models explain why the OECD did not experience explosive growth given its devotion to human capital levels and rates of accumulation.

Another class of models draws attention to macroeconomic stability, abiding by a set of international prices and the respect for property rights that provides a set of incentives for resources to be allocated efficiently and for long-term investment to be encouraged. Such prescriptions are to be commended, but do not distinguish East Asia from many other nations, mature or otherwise, that have not enjoyed explosive growth despite respect for macroeconomic stability, relative prices and property rights.

In many ways, existing growth theory is too broad and too general in that it only encourages observational equivalence. Several major faults of existing growth theory include its preoccupation with the long run, technological progress being the only engine of growth, all variables couched in terms of 'reals', only one price level, a presumption of a closed economy and little attention paid to the (illegal) imitation of goods and design. In contrast, much of the East Asian growth experience needs to be explained in terms of a developing open economy framework, as export-led growth has figured more prominently than both old and new growth theory give recognition. Moreover, the production-theoretic approach that focuses on real variables needs to be reconciled with the financial shadows of those same variables that generate an explosive value of the MPK and so super-profits. While export growth will not yield sustainable long-run growth (because of ultimate convergence), it can yield medium-run explosive growth. And the medium run may be the long run.

The major thrust of Chapter 4 is to examine the determinants of East Asian export growth into mature economy markets. The sometimes massive and phenomenal export growth rates, particularly of manufactured goods, require explanation. The literature points to 'fortuitously' high income elasticities in the light of the widespread belief that price elasticities are low. That is, for some unspecified reason, the 'income term' dominates the analysis, meaning the change in United States or mature economy income is the major catalyst of East Asian export growth. Evidence to date appears to support the notion that the income elasticity estimates are overstated, capturing explanatory power that belongs to some other force. At first glance it appears that the *higher income level* (rather than change in income) in a mature economy is that 'hidden' driving force of Asian export growth. However, an equally plausible explanation is that of the *higher price level* performing the same signaling function as that of the high income level, as one is the shadow of the other. This translates into the low level of the real exchange rate as being the catalyst of export volume growth, within the confines of the model used. This chapter tests hypothesis two, that East Asian exports are driven, in part, by foreign income or price levels, a semi-exogenous force in a world of unequal partners.

In Chapter 5, the impact of exports on economic growth is examined. Given the dichotomy between real and financial forces of growth, there is a need to explore the link between super-profits, super-export growth and super-economic growth as in the East Asian experience. A divergence of price and marginal cost in a world of unequal partners generates above normal profits and above normal savings rates. The

World Bank (1993) claims that income growth drives savings growth in the Granger causality sense and not vice versa. Hence, the direction of causation may well run from exports to income to saving to investment to exports, a virtuous circle of income growth driven by a semi-exogenous force of higher mature economy income and price levels.

The challenge is to develop a model that captures the centrality of export externalities on economic growth, but in a framework that recognizes rates of return and the value of the MPK. A young nation's stage of development is more reliant on the influence of financial forces of growth whereas a more mature nation's stage of development becomes more reliant on the effect of real variables on growth. This chapter tests hypothesis one, that export-led growth exists for East Asia. It also examines hypothesis three, that TFP growth is export driven.

In Chapter 6, the crucial role played by 'hard currency' is examined. Although monetary neutrality may hold for developed economies there appears some potency for developing economies. Not only is financial intermediation and financial sector maturity associated with economic growth but also the acquisition of hard foreign currency by allowing significant domestic credit creation. Not only is domestic allocative efficiency stimulated but international allocative efficiency as well by supplying credit constrained export companies with investment funds. Higher rates of return are thus captured by export orientated East Asian economies. Sizeable foreign exchange reserves also adds credibility to the central bank and its monetary policy.

The focus of Chapter 7 centers on the financial firestorm that hit the region in 1997. The financial forces that drove East Asia's 'growth miracle' were the *same* financial forces that caused its demise. In some ways East Asia was victim of its own success in that export growth, super-profits, liquidity and the associated attraction of foreign investment sowed the seeds of an eventual crisis or collapse. Constraints were binding, in that human capital, public infrastructure and productivity levels acted as a drag on export profitability over the long run. Institutions were also growing in maturity but nevertheless inadequate to cope with enormous flows of foreign capital and the pressures of greater openness. Internal causes of the crisis are evident but so too are external causes that may have 'triggered' the collapse of financial sectors, confidence and spread contagion throughout the region.

The role of the IMF in dealing with the crisis is surveyed in Chapter 8. Heavy short-term debt obligations, a lack of foreign exchange and the threat of continued speculative attack forced Thailand, Korea and Indonesia to the bargaining table of the IMF. Early IMF initiatives were regarded as being too austere, as they concentrated too heavily on balance, contraction and currency stability. Later IMF initiatives focused on orderly debt workouts with creditors, some fiscal flexibility and less haste in overseeing bank closures. Despite some moderation in approach, the IMF has endured much criticism for recommending high interest rates and economic contraction at a time of financial collapse and rising unemployment. Other policy alternatives are canvassed in this chapter as well the heated clash over policy prescription between the IMF and the World Bank.

Chapter 9 places the spotlight on Japan and its financial sector crisis. The origins of the asset price bubble and the government's policy response are considered. Japan's capture in a quagmire of financial collapse and disintermediation should serve as a warning to the rest of Asia of the seriousness of a bursting asset price bubble. Traditional monetary and fiscal policies failed to lift Japan out of the mud as the damage to corporate, financial sector and household balance sheets was great. These adverse wealth effects sentenced Japan to 10 years of stagnation. Similar forces have been at work in East Asia as the financial sectors have lost confidence, contracted credit and sought to recover non-performing loans. Financial disintermediation threatens to suffocate Asia's recovery. Government policy responses may be critical in order to illicit a robust economic revival.

Chapter 10 seeks to outline the challenges facing East Asia post crisis and the kinds of responses that might be appropriate under such difficult circumstances. The philosophic debate is examined along with the complex policy dilemmas facing EA in the aftermath of the crisis. There are old and timeless constraints to consider – such as low but growing levels of human capital, public infrastructure breaking key bottlenecks for the private sector and fragile economic and social institutions that inhibit recovery in the near term. Immediate complexities associated with collapsed asset values are both vicious and compounding in nature. Over coming financial challenges holds the key to overcoming immediate economic challenges.

Chapter 11 provides an assessment of the economic recovery as of the year 2000. There are strong signs that the worst is over in Thailand, Malaysia and Korea and possibly Indonesia. Taiwan, China and Singapore were to some extent exempt from the financial collapse and reveal a return to solid economic revival. Nevertheless, the robustness of the US economy still holds the key to world growth and so the vitality of US stock markets will play an important role in maintaining investor confidence. To a lesser extent Japan could do the Asian region a favour by returning to the growth performances of the 1980's. Exports still remain a vital lifeline for economic development for East Asia as does foreign capital. Both economic and financial reforms will assist the economic recovery in the long term but the immediate return to prosperity depends on the success of the IMF intervention, the return of foreign capital and the US economy posting several more years of robust growth.

Chapter 12 seeks to tie the forces of ascent and demise together. Just as East Asia's 'miracle' had a strong financial foundation in terms of acquiring super-profits via exploiting its international competitiveness via exports, so too did the deterioration of such forces lead to East Asia's financial collapse. Financial leverage and liquidity acted as boosters on the way up but also acted as lead balloons on the way down – as a severe credit firestorm . swept through the region in 1997. Thus, a reinterpretation of East Asia's miracle is warranted as the crisis was financial and not economic in nature.

Chapter One

East Asia's Economic Performance

1-1 Introduction

For over forty years the economic performance of East Asia was referred to as a modern 'miracle.' Key economic indicators revealed rapid economic growth, at twice the OECD rate, combined with relatively low inflation and unemployment. Even before the crisis of 1997 there were few signs of any serious macroeconomic imbalances as budget and current account balances were within 'normal' bounds. In short, macroeconomic management by policy makers was considered to be both competent and of appropriate standard. So what went wrong? Why did East Asia succumb to a sudden and violent firestorm? Was there no miracle to begin with? Has the super-growth experience of East Asia come to an end? Chapters Two and Three offer an explanation of East Asia's successful growth record. This chapter examines the key indicators of economic performance.

1-2 Economic Growth

Most East Asian nations experienced super-growth after the 1950's. In fact, economic growth rates were roughly double that of the USA in the same period. Even when the US and OECD were in recession, bordering on zero output growth, East Asia's growth rate was still positive - at around 4%. Rescilience was a common feature of East Asia's growth record.[1] As Table 1-1 reveals, the growth rates for the 1990's was still very robust. China grew at close to 10%, Singapore, Thailand and Korea at around 8%. Japan was the obvious exception that languished at below 2% for the decade. With the onset of the crisis, Thailand, Indonesia and Korea were the hardest hit and experienced negative growth rates. Nevertheless, East Asia's growth record to date has been consistent and of a catch-up nature. As discussed in Chapter Two, the major reason for East Asia's super-growth was the integration with world markets and so acquisition of world knowledge, profits and foreign exchange. As stated above, growth rates have been far faster than that of the OECD, revealing the closure of the economic maturity gap with the OECD. Incomes per head mesaured in $US for Japan, Taiwan, Hong and Singapore have approached US levels.

1-3 Internal Balance

A traditional Phillips curve relationship postulates an inverse relationship between inflation and unemployment. Low unemployment and high output growth rates aggravate inflation. That is, rapid growth generally causes inflation to accelerate. Moreover, inflationary expectations may cause the Phillips curve to shift rightward causing the 'trade-off' to become more expensive. East Asia has not suffered from this Phillips curve curse as it managed to generate output growth without the associated theoretical inflationary expense. As Western (1996) points out, the economic cruise speed of East Asia was far higher than that of OECD nations.[2]

Unemployment

Measuring unemployment is always difficult and no less so in the developing economies of East Asia. There is 'under' and as well as unemployment. There is hidden unemployment as housewives, the elderly in 'retirement', those in the 'informal sector' and family businesses help conceal those that are actually full-time employed. Even so, most East Asian nations lack any sophisticated social welfare net, private insurance cover or strong unions and so there is a strong stimulus to work. An auction type labour market exists whereby the forces of supply and demand dictate wage outcomes. Hence, the labour market clears at the going wage rate and observable unemployment is low by OECD standards.

Table 1-1

GDP Growth Rates

	1992	1993	1994	1995	1996	1997	1998
China	14.6	13.9	13.0	10.7	9.6	8.8	8.0
H.Kong	6.3	6.1	5.4	4.6	4.7	5.5	2.5
Indonesia	7.2	7.3	7.5	8.2	8.0	5.0	-10.0
Japan	1.1	0.1	0.4	0.9	3.6	0.9	1.0
Korea	5.0	5.8	8.4	9.0	7.1	5.5	-2.5
Malaysia	7.8	8.4	9.4	9.4	8.6	8.0	3.0
Philippines	0.3	2.1	4.4	4.8	5.5	5.1	3.3
S'pore	6.3	10.4	10.3	8.9	6.9	7.8	2.8
Taiwan	6.8	6.3	6.5	6.0	5.7	6.8	6.5
Thailand	8.1	8.3	8.8	8.7	5.5	-0.4	-1.5

Source: World Bank (1998) and Asian Development Bank (1999)

Inflation

Given a passive labour market and wage rises in line with productivity, there have been few pressures on prices from this source. Inflation is provoked from other sources such as rising oil and commodity prices, loose credit policies and poor fiscal management. Currency instability, in part a response to weak economic management, also may generate inflation. East Asia, by and large, has avoided any serious inflation difficulties. At face value, macroeconomic management has been sound and labour productivity on the rise over the last forty years.[3] More importantly, inflation has been subdued considering the economic cruise speed that East Asia has achieved - around 8% for forty years. In short, inflation has not been far above OECD rates while growth has been far above the OECD average.

Table 1-2

Unemployment Rates %

	1991-1995	1996	1997	1998
China	2.6	2.9	3.0	3.1
H.Kong	2.2	2.8	2.2	4.7
Indonesia	3.9	4.9	4.7	5.5
Japan	2.6	3.4	3.4	4.1
Korea	2.3	2.0	2.6	6.8
Malaysia	3.3	2.5	2.6	4.9
Philippines	8.7	7.4	7.9	9.6
S'pore	2.5	2.0	1.8	3.2
Taiwan	1.6	2.6	2.7	2.7

Source: Asian Development Bank (1999)

1-4 External Balance

Not only must policy makers adhere to the principle of internal balance, and its associated growth 'constraints', but also to external balance and so the need to pay for imports, technology and services. Any deterioration in competitiveness stemming from domestic cost rises and/or currency appreciation places stress on the trade account balance. Low productivity, or a slow productivity growth rate compared to trading partners also may contribute to current account deficits.

An alternate view of the cause of persistent current account deficits rests with the volume of capital inflows. Disturbances to foreign investor confidence affect foreign capital flows and indirectly the current account balance. Any significant imbalance or gap between domestic savings andinvestment requires foreign capital inflow to cover the gap- which in turn causes the current account to register a deficit. That is, domestic spending exceeds domestic savings. Developing Asia may endure account deficits for a time while it undergoes much needed structural transformation and modernization. Hence, current account deficits are not evil per se. Such deficits are the result of domestic productivity, capital flows, government policies and intertemporal choice exercised by economic agents.[4] However, over the longer term, a lack of external balance is a problem for developing economies that can not pay their way in the world.

Table 1-3

Inflation Rates %

	1991-95	1996	1997	1998
China	12.5	8.3	2.8	-2.6
Indonesia	10.5	6.5	11.6	60.0
Japan	1.5	0.1	1.8	-0.5
H.Kong	7.3	6.0	6.8	2.6
Korea	6.3	4.5	4.7	3.6
Malaysia	4.0	3.5	2.6	5.3
Philippines	9.7	8.4	5.1	9.4
Singapore	3.1	1.4	2.0	2.1
Taiwan	2.4	3.1	0.9	3.0
Thailand	4.8	5.8	5.6	4.8
USA	3.8	2.8	2.0	2.0
Australia	7.0	1.8	1.3	2.0

Source: Asian Development Bank (1999)

Current Account Outcomes

What is evident from Table 1-4 is the fact that those nations such as China, Singapore and Taiwan registering current account surpluses did not endure any deep, persistent havoc of the recent crisis. A lack of dependency on foreign borrowing and more reliance on FDI and domestic savings somewhat insulated these nations from instability. Conversely, those nations that borrowed heavily did witness current account deficits and so the need to attract capital after hot money flowed outward.

In East Asia's experience the size of the current account deficit as a percentage of GDP was not near the 'danger mark' of 8% of GDP. There were exceptions such as Malaysia in 1995 and Thailand in 1995 and 1996. The justification for such 'large' current account deficits was the importation of capital goods for development, the exercise of choice by rational economic agents and the desire to adhere to the United States quest for a more open world economy. More trade, rather than less, was seen to raise world welfare and efficiency. Financing such deficits via foreign borrowing and foreign investment was not a problem in 1980's or 90's. Besides, respected economic theory dictates that the capital account drives the current account and not vice versa.

With the advent of the crisis of 1997, the respected wisdom that current deficits and foreign capital flows were 'optimal' came under fire. In practice, economic agents did miscalculate and borrowed un-hedged foreign funds with dire consequences for debt repayment. Financing the current account deficit did become a problem as hot foreign money exited East Asia. Governments were forced to reduce domestic absorption with the intent of curtailing imports. Hence, external balance assumed greater priority than during the boom years of the early 1990's. Policies focusing on 'growth at all cost' had to be abandoned in favour of IMF led policies for more balance and stability.

1-5 Government Budget Outcomes

Crises that occur in many developing countries are often blamed on government fiscal imprudence. A temptation by policy makers to over-spend, over-borrow, print money and so placate the masses. This was not

Table 1-4

Current Account (% of GDP)

	1992	1993	1994	1995	1996	1997	1998
China	1.3	-1.9	1.4	0.2	0.9	2.1	3.1
H.Kong	5.8	7.2	2.3	-2.6	-2.5	-6.8	4.1
Indonesia	-2.0	-1.3	-1.6	-3.5	-3.4	-3.6	4.1
Japan	3.0	3.1	2.8	2.2	3.8	2.6	3.2
Korea	-1.3	0.3	-1.0	-1.8	-4.8	-3.2	12.8
Malaysia	-3.8	-4.5	-5.9	-10.2	-4.9	-4.7	12.9
Philippines	-1.9	-5.5	-4.6	-2.7	-4.7	-4.0	9.1
S'pore	11.3	7.3	16.2	18.0	15.0	15.2	20.9
Taiwan	3.9	3.1	2.5	2.0	3.8	2.5	1.3
Thailand	-5.7	-5.1	-5.7	-8.1	-7.9	-2.2	12.7

Source: World Bank (1997) and Asian Development Bank (1999)

the case in East Asia. Government budget deficits, as can be seen from Table 1-5, were quite modest as a percentage of GDP and certainly no cause for alarm. Japan has run budget deficits for good reason, to offset a collapse in business and consumer spending. Thailand registered a budget deficit in 1997 as the crisis reduced the tax base and increased pressure on social welfare spending. Moreover, many of these nations, for much of the period, actually registered budget surpluses. Hence, the notion of irresponsible governments over-spending, creating a crowding out environment for private investment and aggravating inflation does not accord with the evidence on budget stance. However, deeper issue on the efficiency of government spending remains. Were government-backed projects wise strategic investments?[5] It also should be noted that the boom conditions of the 1990's made it easier for governments to run budget surpluses; a cyclical phenomenon. Nevertheless, from a macroeconomic management perspective, there appeared a degree of prudence and competence by the civil service in maintaining fiscal balance.

Table 1-5

Budget Outcomes (% of GDP)

	1992	1993	1994	1995	1996	1997
China	-1.0	-1.0	-0.5	-1.0	-0.8	-0.7
H.Kong	0.9	-0.2	0.7	2.6	1.5	2.6
Indonesia	-0.4	-0.6	0.2	0.3	0.0	1.0
Japan	1.4	-1.6	-2.1	-3.1	-3.9	-3.7
Korea	-0.5	0.6	0.3	-0.2	-0.2	0.3
Malaysia	-4.2	0.2	2.4	1.0	0.7	1.8
Philippines	-1.2	-1.5	1.1	0.6	0.3	0.1
S'pore	12.6	15.5	12.1	13.3	13.9	2.8
Taiwan	4.5	5.0	4.6	2.8	1.6	2.2
Thailand	2.8	2.1	1.8	2.6	2.3	-1.5

Source: World Bank (1997) and Asian Development Bank (1999)

1-6 How Serious is the Current Economic Downturn?

When the crisis broke there was much financial distress for households, private corporations and financial institutions as spending flows collapsed and debt burdens increased the prospects of bankruptcy. What appeared as a financial and currency crisis threatened to spill over into the real economy, and it did, albeit with lags - but not to the draconian degree expected. Unemployment rose and many suffered from the associated poverty of job loss. Others feared job loss. Consumption spending fell heavily as a result of rising unemployment and rising interest rates. Inflation increased dramatically as crashing currencies caused rising import prices. The fear of shortages (accelerating inflationary expectations) drove people to 'purchase in advance' where possible.

A severe decline in profitability and asset prices caused much distress for corporations in terms of debt repayment. Investment also fell in response to higher interest rates and an outflow of foreign capital. In short, aggregate demand was in free-fall in 1997 with investor and consumer confidence severely shaken. Fiscal stimulus by government was weak and uncertain in 1998 as a result of IMF 'conditions' on its loan assistance. Besides, government revenues had shrunk and so the ability to refloat the economy somewhat diminished.

Despite the spillover of financial disaster into the real economy and the drastic affect on basic consumption there was a degree of containment in that economies did not come to a standstill. Indonesia, however, did come close with riots and widespread discontentment. Since 1997 there has been a rebound in economic indicators such as inflation subsiding, currencies stabilising and current accounts turning into surplus. Consumption spending and economic activity has also picked up. Such economic responses are in part due to turnaround in financial variables such as stock market indeces, asset prices and monetary liquidity provided by the banking system.

1-7 Conclusion

It is undeniable that East Asia achieved some kind of economic miracle - at least a generation of super-growth for many years. Key economic indicators reveal a superior economic performance to that of the OECD. East Asia's economic cruise speed was exceptionally high, as growth did not ignite any serious deterioration in inflation rates, current accounts or international competitiveness. Hence, problems of internal or even external balance did not arise in any systematic manner - at least until 1997. *Why* East Asia was so successful is examined in Chapter Two through Six.

Nevertheless, such a smooth economic cruise speed came to an end in 1997. Although the nature of the crisis was financial and currency in origin, it did become a real crisis that affected real activity and created social misery for a time. Make no mistake concerning the severity of the crisis, as it was akin to a fierce firestorm passing through the region. Bankruptcies are widespread and on the rise, unemployment has ballooned, financial sector confidence severely shaken and credit far more costly. Fortunately, the worst appears to be over as several financial and economic indicators point to an economic recovery. The prospects of economic recovery are examined in Chapter 11.

Chapter Two

The Western Shuttle Model
of Economic Take-Off

2-1 Introduction

When the now developed world ascended to prosperity, it did not have the benefit of 'rich neighbours' providing trade or knowledge opportunities in propelling its own economic take-off.[1] Much of the OECD's development achievement was derived from supply-side factors such as research, invention, innovation, productivity, the building of capital stock and pro-growth choices of sweat and sacrifice. A concomitant of long-run growth was the sustained commitment to the construction of both a human and physical capital stock. Its economic flight path to maturity was supply-side driven. East Asia, however, did and still does, enjoy the benefit of living alongside 'rich neighbours' - and so the advantages of backwardness (Gerschenkron,1962). There are vast trade, profit and knowledge opportunities for EA in achieving greater growth acceleration than the lower trajectory OECD flight path. It has been an exogenous, foreign-demand led force that has been the major catalyst of East Asian growth and indirectly, of development. This chapter outlines East Asia's dependence on the wealthy US market, expounds the Western Shuttle Model of economic take-off and highlights a different path to economic maturity than exists in the current development literature.

2-2 Thurow's Insight

It was Lester Thurow (1996,p118) who highlighted the central importance of the US market for aspiring nations. "Having America as a large, open, rich market was particularly important, since it was far easier to become rich selling to wealthy people than by selling to poor people. Since there was only one large group of rich people on the face of the earth after WW II, access to the US market was a prize worth winning."[2] Thurow (1996,p118) therefore makes the point " If one looks at countries that have become rich since World War II, *all of them* have gone through a period of time when their exports focused on the American market" (italics added). The key hypothesis of this book is to empirically test the validity of this exogenously driven, high trajectory flight path of economic take-off. Those nations that have exported strongly to the large, rich US market have defied the laws of gravity (poverty).

2-3 East Asia's Dependence on the US Market

Given that many EA nations lacked an abundance of natural resources and given the chill of the Cold War, there was a strong desire for a warm friendship with the USA. Such a friendship included preferential tariff treatment and 'most favored nation status' for EA exports, a 'trade follows aid' strategy whereby EA nations were encouraged to achieve self-sustained growth on the back of the US economic rocket launcher. As Table 2-1 reveals, all EA nations relied heavily on the US market during early stages of economic take-off.

Not only did EA export strongly, but it also penetrated the US market for manufactured goods very successfully. As Table 2-2 reveals, in 1965 EA accounted for 26% of total manufactured goods imports in the US, but to a massive 47% by 1995. While Japan's percentage remained relatively constant, many other EA nation shares rose dramatically, particularly that of China. It is also obvious that EA nations experienced a high share of manufactured exports to their own GDP as revealed in Table 2-3.

Table 2-1

East Asian Manufactured Exports to USA

(as a % of own total exports)

	1965	1975	1985	1995
China	0	6.4	18.2	24
H.Kong	32.9	31.4	36	20
Indonesia	20	27	39	23.4
Japan	31.9	25.6	35.5	29.3
Korea	45.8	38	46.3	23.1
Malaysia	8.6	28.9	40.9	27.6
Philippines	85.5	49.1	55.4	45.9
S'pore	8.6	25.9	37.6	25.7
Taiwan	29.9	42.1	53.2	27.2
Thailand	9.4	13.6	31.9	26

Source: UN Data, IEDB, Canberra, Australia

2-4 Growth Catalyst Differentials

Given a world of unequal partners in terms of wealth, income and knowledge, several key differentials present themselves as catalysts of economic growth. Such forces reflect a type of catch-up growth potential with wealthy nations and the USA in particular. Firstly, the vast differences in income between EA and the USA, (Y^{EA}/Y^{USA}), is one catalyst that has a central place in existing growth theory, in terms of being a proxy for K/L ratios and productivity levels. Hence, income disparities serve as a proxy for differing K/L ratios. The relatively low income nations of EA possess low K/L ratios, and so a potentially explosive MPK. Hence, a dichotomy in the MPK between developed and developing nations is a by-product of such differences in levels. This is a *productivity differential version* of catch-up growth.

Secondly, another catalyst of growth is the vast differences in costs, both labor and unit costs, (C^{EA} / C^{USA}). This term has its expression in the Hecksher-Ohlin trade model and some competitiveness models of growth. From a theoretical perspective, relative costs and relative competitiveness are more embedded in the trade than the growth literature. This is a *cost differential version* of catch-up growth via exports.

Table 2-2

East Asia's Manufactured Exports

(as a % of US Manufactured Exports)

	1965	1975	1985	1995
China	0.004	0.12	1.03	7.0
H.Kong	3.15	2.97	3.41	1.77
Indonesia	0.02	0.02	0.22	0.85
Japan	20.7	21.3	27.3	21.6
Korea	0.4	2.64	4.01	3.53
Malaysia	0.08	0.47	0.72	2.46
Philippines	0.62	0.33	0.78	0.96
S'pore	0	0.83	1.62	2.72
Taiwan	0.55	3.63	6.74	4.88
Thailand	0.04	0.10	0.37	1.51
Total	25.6	32.4	46.2	47.3

Source: UN Data, IEDB, Canberra, Australia

Table 2-3

Manufactured Exports as a % of Own GDP

	1965	1975	1985	1995
China	1.11	1.65	4.61	3.5
H.Kong	37	53.2	73.5	38
Indonesia	0.2	0.2	1.8	11.4
Japan	7.6	10	13.3	8.8
Korea	3.1	17.4	23.6	22.6
Malaysia	3.4	8.4	16.4	71
Philippines	1.3	2.6	10.1	18.3
Singapore	9.3	30	59.4	83.8
Taiwan	1.1	2.6	7.4	22.8
Thailand	7	28.5	49.8	41.8

Source: UN Data, IEDB, Canberra, Australia

Thirdly, vast price differentials between EA and the USA, (P^{EA}/P^{USA}), is another catalyst of catch-up growth via trade. Such price differences (as well as cost differences) yield wide profit margins for EA exporters. This is a *profit differential version* of catch-up growth via exports. EA entrepreneurs face high world prices in mature economy markets on one side and yet developing world costs on the other. Several reasons shall be examined later as to why prices may differ between nations.

Fourthly, unequal distribution of wealth between East Asia and the USA, (W^{EA}/W^{USA}), has acted as a strong attraction for trade in manufactured goods, a *wealth differential version* of catch-up growth. Such a foreign market is large in terms of depth and variety, acting as a permanent market of attraction, like a constant sounding bell.

This research tests the importance of catch-up growth in the EA experience. Moreover, the nature of such catch-up growth is trade-rooted and exogenous in origin. This is not to deny the importance of competing models of human capital, investment, positive externalities, invention or role of government in creating a stable economic environment in which trade flourished. However, strong growth in manufactured good exports was a common feature of EA economic development and so the question remains as to *why* such export growth was such a catalyst of economic take-off.

2-5 Catalyst Versus Fuels of Growth

As noted above, the USA has never in recorded history, sustained growth rates of 8 percent or more.[3] Rapid spurts of growth were evident for short periods of time, but never sustained at such a pace. Why did the USA or OECD never achieve such super growth speeds as those of EA? Did it not have the world's best research facilities, scientists, university graduates, human capital and vintage capital stock, innovative power, wealth and saving to push up productivity growth rates so rapidly that super economic cruise speed would result? Possessing the world's best human and physical resources could *not* cause productivity growth rates (either labour or total factor productivity - TFP) to be the catalyst of super growth in the USA's heyday of development! But could EA, far inside the world production possibility frontier (and so world best practice), often with minimal natural resources, with relatively low levels of human capital formation and with little physical capital or foreign exchange reserves achieve super-growth? Is this a story of how EA raised its productivity growth rates far above those of the USA, despite lacking any plausible prerequisites or preconditions for take-off? No, this is a false and misleading story. What appears to be 'productivity' is nothing but false perception, as increases in output per worker are driven by super profits from export sales to wealthy markets. Thus, introducing 'value' into productivity measurement, because of the exploitation of world prices (in $US) from domestic costs (in local currency) tends to reduce the 'productivity story' to a 'profitability story'. Or inversely, productivity assumes greater importance and profitability less importance as an exporting, developing nation nears economic maturity.

The USA could never emulate such super-growth without a set of rich neighbors living alongside, despite its outstanding productivity achievements of the last 100 years. Therefore, the sources of growth for EA may be significantly different from the environment in which the USA achieved economic take-off and high living standards. *The search is for a growth stimulus that was NOT COMMON to both EA and the USA (OECD).* Such a catalyst of growth rests in the above section 2-4. Therefore, the present inquiry tests the hypothesis that the driving force of catch-up growth has its origin in manufactured exports. It is this crucial link between super export growth and super economic growth that yielded the cold hard cash so necessary to break the vicious circle of poverty.

2-6 International Competitiveness: Changes or Levels?

As the world has shrunk to the size of a global village, so has the need for every nation to become internationally competitive in producing and marketing goods and services. Failure to tap foreign markets or retain domestic market shares may result in higher domestic interest rates, balance of payments constraints, a lack of foreign exchange reserves, loss of technical skills and a falling behind in product quality. Whilst the quest for international competitiveness is desirable for developed nations for reasons of *stabilization*, it is essential for developing nations for reasons of *growth*.

An often used measure of international competitiveness is that of unit labor costs (ULC) -

$$ULC \quad = \quad f(e, w, y/l) \tag{2-1}$$

$$e \quad = \quad \text{nominal exchange rate}$$

$$w \quad = \quad \text{wages}$$

$$y/l \quad = \quad \text{labour productivity}$$

This measure may be used to determine export supply but needs to be modified to accommodate the interaction with the foreign nation via relative ULC's. Using p^{EA}/p^{USA} to represent relative prices does not alter the measure in any material way, providing profit mark-ups remain constant and stable. It also should noted that $(e \cdot p^{EA}/p^{USA})$ represents the real exchange rate.

One perspective of international competitiveness is a *changes model* (with assumed equilibrium in levels), expressed in lower case letters, as follows:

$$\text{Exports}_{\text{supply}} = f\left[(e \cdot p^{EA}/p^{USA}) \cdot (y/l)\right] \qquad (2\text{-}2)$$

where

$$p^{EA}/p^{USA} = \text{relative prices}$$

$$e \cdot p^{EA}/p^{USA} = \text{real exchange rate}$$

For a nation to increase exports, it seeks to lower its nominal exchange rate, lower its inflation rate or raise its productivity (ie output per worker). Strictly defined, the *inverse* of labour productivity variable *lowers* unit costs.

Developed nations, competing amongst themselves, are ever conscious of changes at the margin in any of the above terms, as they are basically on similar income, price and technology levels. Developing nations, are rivals in rich foreign markets and so too are ever conscious about changes in their competitiveness; being on similar income, price and technology levels. In reality, developed nations experience slower growth rates of productivity than developing nations because of higher productivity levels.[4] The same applies to prices or inflation rates, as they too, are an inverse function of price levels. Hence, the very nature of and quest for greater international competitiveness is very different for developed and developing nations. For the former developed group, raising productivity growth rates is very difficult to achieve, while for the developing latter group, lowering inflation rates is likewise a difficult task. It therefore follows that such a changes model loses reliability and predictive power when such *levels* are mixed together with *rates of change*, such as when developing nations interact (trade) with developed nations. It is *not* changes in relative price, the nominal exchange rate or - the productivity growth *rate* that truly reflect underlying competitiveness, as these are side-shows in a world of vastly unequal levels.

Hence, a *levels model* of international competitiveness may be more appropriate, expressed in upper case letters.

$$\text{Exports}_{\text{supply}} \quad = \quad f(E \cdot P^{EA}/P^{USA}) \cdot (Y/L) \qquad (2\text{-}3)$$

In this levels model, allowance is made for disequilibrium in exchange rate, price and productivity levels between nations. Hence, nations such as the USA may have higher productivity (technological capability) than say Germany or Japan, far more than middle ranked nations like Taiwan, Korea, Hong Kong and Singapore and certainly more than a poor but growing China.

But the USA, has in some manufacturing industries, higher prices than Germany or Japan, and certainly higher than East Asia. When the USA's international competitiveness is estimated via this levels model, it becomes obvious that the USA relies heavily on its superior productivity level to offset its inferiority, at times, in its high level of the real exchange rate. The reverse is true for EA, as it relies on the low level of its real exchange rate (lower price and cost levels) to overpower its relative disadvantage in low productivity levels. Therefore, international competitiveness changes its composition and complexion over stages of economic development. The confusion of changes and levels often leads to poor policy advice, and unfortunately, even poorer econometric analysis.

For EA, it becomes clear that the generator of international competitiveness stems from relatively low levels of both prices and the nominal exchange rate – denoted by $(E \cdot P^{EA}/P^{USA})$. Even though the rate of productivity growth is rapid, denoted as y/l, its level is relatively low. Nevertheless, EA has been and still is, very competitive via its low unit costs in most labor intensive manufactured goods.

$$\text{EA Exports}_{\text{supply}} \quad = \quad f(E \cdot P^{EA}/P^{USA}) \cdot y/l \qquad (2\text{-}4)$$

We are left with a *disequilibrium and unequal levels* equation (2-4) of international competitiveness. A developing nation relies heavily on a low level of $(E \cdot P^{EA}/P^{US})$ in early years to compete but aspires to raise y/l rapidly in order to achieve a high level of Y/L in maturity. Hence, the nature and complexion of international competitiveness changes over the life cycle of a nation, along the path to maturity, as price competitiveness declines and productivity competitiveness increases.

2-7 Stage of Development and Disequilibrium

While no one doubts the myriad levels of development among nations that is reflected in a vast diversity of poverty, calories per day, health standards and life expectancy, there is less agreement amongst economists as to what constitutes 'equilibrium.' Economics 'by assumption' states that the developed world is in some kind of equilibrium or it least should be. Whilst markets such as goods, labour and finance markets in developed nations may approach or surround equilibrium, those of developing nations do not. The believers of one world price and one interest rate must accept that the family of nations is currently in gross dis-equilibrium with regard to wage, cost and profit rates.[5] The transition to maturity is but a reflection of dis-equilibrium in both labor and goods markets, developed country wage and price levels. In a world of unequal partners, there are vast opportunities to realize dis-equilibrium quasi-rents via exports to mature economy markets. As convergence in prices and wages proceeds, these quasi-rents dissipate on the path to maturity. It is now possible to build a model of EA economic take-off.

2-8 The Western Shuttle Model of East Asia's Takeoff

Given the wide cost and wealth differentials that exist between EA and the USA, this model characterizes EA economic take-off in terms of hitching a ride on the exogenous rocket launcher of the US market. The launch pad is international competitiveness, while the rocket itself is the selling of manufactured goods to the USA. Economic take-off is initially propelled by the twin rocket boosters of cost and wealth differentials, being fueled by the accumulation of capital and labor in EA. Mid-atmosphere propulsion is derived from the twin rocket engines of super profits and hard currency, being fuelled by allocative and technical efficiency. This first of this two-stage economic take-off is exogenous efficiency. This first of this two-stage economic take-off is exogenous and catch-up in nature but fades during the second stage as EA cost and income levels converge on those of the US.

Upon convergence, the EA shuttle disconnects from its rocket, as both the rocket and rocket booster engines and fuels have outlived their usefulness. Now the cruise economic speed of the shuttle depends upon the twin engines of technological progress and productivity growth. These fuels are different from those of the economic take-off fuels, being more orientated toward human capital, research and development, innovation, property rights and vintage capital. Sustainable, endogenous steady-state growth of the EA Shuttle depends on these fuels.

There is a role for the control center (EA governments) to ensure a smooth take-off, acceleration, flight path and shuttle speed efficiency.

The Rocket Launcher Pad

It is the exploitation of international competitiveness that generates economic take-off. Super-export growth drives super economic growth in an EA context. As equation (2-4) suggests, EA has experienced considerable price (and unit cost) competitiveness in producing and exporting manufactured goods. This is the low level of the real exchange rate igniting take-off.

The Launcher Rocket

The rocket itself is the selling of manufactured goods to rich markets, such as the USA. Greater acceleration and a steeper trajectory path to economic maturity are achieved via exports than by the traditional 'invention' rocket used by the USA shuttle for its economic take-off. However, propulsion in this development model is derived from super-profits and hard currency from exporting to the wealthy US market. Less emphasis is placed on the traditional growth literature forces of technological progress and productivity.

The Rocket Boosters

The first rocket booster is cost differentials. Several forces are at work. One is the relatively high price of US labor that places a *high floor* on world prices, a kind of benchmark that conditions consumers into believing what constitutes 'normal prices'. On the demand side, US

Figure 2-1

<u>THE WESTERN SHUTTLE MODEL:</u>

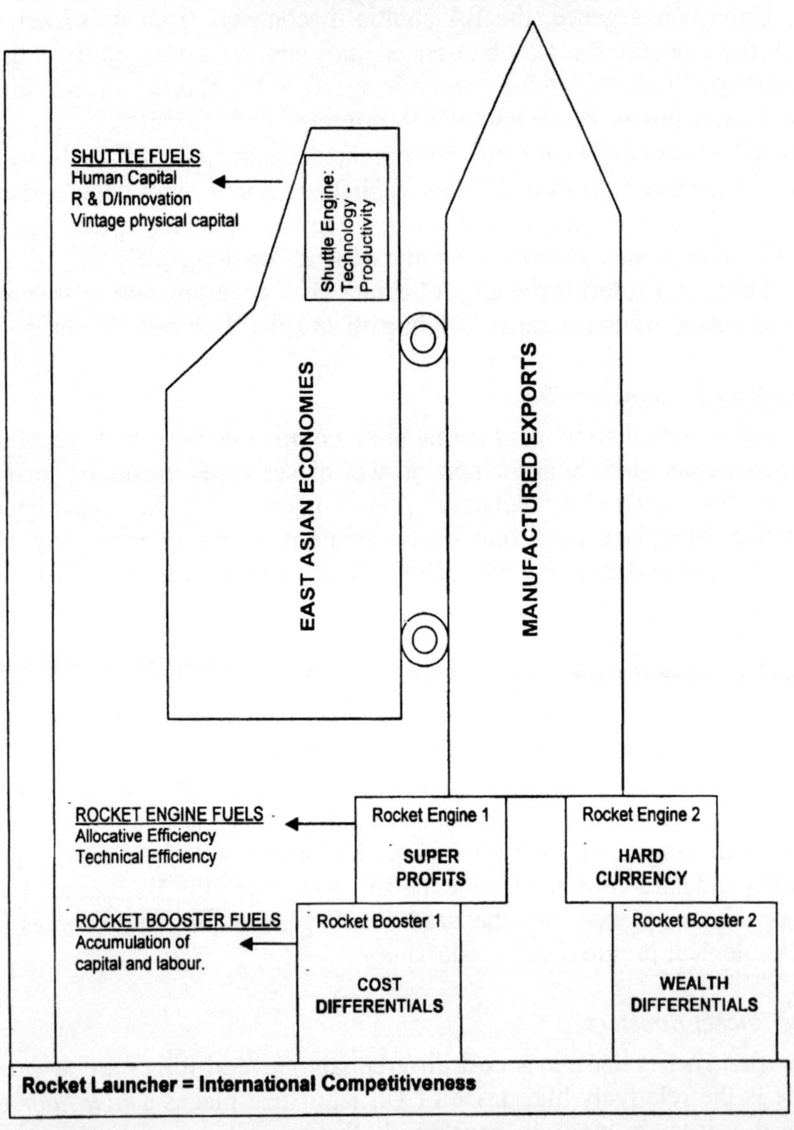

consumers suffer from a type of 'price illusion' and are sluggish to adjust to a world market place that is integrating rapidly. Such consumer inertia in price expectation adjustment also supports a high world price floor. This price floor is also supported by high US income and wealth levels and positive-feedback income effects from trade. However, it should be noted that the US price level for manufactured goods, in *real terms* has fallen from a great height, albeit slowly. On the supply side, high US unit costs in some manufactured goods are driven by high wages and their effect on costs; for example, superannuation, workers compensation, sick leave, the power of unions, a lack of commitment to employee skill and human capital accumulation and government regulation over working conditions and the environment.

A second major force driving wide cost differentials is that EA producers enjoy a high degree of unit cost competitiveness via surplus labour in the non-traded goods sector. Abundant labour implies relatively low wage rates. Given that EA production costs are mainly denominated in local currency while foreign sales are mainly denominated in $US, profit margins are super-normal. Low domestic unit costs imply that EA exporters can set prices far above domestic market prices and yet below world (US) prices. Monopolistic profits of a type are extracted because of the low level of EA's average cost curve, in contrast to the high level of the US foreign demand curve.

The second rocket booster is wealth differentials. It is the sheer wealth, market size and depth of the USA that acts as a strong, sustained magnet of attraction for EA manufactured goods, that stimulates both large export volumes and rates of growth. As penetration of the US grows, EA producers are able to harness economies of scale and suppress unit costs. Saturation of such foreign markets in the early years of development was never a constraint.

The Rocket Booster Fuels

In order for the above two 'demand side' rocket boosters to function, a supply side response is required. The accumulation of capital and labour are essential fuels for economic lift-off, in terms of raising K/L ratios, skill levels, social competence and breaking critical thresholds.[6] Preferences of work over leisure and saving over consumption play important roles in this accumulation process. More inputs into the production process are important for reasons of *domestic allocative efficiency* as more resources are devoted to the manufacturing sector. Hence, drawing upon underemployed resources and reallocating resources according to comparative advantage represent the loading of fuels into the two rocket boosters. However, in the initial stage of take-off, the accumulation process is directed at very simple, labour intensive manufactures.

The Rocket Engines

As explained in Section 2-6, EA producers have been able to exploit super-profits from vast differences in both labour and unit costs compared to the USA. Super profits are the first rocket engine. Monopolistic profits are international in nature and obtained mainly through the manufactured-good export link to the USA, not through selling to the domestic market or overseas poor. Gaining such funds breaks several bottlenecks of growth; such as using retained earnings for investment and so exploiting a powerful marginal physical cost of capital (MPK). Provided that super-profits are re-ploughed back into the export drive, rapid acceleration of the rocket continues. Yielding to temptation in the form of domestic consumption or waste in the non-export sector causes rocket acceleration to decrease.[7]

The second rocket engine is that of hard currency. Most transactions in the world may be carried out in \$US, and if not, then in Yen, British Pounds or Deutsche Marks. Obtaining respectable foreign exchange is essential to catch-up, in a technical sense, to the modern world. Purchasing capital imports, patents, licenses and foreign technicians is critical for rapid economic flight and can only be achieved by payment in hard currency. Whilst foreign aid and government overseas borrowing are avenues for gaining hard currency, they are not optimal. Exports to the USA represent the most preferred way of securing hard currency, breaking domestic bottlenecks and so the vicious circle of poverty. The potency of this rocket engine in sustaining altitude and rocket acceleration should not be underestimated.

The Rocket Engine Fuels

International allocative efficiency is the first rocket engine fuel. Moving unemployed resources into use or resources out of the rural sector into the manufacturing sector yields efficiency and visible output gains, moving output gains closer to the production possibility frontier (PPF).

However, such a reshuffling of resources into the export sector yields even higher efficiency *and* profit gains via higher world than domestic prices. Super profits result. This is analogous to EA moving to an international steady state rather than to its 'own' steady state. The intersectoral allocation of resources in EA is a powerful force, once married to the depth and variety of the US market. This second stage of take-off is partly achieved by the second-leg of allocative efficiency; that is, raising product quality and product variety, moving up these respective 'ladders' of sophistication, and so further penetrating wealthy foreign markets such as the USA. This is above and beyond the first-leg of allocative efficiency that concentrates on domestic efficiency gains and simple manufactured good exports. Technical efficiency is the second rocket engine fuel. The acquisition of foreign knowledge is not a major obstacle for EA to overcome. Producing labour intensive manufactured goods in early years of development required little by way of technical knowledge. In later years, more sophisticated manufactured goods required deeper knowledge transfer that is partly facilitated by its 'public good' or 'free good' nature. Given that EA is well inside the world production possibility frontier, and so world best practise, it can readily draw upon foreign knowledge.[8] Imitation and innovation rather than invention was and still is a useful fuel of rocket acceleration.

The EA Shuttle

After the two-stage lift off has been completed, the EA shuttle disengages from its rocket. Manufactured exports no longer offer rapid acceleration along the flight path, as the potency of both allocative and technical efficiency are exhausted. Hence, super- profits no longer exist via the export channel, and hard currency ceases to be a constraint on growth. Likewise, the basic accumulation of capital and labour ceases to be an important fuel of take-off, as cost and wealth differentials converge on US levels. In short, as economic maturity is reached, the forces of gravity (poverty) are denied and so the EA shuttle achieves a long run 'steady state' economic cruise speed that resembles that of other shuttles (mature economies) in outer space (prosperity).

Such a cruise speed is derived mainly from the traditional shuttle twin engine model of technological progress and productivity. The fuels are also more traditional in nature reflecting 'real factors' and supply side stimuli. In the international steady state, all shuttles (mature economies) are aware of the importance of maintaining international competitiveness via the creation of new ideas and knowledge. Hence, productivity-driven shuttle acceleration takes over from profit-driven rocket acceleration.

2-9 Old Flight Paths

Old development theory, espoused by Rostow (1960), emphasizes 'successive stages of development' through which all nations must pass. Nations that are in the 'traditional society' or 'preconditions' stage, had only to abide by a set of rules for economic take-off. However, mobilizing resources, is more of a necessity than the 'assumed' sufficient condition for economic take-off. Rostow assumed that all nations would follow this *same* flight path.

Another school of thought, led by Lewis (1954) highlights the importance of structural transformation and surplus labour in the rural subsistence sector. The modern sector accumulates more than normal profits via labour migration and cheap wage rates and so achieves self sustained growth. Lewis assumed that such a transition was a *typical* flight path for most developing nations.

A third flight path is espoused by the neo-classical school that favours free markets, less government regulation and openness. Their argument is that developing country resources are being used poorly and prices do not reflect scarcity. Hence, gross inefficiency and heavy state involvement in economic activity leads to a sub-optimal growth performance. The solutions rest in privatization, de-regulation and opening doors to trade and knowledge. This flight path of *openness* entails moving from a closed to a more open economy with market driven allocative efficiency improving along the way.

Comparing the growth characteristics and economic structure of mature nations with developing nations is fraught with difficulty and so allowance is made for metamorphosis along the development path.

2-10 Rocket-Shuttle Flight Path

The Western Shuttle Model does not neglect the 'stages' concept, the 'structural transformation' concept, the 'resource re-allocation' notion or the 'openness' prescription of the existing development literature. Where this model differs from most other models is in its emphasis on hitching a ride, indeed, leapfrogging, the initial endogenous energy required for economic lift-off. The exogenous force of the wealthy US market, which acted as a circuit breaker of some ferocity in providing the surplus funds, in hard currency form, is so essential for rapid growth acceleration.

During the two-stage take-off, it is the profitability of the marginal efficiency of investment (MEI) that accelerates growth. This eventually dissolves into the commonly known MPK, once the Shuttle disengages from its rocket. International competitiveness is essential for lift-off, as super profits from exports promote growth acceleration. However, competitive advantage (of the shuttle) overpowers the importance of comparative advantage once the rocket loses its thrust.[9] That is product differentiation, where product quality and strategic marketing assume greater importance than just low unit costs as stated by Porter (1990). Table 2-4 summarizes the specifics of the Western Shuttle flight path.

2-11 Massive Profit Opportunities: The Control Center's Response

The above model implies that selling manufactured goods to the wealthy US market (the rocket) creates a very steep trajectory for the EA shuttle. Even though the physical rocket is in place, together with its rocket boosters and engines, the fuels required for take-off do not accrue automatically. It is the control center's responsibility to ensure that the fuels of accumulation and allocative and technical efficiency are employed so as to ensure a successful take-off and smooth flight path. Likewise, in maturity (space) the Shuttle requires guidance and monitoring.

Whilst the EA nations flirted with import substitution strategies in the 1950's, the drawbacks of such strategies became obvious by the 1960's in terms of balance of payment constraints, lack of hard currency, foreign debt repayment and stagnant product quality. Policy reorientation included moves toward export-led growth, which in some ways may be interpreted as more openness. The basic *dual objective* was to expand market opportunities and so sell in volume to foreign markets, thereby restraining rises in domestic unit costs and secondly, exploit large monopoly profits via the historical wedge between world prices in $US and domestic costs in local currency.

How did EA governments seek to exploit such massive export opportunities in manufactured goods? More concisely, how did EA governments seek to exploit their cost competitiveness with wealthy markets?

Table 2-4

The Rocket-Shuttle Flight Path

	1st Take-Off	2nd Take-Off	Shuttle Speed
Competitiveness	Cost Driven	Allocative	Productivity
		Technical	
Growth Force	Exogenous	Both	Endogenous
Dynamics	P^d/P^f	MEI_x	MPK
Acceleration	Cost	Super Profits	New Knowledge
	Differentials	Hard Currency	
Fuels	Accumulation	Allocative	R and D
		Technical	Human Capital
Altitude	Levels Matter	Both	Changes Matter

Firstly, as the World Bank (1993,p84) points out, government policies were by and large 'market friendly'. The objective was not to oppose the role of market forces in allocating resources efficiently but to reinforce and accelerate such a role.

Secondly, more tangible assistance was in the form of a protection policy in that tariffs were relatively high on consumption goods up until the 1980's. Quotas were also used to protect local industries. However, tariffs on imported inputs were generally low or exempt. This umbrella period purchased time for local producers to attain world product quality. Such a revisionist view, is proclaimed by Amsden (1989) and Wade (1990), that relative prices were deliberately and significantly biased.

Thirdly, industrial policies were widely used, with mixed results, in that subsidies and bounties were directed mainly at export and export-potential industries. The major intermediate objectives were to assist industrial restructuring, climb product ladders, raise product quality and sophistication and contain unit cost rises in the short run. The ultimate objective was to improve international competitiveness. However, the World Bank (1993,p316) remains skeptical of the effectiveness of such policies, as distinct from natural market outcomes, in EA.

Fourthly, governments also indulged in the habit of directing credit (often below market rates) to capital-starved export industries in the early years. More available capital and its lower cost did stimulate exports - so vigorous was the push of EA governments. EA exporters understood the 'rules of the game' in that refinancing and further credit applications were dependent on verifiable export success.

Fifthly, EA governments often supported dual exchange rate systems. A higher exchange rate was employed to discourage imports and require foreign investors to pay a 'premium' for the right to invest in the domestic economy. A lower exchange rate was aimed at encouraging domestic resources to flow into the export sector. As the World Bank (1993,p125) states, there were 'deliberate under-valuations' in order to stimulate exports.

What becomes evident, in the case of EA, is the effectiveness of the 'control center' in subcontracting and commissioning the construction of the launch rocket and its fuels. Manufactured exports were seen as the catalyst for economic take-off, and there was a high degree of unanimity between business leaders and governments as to what immediate strategic objectives were to be pursued.

2-12 The Western Shuttle Paradigm

In short, vast cost differentials between East Asia and the West drove super-export growth which drove super-profits which in turn generated super-growth. The accumulation of capital and labour was as much the result of this exogenous super-export force as it was the cause of it. Preferences 'appeared' to be biased toward sweat and sacrifice but so too were super economic incentives to save, invest and profit from interaction with the West. Hence, the WSM emphasis on 'hitching a ride' on the wealth of the West – a semi-exogenous force driving growth in EA.

2-13 Conclusion

This chapter unveiled the Western Shuttle model of EA economic take-off. In many ways this model is a reaction against the failure and misdirection of the current trade and growth literature's focus on *changes* in real exchange rates, foreign income and productivity. The labor and goods markets of this global village are not in equilibrium. Vast differences in wage, price, and productivity *levels* among the developed and developing world imply the persistence of super-profits while such gaps remain. It is the wealth and high income levels of the USA that has acted as a permanent magnet of attraction for EA exporters and as a long-term motive force for economic growth.

However, such super profits have not and do not accrue automatically to EA. Vast profit opportunities must be both seized and realized via manufactured exports to wealthy markets. A high degree of international competitiveness, as measured by the low level of the real exchange rate is impotent for economic growth if it is not married to the selling of manufactured exports to wealthy markets. The potency of international price competitiveness is realized when super-export growth yields super-profit growth which in turn drives super economic growth. Therefore, profit - not productivity growth - holds the key to EA take-off. Whilst economic incentives, and to a large degree adventurous entrepeneurs finessed export growth, so too have EA governments been active in stimulating an outward looking export strategy.

This chapter presented the Western Shuttle Model of EA economic growth in basic form that will be refined in the remaining chapters. It will become clearer how this model differentiates itself from existing growth, trade and development theory in Chapter 3. Points of departure from traditional models will be further discussed.

Chapter Three

Growth Theory: Multiple Flight Paths

3-1 Introduction

This chapter examines the relevance of both 'old' and 'new' growth theory in explaining East Asia's rapid growth experience. Traditional channels of economic growth, such as investment, low capital-labour ratios, stable macroeconomic policies, economic fundamentals, preferences and technological progress are considered in the light of East Asia's growth record. The not-so-traditional determinants of growth, such as innovation, quality ladders, increasing returns, externalities from both human capital and technology and monopoly pricing are also surveyed. The search is for the relevant engine(s) of growth for East Asia from existing growth theory.

Despite the strength of growth theory in explaining the growth experience of developed nations, it has met with less success in explaining the growth experience of developing nations. Clinging to a production theoretic framework, as growth theory still does, has its costs in terms of omitting valuable financial variables. These variables include super profits from openness and exports, a divergence between international prices and domestic marginal costs, international relative price signals stimulating allocative efficiency, the bottleneck-breaking ability of 'hard currency' and the value of the marginal productivity of capital (MPK) being greater than its physical product.

This chapter seeks to identify the strengths and weaknesses of existing growth theory in an East Asian context. It is argued that the production-technology channel of existing growth theory is not capable of a satisfactory explanation of East Asia's rapid growth experience. While new growth theory has two key points of departure from old growth theory, in the form of increasing returns (P>MC) and externalities (social returns greater than private), this chapter focuses on another point of departure, this being a divergence in unit costs (price differentials) between developing and developed nations creating a monopolistic profit channel via exports. This growth engine contains explanatory power of East Asia's economic performance.[1] Whilst the power of technological progress generating growth in the long run is undeniable, the forces driving growth in the transition period to the steady state are contestable. What is required is a marriage or synthesis of macroeconomic theory with development and trade theory in order to explain economic take-off to maturity.[2]

3-2 Old and New Growth Theory

The Solow Model

This neoclassical model represents a traditional approach to explain increases in per capita output. There are constant returns to scale, Inada conditions apply and so the MPK declines as capital is accumulated. Embedded in this model is consumer and producer optimization subject to resource constraints, along with a competitive general equilibrium approach to growth.[3] The shift factor, A, from equation 3-1, represents technological progress, the long-run *engine* of growth in this model.

$$Y = A K^\alpha L^{\alpha -1} \tag{3-1}$$

There are three main channels generating 'growth' in this model. The first channel relies on the accumulation of capital and labour inputs (capital widening) in generating increases in output per head via lower dependency ratios. Preferences of economic agents with regard to the labour-leisure and the consumption-saving trade-offs are important in supporting increased participation rates in the labour force and savings rates supporting investment. Such pro-sacrifice choices underpin the accumulation of capital and labour in the short run. However, diminishing returns to the factors of production eventually set in and cause the effectiveness of the accumulation drive to stall.

The second channel of a *low* capital-labour ratio (K/L) implies a high growth of output per worker in the transition phase of the Solow Model (capital deepening), the short-run *dynamic* of the model. The marginal productivity of capital (MPK) is high so long as the K/L ratio is relatively low, compared to its steady state ratio. Such an increase in output per capita is often referred to as 'level effects' rather than 'growth effects,' as the K/L ratio eventually reaches its own steady state or mature economy level. In the transition phase the growth in output per head is only transient. The reason for this occurrence is that the marginal productivity of capital declines as the capital-labour ratio rises and so induces investment and growth to fall back to its original steady state growth path. In the steady state, transitional 'growth' comes to an end.

However, Jones and Manuelli (1990) employing a standard neoclassical model, provide solid arguments as to why the MPK does not fall to zero, but is bounded from below. This explanation does not rely on externalities, increasing returns or human capital formation in generating *endogenous* growth. A standard convex production technology can generate growth. The key is for the interest rate to exceed the inverse of the discount rate, thereby encouraging consumption in the future. To guarantee 'unbounded growth,' it is necessary to prevent the interest rate from falling to the level of the inverse of the discount rate $(r>1/\rho)$. In the case of East Asia, the 'interest rate' or the rate of return from investing (eg exports) has been so high, that meeting this unbounded growth condition has not been difficult.

The third channel is total factor productivity (TFP) driven by disembodied technological progress, represented by the shift factor A in equation (3-1), that generates long run sustainable growth in the steady state.[4] It is this force that offsets the debilitating nature of diminishing returns. While TFP may have many driving forces besides technological progress, there is some consensus amongst economists that economic prosperity, over the long run, has indeed been driven by technological progress.

Empirical research has confirmed, to a large degree, the central importance of technological progress in explaining economic growth. For example, work by Solow (1957) suggested that 7/8 of growth in real output in the US economy between 1909-1949 was due to technical progress. A study by Boskin and Lau (1990) of France, UK, Germany and the US asserted that technical progress accounted for 50% of the growth since WWII. These studies undermined the importance of the 'blunt instruments' of growth, namely increases in capital and labour inputs in favor of the 'sharper instrument' of technological progress for developed nations.

Given that the Solow Model has its weaknesses, how well does it explain the East Asian growth experience? Economists such as Krugman (1994) and Young (1994) claim that the rapid accumulation of inputs can explain much, if not all, of the growth in East Asia over the last forty years. Labour has been drawn from rural sectors and labour force participation rates have soared. Structural change, in the form of resources moving into areas of comparative advantage (eg manufacturing), has also been a contributing factor.

These authors also point to the relevance of diminishing returns setting in as accumulation reach saturation, so causing the rapid growth process to end. Moreover, the 'sweat and sacrifice' of high labour productivity and high saving could not be sustained indefinitely as preferences would eventually have to turn pro-consumption and pro-leisure – as income levels rose. By contrast, a developing nation competing on world markets at the lower end of product sophistication can still find growth from the traditional inputs of capital and labour. Therefore, it is not surprising that the World Bank (1993,p48) estimates that 'accumulation' of such factors contributed to around two thirds of East Asian growth. In other words, the application of the accumulation channel of the Solow Model to the Asian growth experience has support.

The transition phase of the Solow Model also has some applicability to the Asian experience. Capital deepening and an explosive MPK has provided a reliable avenue for many East Asian nations to push resources into their manufacturing sectors and take advantage of relatively cheap labour costs. The power of investment should not be underestimated, as DeLong and Summers (1991) find evidence of a more specific relationship between growth and equipment investment. The explanation given is that this type of investment contains or embodies substantial external benefits and thus propels productivity growth. Specifically, they find that GDP rises by 0.26% for every extra one percentage point of total GDP devoted to machinery and equipment investment. They also estimate the social rate of return on this type of investment to be as high as 30 percent (while the private rate of return averaged around 10%). De Long and Summers (1992) provide solid arguments as to why causation runs from investment to output, as high investing countries pay low prices for equipment. If high output and demand drives investment, then high prices for equipment would be evident. De Long (1992) argues that machinery investment is such a key element of growth because it embodies modern technological know how and it has been indispensable for industrialization in the past.[5] However, a major externality, as a by-product of investment may not be the only plausible explanation of investment's potency in explaining growth. Other important factors may drive growth, such as openness to trade, an improvement in work skills and changes in the exchange rate also may be present while large amounts of investment are being undertaken. By omitting these other variables, the supposed potency of investment may be over-stated.

Nevertheless, there are other authors who lend support to the importance of physical investment. Romer (1986) makes the claim that the classical model underestimates the contribution of physical investment in accounting for growth. The share of capital in total income is larger than its nominal (national accounts) value because of the positive externalities generated.

Applying technological progress to the East Asian growth experience meets with less success. There is little evidence of any Asian nation creating new inventions or new horizon goods over the last forty years, with the possible exception of Japan. Asia has been well within the production possibility frontier (PPF) and well below world best practise for much of this century. While improvements in technical efficiency, adaptation and imitation have been widespread, there is no evidence of pure technological progress. Therefore, the long-run driving force of the Solow Model has been absent in case of East Asia. According to authors such as Krugman (1994), Young (1994), Collins and Bosworth (1996), TFP has been a minor force in East Asia's development. According to these authors, East Asia may experience a 'window of exposure' until human capital and productivity catch up to OECD levels.

The AK Model

This type of model assumes that all inputs take the form of reproducible capital, either physical or human. This broad measure of capital is used by Rebelo (1991) whereby the production function retains the property of constant returns to scale but the diminishing returns to capital assumption is abandoned. Labour is held fixed and so variables are expressed in per capita terms.

$$Y \quad = \quad A\,K \tag{3-2}$$

The *engine* of growth in this model is the employment of capital goods that can be produced without limit, such as *reproducible* human capital and the stock of knowledge that in turn generate externalities. The end result is that an ever-increasing capital stock per capita is possible and steady state growth. There is no difference between the APK and the MPK, so there are no transitional dynamics. Moreover, the shift-factor, A, is not essential in driving steady state growth. In this model, raising the savings rate becomes a fair target for the policy maker to pursue. The *dynamic* of this model is the incentives to save and invest, altering the capacity to grow in the long run. Government intervention becomes a legitimate policy option, as King and Rebelo (1991) re-emphasize the crucial role played by national policies in affecting incentives for individuals to accumulate both human and physical capital. They claim that small open economies, subject to capital mobility, are particularly vulnerable to taxation policies that can generate both 'growth miracles' and 'development traps.'

The Lucas Model(s)

Human capital is the emphasis of the Lucas (1988) model as the representative agent chooses between work, u, and building human capital, 1-u. The production of human capital is assumed to be linear (constant returns to scale) and there is an externality derived from the average level of human capital.

$$Y \quad = \quad A\,K^{\alpha}\,H^{\alpha-1} \tag{3-3}$$

$$H \quad = \quad Lh$$

$$L \quad = \quad \text{quantity of workers}$$

$$h \quad = \quad \text{quality of workers (human capital)}$$

While an increasing L may be a source of diminishing returns, there are offsetting influences from both the accumulation of K and h. It is human capital that is the *growth engine* of this model via both externality and accumulation and so the *dynamic* is the representative agent's choice to sacrifice work time for formal education or learning by doing. A social planner may increase society's output and welfare by creating incentives that encourage human capital accumulation. Externalities imply a role for the social planner.

Lucas (1993) employed a 'learning by doing' model in trying to explain the rapid economic takeoff of Korea compared to the Philippines in recent years. His engine of growth is human capital differentials. The model's dynamic stems from a vast array of product lines that represent higher quality (a higher world price) and productivity potential in each product line. Shifting the work-force into new product lines increases productivity potential as worker productivity rises with experience and learning by doing. As each product line is 'exhausted' – as diminishing returns set in – and so the impulse is given to move up to a higher product and quality ladder. Lucas claims that Korea's consumption and production mix were different through trade, that expanded the opportunity set for learning by doing. Lowering unit costs via trade is essential – but with this 'technology gap' model. Catch up growth is not only dependent on the pool of domestic human capital but on the pool of world knowledge. This is a profitability story but couched in terms of human capital differentials. Equally, it could be an export-led growth model that exploits low unit costs and progressively higher world prices – albeit in different product categories – generating super-profits as P>ATC.

Barro and Lee (1993a) find evidence that suggests growth rates are strongly driven by the pre-existing stock of human capital in the male labour force. Another year of schooling is estimated to raise GDP growth by more than 1% point. However, Gapinski (1997a,1997b,1999) finds that human capital matters little in an EA context.

Canterbery's Vita Theory and Product Cycle Model

This theory centers around specific human capital and segmented labour markets. Each worker is endowed with a birth vita according to sex, racial background, religion, national origin, inherent mental and physical capacity, inheritances and family background. A birth-market vita may be augmented via learning by doing and formal education. Demand for human capital (in its various categories) may be disturbed by changes in tariffs and exchange rates and ever-evolving trade flow patterns. Enter the product cycle model, whereby production may shift to other lower cost producers, and so the demand for labour shifts in both countries. Moreover, as standardized production technology is transferred to lower-wage countries, the higher wage country can lose its comparative advantage in that production. Long-term real dislocations follow and as Canterbery (1994,p 8) notes "tariffs and exchange rates can change faster than workers can be retrained." Hence, there is a role for commercial and human capital policies to smooth over the painful adjustment process. Growth in the developing country is very much a function of how the now-standardized technology can be used to produce the now - standardized product. The strength of this model rests in its stress on mark-up pricing based on product differentiation so that quasi-profits are generated in a dynamic general equilibrium *trade* setting.

The Barro Model

This model concentrates on the potency and complementarity of government expenditure (public services) in stimulating the growth of private sector inputs. An increase in G offsets diminishing returns stemming from the accumulation of K, raising the marginal products of both K and L, which in turn allows endogenous growth.

$$Y \qquad = \qquad A\, K_i^{\alpha}\, L_i^{\alpha-1}\, G^{\alpha-1} \qquad\qquad (3\text{-}4)$$

If the exponent on G exactly equals $\alpha - 1$ then constant returns to scale apply. However, it should be noted that additional public services require funding, so increased taxation may have adverse effects on growth via disincentives to work and save. Hence, the MPK is positively affected by an increase in G, but adversely effected at some threshold level of public services. Hence, there is some theoretical optimal size of government.

There is evidence, for the US at least, by Aschauer (1989), Easterly and Rebelo (1993) and Lynde and Richmond (1993) that public investment (infrastructure) has played a significant complementary role to private investment and productivity. Dowrick (1993) claims that government consumption is non-linear, as rises in government consumption increase growth up to a critical value of about 12% but detract from growth thereafter.

The Romer Model

In many ways the work of Paul Romer has sought to address the deficiencies of the Solow Model. Romer (1990) questions the wisdom of relying on perfect competition, marginal cost pricing, exogenous technological growth, abstract science generating innovation and constant returns to scale.

$$Y = (A\,L_Y)^{1-\alpha}\ \Sigma\,(X_{ij})^{\alpha} \qquad (3\text{-}5)$$

Endogenous growth models, particularly Paul Romer's (1990) model, emphasize the importance of investing in human capital and research and development that in turn create 'new' knowledge; the *growth engine* of this model. It is a product variety model, whereby new type goods are rewarded in the market place for being first. The X's represent specialized intermediate goods, the *dynamic* of the model, which if they increase in number (variety) tend to offset diminishing returns.

The shift factor A (new knowledge) in equation (3-5), has a 'non rival' component that resembles a public good that is available to all economic agents at zero cost. It also has a rival component that private firms can appropriate and protect, the driving force of monopoly profits in the short run. There is an obvious trade off or conflict here. Society wants as much public knowledge and spillover benefits as possible, while the private sector or firm wants as much 'private information' as possible in order to preserve market position and so monopoly power.

Therefore, a delicate balance exists between the components of new knowledge - private enough for it to be produced in the first place and public enough for the benefits to be shared throughout the community. Not only is balance important but so is the length of time it takes private knowledge to become widespread public knowledge (ie, filtrate through the community and to competitors). Another dimension of the spillover process is that the ongoing production of new knowledge builds or adds to the stock of existing knowledge (a cumulative process) that enhances the

The growth of A, is determined by the number of researchers L_a and the rate at which they discover new ideas δ. This is the *dynamic* of the Romer model, the origin or catalyst of growth.

$$\dot{A} = \delta\,L_A\,A \qquad (3\text{-}6)$$

Romer assumed that the productivity of research is proportional to the stock of new ideas: $\bar{\delta} = \delta A$. Therefore, the productivity of researchers may rise even in the absence of an increase in their numbers.

It is new knowledge that creates wealth, as any advantage a firm gains over its rival can generate monopoly profits in the short run. Romer emphasizes the importance of imperfect competition and the divergence of price and marginal cost that encourage firms to seek above-normal profits. Large up-front investment (fixed costs) imply that average cost pricing should prevail as output rises. Increasing returns are the result of the non- rival nature of ideas and the spreading of fixed costs over a wide range of output.[7] Hence, there is an emphasis on securing a competitive edge and first-mover technological advantage.

According to Romer's model there are important implications for public policy. For example, there may be a role for government in providing incentives for research and development and legal protection of property rights via patents, copyrights etc. There is also the question of the optimality of market outcomes, as externalities are prevalent and monopoly profits exist. Moreover, rapid economic growth does not just come along for some exogenous reason, as in the Solow model, but rather occurs as the result of deliberate decisions made by rational profit seeking economic agents, that is, an outcome of market forces which may also be spurred by government incentives. In other words there is an explanation of 'how' and 'why' economic growth occurs.

How well does a Romer type model fit the East Asian growth experience? There is very little evidence pointing to pure research in East Asia in terms of new inventions, breakthroughs or methods, so little technological progress purely defined. Existing economic incentives are such that EA producers and entrepreneurs can free ride or imitate the stock of current world knowledge at low or near zero cost. It is the 'publicness' of knowledge, in the Romer sense, that East Asia can appropriate and so exploit to make super normal profits. While these profits are not of a monopoly type or protected by patents, they can be enduring as EA sellers capture both economies of scale and low unit costs driven by cheap labour.

Sengupta (1993) applies new growth theory to the East Asian NIC's and Korea in particular. He finds evidence of the importance of increasing returns to scale, a dynamic externality effect and human capital spillovers that flowed from openness and the export sector.

Structural change, a stimulus to investment in manufacturing and technological adoption emanated from exports and increasing returns to scale. Fixed costs are spread over large export volumes, so unit costs are suppressed. Thus, key concepts of new growth theory are supported by these results.

The Grossman and Helpman Model

A model developed by Grossman and Helpman (1991) employed imperfect competition and industrial innovation to generate endogenous growth. In this product-quality model, technological innovation is the *engine* of growth, driven by purposive, profit seeking economic agents. Researchers target the quality improvement of intermediate goods, each having its own 'quality ladder.' First-mover profits exist for innovation up these quality ladders. It is the diffusion of knowledge and its link to international trade that is the major driving force in promoting innovation, the growth of firms and so the economy. In this model, production activities are separated into high technology manufacturing firms that exhibit increasing returns to scale and a traditional manufacturing sector that exhibits constant returns to scale. The former sector depends on research and development to maintain its market position, which is in effect an ongoing process as dictated by ever changing consumer demand for variety. The latter sector, depends on the high technology sector to generate ideas and processes that contain a large degree of 'publicness', embodied in intermediate good inputs. In fact, Grossman and Helpman (1991) stress the importance of the 'cumulative investment' and the vast amount of knowledge embodied in the latest generation of intermediate goods.[8]

How is endogenous steady state growth generated in this model? The *dynamics* include the profitability and cost of industrial research that drives the speed at which intermediate goods move up their quality ladders. Scientific breakthroughs increase the productivity of researchers and so profitability, while an increase in the savings rate lowers the cost and increases financing of research. Continual, never ending improvements in quality contribute to productivity of physical capital and arrest the fall of the MPK to where it is no longer productive. Capital accumulation is thus driven by innovation.

The international flavour of this model is borne out by the interdependence of the global economy. International transactions contain channels through which knowledge externalities are generated, for example, through the flow of non-rival knowledge via technology and the movement of international researchers. Newer innovative goods also contain information, signal success and provide rewards for being first. Grossman and Helpman (1991,p39) clearly point out that "It may be that the high technology products manufactured in one country can be improved as readily by research labs in a foreign country as they can by labs located nearby." These technological spillovers are international in flavor and imply that foreign countries can absorb and build upon the stock of world knowledge.

This model predicts that nations may diverge in per capita income. While trade and openness offer the opportunity for technological diffusion, provide feedback on product quality, and increase the size of the customer base, there are drawbacks to consider. A nation with comparative advantage in unskilled labour may get caught in a low growth trap through specialization and openness to trade as resources are attracted away from human capital formation and research to the detriment of innovation. Such a low growth trap may exist in small countries that have only a limited research base with which to compete with research giants. According to Grossman and Helpman (1991) international knowledge flows and absorption are not cost-less, and so a nation that is relatively endowed with skilled labour will specialize and export human capital intensive goods. Local spillovers may cause a whirlpool process of ideas which ensures that a technological lead can be sustained indefinitely. In this case local technological spillovers may outweigh any advantage flowing from factor endowments. Hence, this model supports per capita income divergence based on growth poles and traps.

The Pack and Page Model

While a low K/L ratio yields a high MPK along the existing production function, Pack (1994) points out that developing countries operating on a lower production function have an opportunity to embrace technological diffusion, borrow more productive technology, exploit a type of catch-up growth and so move to a higher production function. It is the distance of the gap between actual practice and world best practice that dictates the speed of this catch up growth. The shift factor, A, in the production function is not similar among nations and there are wide differences in the contribution and growth of TFP to economic growth. Even though the distance from world best practice is wide and so the opportunity large, exploiting or realizing catch-up growth through the technological transfer is not cost-less in terms of purchasing equipment or knowledge. The channels to acquire world best practice include licensing, consultants, foreign direct investment, technical literature and informal person-to-person contact. This model emphasizes the importance of international trade, and in particular exports, that allows the above channels to become effective. Knowledge transfer, the commitment to costly adoption and the ability to adapt to local needs all require a degree of absorptive ability. Thus, the interaction between exports and the level of human capital (formal education) is an important ingredient in securing the inter-sectoral re-allocation of resources (structural change) in order to achieve dynamic economic growth. As Pack (1994,p62) points out about the dynamic of this model "the level of technology is changing with the allocation of resources between domestic sales and exports, partly offsetting any effect of diminishing returns to capital." For a developing country, raising technical efficiency and technology transfer via exports is the engine of growth in this model.

The production function in Pack (1994) is

$$Q(t) = Q^f e^{u(t)} = F[Z(t); t] e^{u(t)} \tag{3-7}$$

Here the $Q(t)$ represents potential output at best practice for a vector of inputs $Z(t)$; and $u(t)$ is the level of technical efficiency. The derivative in logs of equation (3-7) is:

$$\frac{\dot{Q}(t)}{Q(t)} = \frac{F_z \dot{X}(t)}{X(t)} + F_t + \dot{u}(t) \tag{3-8}$$

where F_z and F_t are output elasticities with respect to $Z(t)$ an d time

The first term of this equation represents accumulation of inputs, the second term, F_t, is the rate of technological progress of the world best practice frontier and $\dot{u}(t)$ is technical efficiency change. TFP is regarded as a combination of these last two terms. While developed countries are operating on the best practice frontier ($\dot{u}(t) = 0$), developing countries are not, and so u(t) is positive. This model claims that technical efficiency from export-led growth is the key channel driving 'TFP', as most Asian nations are inside the world PPF and below world best practice.

There are several channels through which exports can cause technical efficiency to rise. De Long and Summers (1991) point out the importance of equipment investment in cross section growth studies. It may be that additional investment captures and exploits the high marginal productivity of capital from a low base. Such capital also embodies new ideas and technology itself, so an implicit transfer of productive power takes place via imports in an Asian context. Secondly, direct foreign investment (DFI) sometimes provides the essential know-how for specific commercial, industrial and marketing tasks to be completed that is non-resident in the domestic economy. Positive spillover benefits are also likely from foreign firms. Thirdly, there may be more technical knowledge acquired by searching the trade and engineering literature at a low cost, using patents and licenses at a fee, and transferring of knowledge from purchasers that have intimate knowledge of other more technological advanced suppliers. Fourthly, there may be some stimulus to domestic research, as profits from trade are re-employed into an industrial upgrading drive, that implies a move up the product ladder.

Pack and Page (1994) employ a modified Solow model that incorporates transitional dynamics and human capital. This model specifically uses a catch-up variable, the relative gap between Asian and US income in 1960, a shift variable that captures technical efficiency or movement to best practice. This interpretation holds on the basis that technological progress for all nations is constant. However, this shift variable may *also* be explained by structural change, as developing Asian nations have re - allocated labour from agriculture to industry and from low paying, low productivity employment to higher paying, higher productivity employment. Hence, as Pack (1992) points out, this variable incorporates intrasectoral and intersectoral re-allocation of factors that raises productivity, reflecting mainly *domestic* allocative efficiency.

A key conclusion of Pack and Page (1994) is the central importance of exports in driving technical efficiency. Two measures are used, manufactured exports as a share of total exports and share of manufactured exports in GDP. It is the former measure that has more predictive power, presumably because it indicates the importance of more manufactured exports, *at the margin,* in generating more decisive and technical information flow. Although a study by Dollar (1990) reveals a correlation between 'openness' and GDP growth, the manufactured export variable by itself (ie, no imports) also yields a powerful correlation with productivity growth. The temptation is to attribute the stimulus of manufactured exports on growth to technical efficiency alone, in order to explain such *prolonged* GDP growth. Pack and Page (1994) therefore place great emphasis on the knowledge spillover channel of export orientation.

Hence, this interpretation places a secondary emphasis on domestic allocative efficiency as it implies only static gains or 'one shot' experiences and so any export orientation cannot account for the continuing high growth rates of these Asian nations. However, this conclusion may not be valid if the size of the non-traded goods sector is large or if there is a vast pool of unskilled labor ready to migrate to cities and industry, as the transition may be a long one. Also by focussing export attention on large, lucrative mature economy markets, the diminution or exhaustion of these markets for simple manufactured goods is remote in the near term. Thus it is important to recognize the importance of international allocative efficiency in sending signals for the continual shuffling of resources into viable export industries, subject to domestic supply side constraints. Such constraints may be currently reached in Hong Kong and Singapore but this is not to deny the vibrance and fruitfulness of previous commitment to allocative efficiency in the heyday of the 1960's and 70's.

However, Pack and Page (1994,p216) distinguish between those Asian nations which have experienced productivity driven growth from those that did not. With respect to Korea, Taiwan, Hong Kong, Singapore and Japan, they conclude "The component of total factor productivity change which is independent of the initial level of per capita income appears to be driving much of the growth of these economies"; that is, technological progress of some kind rather than just technical efficiency in later years of their sample.

3-3 Estimates of TFP Contribution to Growth

Traditional estimates of TFP for East Asia by World Bank (1993) and Collins and Bosworth (1996) are seen in Table 3-1. For example, between 1960-1994, TFP contribution estimates for Indonesia and Taiwan were 26.6% and 33.6% respectively and for the full sample 35.6%. Kawai (1994) finds similar TFP contribution estimates of 27.3% for the same six East Asian nations between 1970-1990. Drysdale and Huang (1995) find estimates of 20.8% for the same nations between 1950-1988.

Table 3-1

Estimates of TFP Contribution to Growth (%)

	World Bank		Collins- Bos.
	Accumulation	TFP	TFP
H.Kong	44	56	-
Indonesia	60	40	26.6
Japan	82	18	-
Korea	63	37	26.6
Malaysia	87	34	35.9
Singapore	65	35	30.1
Taiwan	58	42	33.6
Thailand	66	34	35.9

Source: World Bank (1993); Collins and Bosworth (1996)

The World Bank (1993) estimates TFP contribution to growth at 34.4% between 1960-1990. These estimates are at the more optimistic end of those on offer and compared to the above results. Even though the major contribution to growth comes from sheer accumulation, these TFP contribution estimates are high by world standards, even comparable to those of the OECD. However, the World Bank argues that their TFP estimates include elements such as allocative efficiency, technical efficiency and technological catch up and therefore 'TFP' estimates presented in Table 3-1 may well be overstated in terms of disembodied technological progress. While the TFP contribution to growth in the OECD is mainly driven by technological progress, extending the best practice frontier outwards, developing nation's TFP is driven by technical efficiency; a movement from inside the international best practice frontier. However, Wu (1998) examines the case of China's regional economies and claims that catch-up to world best practise was all but exhausted by the mid 1990's and so future growth will be more reliant on pure innovation.

Table 3-2

Relative Contributions of the Sources (%) of Growth

	Capital	Labour	H.Capital	Technology
H.Kong	66	22	11	0
Japan	48	6	3	43
Korea	63	25	13	0
Singapore	67	19	14	0
Taiwan	5	14	11	0
USA	23	30	4	43
UK	35	4	6	55
France	3	-1	4	63
Germany	36	-7	5	66

Source: Kim and Lau (1994) and (1995)

More Pessimistic TFP Contribution Estimates

TFP contribution estimates by Young (1995) for Singapore, Korea, Taiwan and Hong Kong between 1966 and 1990 are 2%, 17%, 28% and 32%, respectively, yielding an average of 19.9%. Therefore, Young claims TFP contribution to growth was nothing special.

Kim and Lau (1994;1995) provide even more pessimistic estimates of TFP contribution for East Asia. These authors use a different meta-production approach, that seeks to separate out scale effects from technological progress by employing standard efficiency units of inputs across nine nations. The method is empirically valid for all these nations. The standard assumptions of growth accounting can be rejected; including constant returns to scale, neutrality of technological progress and profit maximization. The results support a purely capital augmenting view of technological progress for both the European and the Asian nations. The hypothesis of zero technological progress was not rejected for the Asian nations. From Table 3-2 the contribution of technological progress to growth was 54 percent for the 5 mature nations and 0% for the 4 Asian NIC's. These results are not surprising for either mature or developing economies, as technological progress is required to offset diminishing returns for the mature economies and not yet 'essential' for the continuation of growth in the Asian countries.

The results of Kim and Lau (1994) reveal a significant degree of pessimism concerning the growth prospects for these Asian economies, a decline in productive efficiency compared to the United States, no closing of the technological gap between the European and Asian nations in this sample and little evidence of technological progress to date. By contrast the mature economies have been heavily reliant on both capital accumulation and technological progress to ensure the maintenance of future growth rates.

Estimates of TFP Growth Rates

Given that the value of α yields different estimates of TFP growth, Sarel (1996) employed values of 0.25 and 0.45 yielding TFP estimates of 3.7% and 2.2% for the years 1960-1975. Using an α of 0.45 for the period 1970-1985 yielded an estimate of 1%, a result similar to that of Young. Results by Harberger (1996), for five East Asian nations, average around 2.74% and are not dissimilar to those of Sarel (1996). Dowling and Summers (1999) further test the sensitivity of results to the value of α used. Their results reveal a tendency for TFP growth estimates to fall as α rises, as displayed in Table 3-3. These authors also claim that after allowing for improvement in qualities (vintage and human capital) the measurement of disembodied technological progress falls. Their average estimates of TFP growth of 1.36%, 1.72% and 2.14% for the relevant

α's, are below those of Sarel (3.7%), Harberger (2.74%), Elias (2.17%) and the World Bank (2.5%) but closer to those of Young (1%).[9] The World Bank (1993) estimates TFP growth at around 2.5% for East Asia.

Table 3-3

TFP Growth Estimates (%)

	$\alpha = 0.4$	$\alpha = 0.35$	$\alpha = 0.30$
China	1.4	1.6	1.9
Indonesia	1.4	1.7	2.1
Korea	1.9	2.4	2.9
Malaysia	1.5	1.9	2.3
Philippines	-0.2	0.0	0.2
Singapore	1.6	2.1	2.6
Taiwan	2.0	2.4	2.9
Thailand	1.3	1.7	2.2
Average	1.36	1.72	2.14

Source: Dowling and Summers (1999)

Given the fact that East Asian nations are inside their PPF (world best practice), it then follows that TFP also subsumes improvements in both technical and allocative efficiency. The World Bank estimates this 'residual' technical efficiency to be around 0.92% for the top 4 TFP driven economies in Table 3-3. The difference between the TFP growth rate and the growth rate of technical efficiency in these five economies is still 2.5%; leaving allocative efficiency as a possible explanation. The bottom three nations in Table 3-3 have experienced negative growth in technical efficiency. From these World Bank estimates, the 'secret' to much of the Asian growth 'miracle,' besides accumulation, is allocative efficiency. In fact for the top five nations above, the contribution of allocative efficiency to TFP is in the order of 75%.

There is some support for this allocative efficiency view of TFP, as Swee and Low (1996,p9) claim that "structural shifts in the manufacturing sector was a major source of higher TFP growth in the 1980's" in Singapore. The Monetary Authority of Singapore estimates that 60% of TFP growth since 1985 has been due to shifts in the composition of output due to the reallocation of capital and labor to more efficient uses. There is also the example of Korea, as policy makers sought to accelerate allocative efficiency by shifting production to more sophisticated, capital intensive goods via all kinds of price distortions such as subsidies, tax deductions, cheap credit, tariffs etc. Although there were costs in transition, the TFP growth rate of Korean manufacturing was still 5.8% between 1966-1985 (Lim,1993).

Table 3-4

TFP Growth Estimates for East Asia

	TFP	Technical Efficiency	Allocative Efficiency
H.Kong	3.65	1.97	1.68
Indonesia	1.25	-1.23	2.48
Japan	3.48	0.98	2.50
Korea	3.10	-0.20	2.90
Malaysia	1.08	-1.77	2.85
Singapore	1.20	-3.45	4.65
Taiwan	3.76	0.84	2.92
Thailand	2.50	0.10	2.40

Source: World Bank (1993)

Regardless of what explains TFP growth in East Asia, the estimate of 2.5%, is well above the average for the OECD of around 1.5%. However, according to estimates from OECD Economic Surveys (1994) the OECD did experience a high TFP growth rate of 2.6% between 1961-1973. It has only been since the 1970's that a TFP growth slowdown has occurred in the OECD. These differing estimates therefore raise the question as to what are the sources of TFP and why East Asian estimates, in particular, are so far above those of the OECD?

To the extent that technical efficiency improvements may be applicable to East Asia then the production-capital channel of growth holds some explanatory power. From the above World Bank estimates this is only a modest contribution. What is more plausible is that these nations have improved their allocative efficiency by pushing resources into high yielding activities such as exports to mature economy markets supporting the financial - trade explanation of catch-up growth. The Solow residuals may be powerful and a major contribution to growth, but may not be either externality or technology driven. In the case of East Asia, these residuals may indeed be exogenous but trade rooted in origin.

3-4 East Asia: No TFP - Just Accumulation?

What is common to the work of the World Bank (1993) and Barro (1991) is that accumulation matters, both physical and human capital explain much of the growth process. A more extreme view is that it is mostly accumulation. Economists such as Krugman (1994) and Young (1995) employ a fairly standard neo-classical explanation of this 'miracle' and claim that the sheer rapid accumulation of traditional inputs, such as capital and labour, is the simple but crucial cause of such a fine economic performance. Hence, the denial of any abnormal contribution of total factor productivity (TFP) to economic growth in this region. Such a denial has been met with disbelief by an array of policy makers and economists alike, as such rapid GDP growth rates, of around 8% for thirty five years, have never been achieved by the West at any stage of its recorded development. For example, Liang and Jorgenson (1998) refute the Krugman hypothesis for East Asia in the 1982-1993 period. Even when the OECD did grow at reasonably rapid rates, by its own standards, it is most assuredly true that the contribution of TFP driven by technological progress extracted more output per unit of input.

Several platforms of the Krugman-Young (KY) thesis need to be critically re-examined. The first platform of this thesis is the notion thata massive mobilization of resources has been undertaken in East Asia.

However, what Krugman-Young (KY) omit to clarify is *why* this mobilization effort was so rapid. One reason offered is of a social and political nature, that of strong authoritarian governments forcing the allocation and accumulation of inputs. This reason is hardly appealing, especially when compared to the 'point of a gun style' so evident in the Soviet Union. The second platform of this thesis is that ordinary worker-savers indulged in sweat and sacrifice, implying a willingness for long, hard hours of work and a willingness to save. Such personal commitment to deferred consumption (a low rate of time preference), underpinned the growth experience by providing a continual pool of workers and funds for commerce and industry. The third platform is that of the importance and inevitability of diminishing returns setting in and causing growth rates to eventually slow and assume more OECD levels. Long run growth can only be achieved via know-how and technological impetus in a KY world. The fourth platform focuses on the notion that TFP growth is in fact driven by technological progress as per the neo-classical model, although not an exogenous force, but one that economic agents can affect. Hence research, property rights, being first and being innovative are the wellspring of TFP growth. The fifth platform is concerned with the prediction that the Asian miracle must soon run out of steam as the simple accumulation process comes to an end and as a technological gulf between Asia and the rest of the developed world still remains. The diffusion of knowledge is not a 'given' and there is some evidence to suggest that technological convergence has not occurred between the Asian NIE's and the developed world. (Kim and Lau,1994) Therefore Asia may not be able to rely on current efficiency gains to drive its future growth process.

However, all of these platforms are contestable. The first of rapid accumulation is not well explained, as to why EA growth was more rapid than the modern world has ever seen. An exogenous driving force is more likely rather than force or coercion and so accumulation may have been as much the result of export growth as it was the cause of economic growth. The second, of preferences driving accumulation and so the 'miracle,' not ordinary sweat and sacrifice, but super-normal preferences for deferred gratification, is also questionable. Such super-human behavior is unlikely, but what is more likely is the molding of these preferences and the response of rational economic agents to a set of super-normal incentives, that agents in the OECD never enjoyed. Super rates of return from exports constitute such incentives. The third, of diminishing returns setting in, is over pessimistic as the MPK is not doomed to fall to minuscule levels. It is the value of the MPK (MRP) via exports that provides the offset, prolonging the delay of diminishing returns setting in. Fourthly, the KY presumption of accumulation being the driving force in the transition, and technological progress in the steady state, as being the only avenues to growth is over simplistic. Neither of these factors are the likely causes of this miracle, as trade is so dominant in response to a unique set of opportunities. In short, the KY attempt of rationalizing Asia's economic triumphs to mere accumulation is nothing but a misguided faith in a Solow model for 'all occasions'. As Knox-Lovell and Tang (1998,p39) point out, it may be that sound macroeconomic management has acted as substitute for productivity growth in East Asia's case and in particular Singapore. They state "It is clear that 1997 was not about productivity growth, but about the quality of macroeconomic management." Whether a super economic incentives, allocative and technical efficiency or sound macroeconomic management, it becomes obvious that the KY thesis is need of reconcilation.

3-5 TFP: Trade Driven?

Given that technological progress is not a major determinant of growth for East Asia, the relatively high TFP growth and contribution estimates by some authors are in need of explanation. Other driving forces may be at work. Exactly what explains the size and chemistry of TFP growth? The traditional reasons given are technological in nature, as know how is transmitted between nations across time. An alternative view is of TFP growth being driven by trade, and in particular exports to the West. There already exists evidence pointing to a strong relationship between exports and TFP growth, as revealed by the World Bank (1993,p324). For example, microeconomic studies from Korea, Taiwan and China display a significant correlation between export growth and the pattern of productivity change. For example, Chen , Hsu and Chen (1998) find that Taiwan's exports have a strong and significant effect on technical efficiency. Dessus (1998) finds that outward orientation and trade via technology laden imports are more closely related to TFP growth in Taiwan.

Pack and Page (1994) pursue this avenue of export-driven TFP and show strong support for such a hypothesis. However, their claim is that technical efficiency from export-led growth and not allocative efficiency is the key channel driving 'TFP' growth. This constitutes a movement inside the PPF and not a shift outward.

Consider the following hypothetical example clarifying allocative efficiency. If Malaysia produces an extra five T shirts in a year and sells them domestically for one Ringgit, then the extra GDP would be measured as an extra five Ringgit (or say 5%). However, if only four of these T shirts are sold domestically for one Ringit and one T shirt is sold to the US market for 6 Ringit, then the measured increase in Malaysian GDP would be ten Ringit (or 10%). Increased *physical* production is the same in both cases, in a closed versus an open economy. In this example, there is no sign of technological advancement, no increase in technical efficiency or T shirt quality and hence no TFP by any strict definition. However, there has been a superior growth performance, measured in domestic currency in the open economy. What can explain this extra 5% of measured growth? The answer rests in a high financial return variable (P>ATC), driven by a high international price level that rests above Malaysia's price level. Hence, international allocative efficiency is the key to understanding the Solow residuals in an East Asian setting. The Krugman-Young view of modest technology growth may be plausible, but an 'unexplained' force is still at work driving either the Solow residuals or the accumulation process.

Hence, the measurement of TFP is biased upwards, as a measure of technological progress, in a world of unequal partners and unequal prices, driven by super profits from exports and the height of international prices. Although a high contribution of TFP to growth in East Asia is driven by these value effects from trade, there is also a massive domestic supply production response. The former is a financial element and the latter real element of the TFP story, but both reflect allocative efficiency. The first occurs by international allocative efficiency and the second by technical catch up efficiency. Instead of an explanation of TFP, the pursuit should be for an explanation of total value productivity (TVP). An emphasis that seeks to incorporate the international price impetus to the value of domestic production and financial returns to the factor inputs, not just the physical dimension that ignores price or profit differences.

A recent study by Gapinski (1997) reinforces the World Bank view of the strong relationship between TFP and trade. In a model that employs trade as the 'shift factor' instead of technology and discerns between the quantity and quality of capital and labour, in vintage terms, the results came down heavily in favour of trade-driven TFP. As can be seen from Table 3-5 the contribution of TFP to growth is 62.5% and quantities 37.5% for the 9 Asian nations under study, on average. The contribution of TFP for the four OECD nations is, on average, around 40% and 60% for quantities. However, the importance of trade driving TFP is far more important for the Asian nations, around 70% and only 30% for qualities. This should not be surprising as mature economies do experience improvement in their vintage capital and human capital over time. By contrast, East Asian economies have relied on trade and allocative efficiency far more than mature economies as 'the offsetting factor' to the constraint of diminishing returns on growth.

3-6 Export-Led Growth

The export led growth (ELG) hypothesis gains support from earlier research efforts by Balassa (1978), Feder (1983) and Michaely (1977) that focus on cross-country data. More recent research, using time-series data, yields more mixed results. For example, Chow (1987) finds bi-directional causality between exports and growth for Brazil, Hong Kong, Israel, Korea, Singapore and Taiwan. Jung and Marshall (1985) find support for ELG in only four countries out of 37 developing countries. Bahmani-Oskooee et al (1991) find limited support for ELG in only five out of 20 developed countries. More support for ELG is found in Chowdrey (1998), who tests 14 Asia Pacific countries and finds that 75% of this sample reveals export-led growth under a final prediction error (FPE) criterion. Research by the World Bank (1993) finds strong evidence of manufactured goods exports being a major contributor to economic growth in the case of 10 high performing East Asian economies between 1960-1985.

From a theoretical perspective, why would exports make a significant contribution to economic growth? By expanding the size of

Table 3-5

Share Estimates of Output and Growth

Country	Output Share Quantities	Growth Due to TFP	Share Growth Qualities	Of TFP Due to Trade
H.Kong	44.4	55.6	18.2	81.8
Indonesia	70.4	29.6	42.7	57.3
Japan	70.5	29.5	62.7	37.3
Korea	68.8	31.2	49.4	50.6
Malaysia	60.6	39.4	33.9	66.1
Philippines	68.6	31.4	28.2	71.8
S'pore	43.3	56.7	12.6	87.4
Taiwan	63.7	36.3	38.3	61.7
Thailand	70.6	29.4	28.1	71.9
USA	64.3	35.7	70.9	29.1
Australia	64.4	35.6	52.5	47.5
N.Z.	51.0	49.0	40.7	59.3
P.N.Guinea	49.5	50.5	18.0	81.9

Source: Gapinski (1998, p. 134)

the market, economies of scale are harnessed and capacity utilization increased, but these are more likely 'one shot,' static gains to productivity. More dynamic gains stem from exposure to international discipline that lifts product quality and variety and by adopting world best practice that interacts positively with human capital. Increased technical efficiency, learning by doing, learning by watching and increased profitability driving domestic savings are also dynamic forces that raise productivity.

However, there are financial benefits from interacting with mature economy markets. Exposure to a higher international price level also raises export sales by value and so stimulates rates of return, with the added benefits of relaxing the foreign exchange constraint and allowing easier access to overseas credit markets. From this financial perspective, super profits drive super growth.

3-7 Income Convergence: Conflicting Predictions

Old growth theory, in the form of the Solow model, predicts absolute income convergence amongst nations due to the property of diminishing returns and the Inada conditions. Poorer nations, with relatively low K/L ratios, will grow faster than rich nations with relatively high K/L ratios. The assumption of the neo classical model is that all nations share similar tastes and microeconomic parameters and by allowing market forces to work nations should indeed converge in income per head over time. This model predicts that an economy will converge to its own steady state and the speed of such convergence is inversely related to the distance from that steady state. As the world has become a global village, access to world markets and the world's technology should only reinforce such convergence.

It should be noted however, that the concept of income convergence is not some automatic force - there are prerequisites. According to the neo-classical paradigm, all nations must possess some type of competitive economy, share similar economic fundamentals and in particular, have access to the same international technology; in short, allowing markets to work and being 'open' (Helliwell and Chung,1991). Other authors, (eg Baily and Schultz,1990) point to similar levels of education, of technology and social systems as being the starting points for convergence. It also should be noted that government policies toward property rights, taxation, money growth, capital and technology flows are key determinants of the above economic fundamentals. A supportive role played by government in fostering private sector aspirations becomes important as stable, well-known rules of the game are crucial for long-term investment.

Not only does the Solow model predict income convergence but so do leader-follower models that rely on discoveries and technological diffusion to filter from richer to poorer nations. Leader nations focus on innovation, while follower nations focus on imitation and adaptation on basis of the costs of the latter being far lower and attainable. It is diminishing returns to imitation, rather than to innovation or capital, that generate conditional convergence. Hence, poorer nations moving to world best practice will cause income convergence.

Endogenous growth models claim that major forces are at work to yield divergence in per capita incomes amongst the nations. In the Romer model, diminishing returns may not occur, if research yields 'new knowledge' and specialized inputs generate lower unit costs and increase productivity gains via knowledge spillovers. Growth may then be a cumulative process, an increasing function of the stock of knowledge and monopoly profits. In the AK model, there are no transitional dynamics, as the exponent on capital is one and the MPK is constant, not diminishing. Both the short run and long-run growth rates are the same, driven by parameters that affect the willingness to save and invest. Government policies and preferences for work over leisure and saving over consumption may cause some nations to grow faster than others. In the Grossman and Helpman model (1991), the concept of 'growth poles' is illustrated, whereby wealthier nations maintain their power, affluence and knowledge at the expense of aspiring developing nations trapped in exporting low value added or price inelastic agricultural goods. According to this view, integration into world trade and capital markets only enhances richer-nation prospects for more exploitation; thus the rich get richer and the poor get poorer.

3-8 The Evidence

At first glance, the evidence on income convergence paints a negative picture; that is, poorer nations have, in general, failed to catch up to richer nations. For example, Dowrick (1992) examined the period 1960-1988, using the Penn World Tables for 113 nations and concluded that some of the poorest world economies have been on a divergent growth path, leading to increased inequality in per capita output. For example, the poorer nations grew by 1.36%, the middle nations by 2.16% and the rich nations by 2.49% during this period. However, this cross-country study did reveal a statistically significant catch up term across the whole sample, but the higher investment rates and lower population growth rates of richer countries may have camouflaged the catch-up tendency.

The convergence hypothesis itself claims that per capita growth rates should be negatively related to the starting level of per capita income – ceteris paribus. Barro (1990) claims that the correlation is close to zero for 98 nations from 1960-85, thereby refuting the hypothesis in its simple form. Further pessimism is raised by Sheehan (1992) when he claims that inequalities in income levels and growth rates for a broad category of nations are as distinctive at the end of the 20th Century as they were at the end of the 19th. However, there are signs of income convergence amongst the richer group of nations, namely the OECD. The major channel appears to have been via technological catch up, meaning higher multi-factor productivity amongst the poorer OECD nations (Helliwell and Chung,1991). Evidence by Baumol (1986) also supports convergence for the OECD between 1870-1979. Most convergence occurred after WW II with divergence before the war.

Lau and Sin (1993) claim that in both the Solow and Romer models the time series of log output and log capital stock per capita should be co-integrated. However, the co-integrating relationship for the Solow model should be trend stationary and for the Romer model it should be stationary without a trend. They find endogenous growth for Germany, UK and the USA, but exogenous growth for Japan. This is not a damning case against income convergence as the first three nations had already roughly converged in income by the 1970's.

There have been signs of income convergence for OECD nations since 1950 as Table 3-6 reveals. For example, Austria's income per head was only 34.4% of US income in 1950 but had reached 72.2% by 1992. Other European nations experienced similar escalations in their percentages of US income by 1992. What of Asian nations? Many of the East Asian nations have enjoyed a marked degree of income convergence with USA as Table 3-6 reveals. For example, Hong Kong's percentage of US income rose from 58.3% in 1960 to 91.8% and Singapore from 46% to 70.5% in 1992. While East Asian nations may not have converged as closely as European nations have by 1992, the speed of convergence in many cases has been faster. This has been 'catch-up' growth at its best.

Table 3-6

Per Capita Incomes As A Percentage Of Us Income

Europe/OECD

	1950	1960	1970	1980	1992
Austria	34.4	52.9	59.4	70.1	72.2
Australia	78.5	80.6	85.8	73.6	80.6
Belgium	52.1	57.1	66.4	75.2	75.1
Canada	74.2	69.0	80.0	94.3	91.2
Denmark	60.9	69.0	76.0	74.4	78.5
France	48.1	61.5	75.6	78.1	77.6
Finland	41.6	54.9	64.8	72.3	66.9
Germany	40.2	67.9	75.1	79.6	82.0
Greece	16.1	21.3	33.2	39.0	38.6
Italy	32.5	47.4	60.3	69.3	70.9
Luxembourg	77.4	82.9	78.6	79.7	93.6
Netherlands	52.9	62.6	72.5	75.0	74.0
N.Z.	76.7	81.0	73.5	68.0	63.3
Sweden	66.6	76.6	83.6	81.4	77.9
Switzerland	81.2	98.5	100.4	97.0	88.5
U.K.	60.2	67.0	60.5	66.4	70.9

Source: Penn World Tables 5.5

3-9 Income Convergence - In Need of a Reconciliation

Barro (1991) finds support for the conditional income convergence hypothesis after adjusting for the initial level of human capital. For a given starting level of per capita income, a nation's future growth rate is positively related to the initial level of human capital. After adjusting for these human capital levels, subsequent growth is then negatively related to the initial level of per capita income. This supports a modified income convergence hypothesis.

But why would one expect the level of human capital to play such a vital role in achieving rapid 'catch-up' growth? Barro (1991) cites reasons of spillover benefits via the generation, introduction and absorption of new ideas. A higher initial stock of human capital is complementary to investment in physical investment. More human capital also tilts the bias in favour of producing goods and more human capital rather than children.

Thus, in Barro's model the initial stock of human capital is the key complementary element to the low K/L ratio in generating growth.

The World Bank (1993,p50) also acknowledges the fact that the convergence hypothesis in its purest form must be rejected by the available evidence. However, they also claim that 'conditional convergence' is a more apt hypothesis and is supported by the evidence. The advantage of backwardness is only a necessary condition for rapid growth, while other sufficient conditions, such as the attainment of education and investment levels, must also be met. The World Bank sees universal primary education as an important initial condition for growth, again supporting Barro's work on human capital.

A somewhat traditional neoclassical model, modified by the inclusion of human capital, is employed by the World Bank. Traditional variables such as the average share of investment in GDP, primary and secondary school enrolments and the economically active population are used. The not-so-traditional variable of relative income per head compared to the US in 1960, as an indicator of catch up growth, is also used.

However, Romer (1994,p10) notes the agreement of researchers concerning the facts, "everyone agrees that a conventional neoclassical model with an exponent of about one third on capital and about two thirds on labour cannot fit the cross-country or cross-state data. Everyone agrees that the marginal productivity of investment cannot be of the orders of magnitudes smaller in rich countries than in poor countries."

Table 3-7

Per Capita Incomes as a Percentage of US Income(Asia)

	1950	1960	1970	1980	1992
China	-	-	-	-	-
H.Kong	-	22.6	35	58.3	91.8
Indonesia	-	6.4	5.5	8.3	11.7
Japan	17.3	31.0	58.9	68.1	84.2
Korea	-	9.3	13.3	20.7	41.2
Malaysia	-	14.6	16.6	25.0	32.0
Philippines	8.8	11.4	10.8	12.4	9.4
Singapore	-	17.5	24.8	46.0	70.5
Taiwan	11.1	14.1	18.7	32.0	46.2
Thailand	9.8	9.5	11.6	14.2	22.0
Bangladesh	-	8.1	7.6	7.3	8.4
India	6.0	6.8	5.5	5.1	7.1
Myanmar	2.4	3.0	3.1	3.1	-
Nepal	-	6.1	5.0	5.5	-
N.Guinea	-	11.5	13.7	11.1	8.9
Pakistan	6.7	6.3	7.8	7.1	8.0
Sri Lanka	12.5	13.1	10.3	12.3	12.3

Source: Penn World Tables 5.5

Romer's major reason for the neoclassical model's poor predictive power is the assumption that the level of technology is identical for all nations.

It is therefore crucial to allow for a divergence between private and social returns, so knowledge spillovers that may be captured at low or zero cost. An increase in K or L has an external effect on the shift factor A in a Romer type model. Firm j has control over variables with subscripts but not those without, as these represent economy-wide totals.

$$Y_j \quad = \quad A(K, L)\, K_j^{\,1-\alpha}\, L_j^{\,\alpha} \tag{3-9}$$

$$A(K, L) \quad = \quad K^{\gamma} L^{-\gamma} \tag{3-10}$$

$$Y \quad = \quad K^{1-\beta}\, L^{\beta} \qquad \text{(where } \beta = \alpha - \gamma) \tag{3-11}$$

The firm only takes into account the private effect α not the aggregate effect $\alpha - \gamma$ when making decisions. In order to make sense of the cross-country data, the theoretical challenge is to explain why labor is paid more than its marginal product and capital is paid less. Romer (1994) employs a spillover model, whereby there are divergences between social and private returns. Increased capital investment, with embodied knowledge, not only raises the stock of physical capital but also the stock of knowledge across all firms in the economy. Conversely, increased labour supply creates negative spillover effects by reducing incentives and stifling the quest for discovering labour-saving innovations. Romer (1994) estimates β, the aggregate effect of employment on output to be around 0.25, an estimate that explains cross-country variations in income more effectively.

Mankiw, Romer and Weil (1992) employ a pure version neo-classical model with strict assumptions, a closed economy, identical technology across nations, depreciation rates and capital shares that are the same for all nations. While the predicted signs on population growth rates and savings rates are correct, the size of α (capital share/elasticity) appears 'too low,' so these estimates could not adequately explain the cross-country data. By introducing human capital, the exponent on the fixed factor (unskilled) labor falls from 0.6 to 0.33, more in line with national accounts data, and so this 'augmented' Solow model is more capable of explaining differences in cross-country income. By including investment in human, as well as physical capital, this kind of model can explain why an enormous amount of investment is not required in a developed country to offset the explosiveness of the MPK in a developing country in order to achieve similar growth rates. In this model, a threefold increase in investment can achieve this result which is in line with the Summers and Heston data set.

Another attempt at explaining the variations of incomes in the cross-country data is made by Barro and Xavier Sali Martin (1992), who employ a model that assumes the level of technology is different amongst the nations, perhaps driven by history and institutions, and is slow to diffuse across national boundaries. Therefore, per capita output may be lower in some countries as technological capabilities are also lower, further reducing the explosiveness of MPK (driven by a low K/L ratio). Transitional dynamics of the Solow model are less potent and less relevant in this 'technology gap' framework, as it is the diffusion of knowledge from the leader to the follower country that causes income convergence. Nations are more likely to converge on their 'own' steady state, dictated by their own level of technology, rather than the international steady state, in the medium term. The reason why capital does not flow to equalize rates of return between nations is because of the significant offsetting influence of lower technology levels (human capital) that impact on realizable and effective rates of return.

3-10 What Are the Weaknesses of Existing Growth Theory?

From a theoretical perspective, there are some major shortcomings of old growth theory. Firstly, the Solow Model presumes a closed economy whereby trade, multinational power and mobile international capital are largely ignored. These are crucial omissions in an East Asian context where many economies are 'open' and trade in volume.

Secondly, the production function assumes diminishing returns to each factor and constant returns to scale. The former assumption may apply in the 'short run,' but in East Asia's case, this transition phase may be very long indeed, as the K/L ratio rises from a very low base. The latter assumption ensures that both capital and labour are paid their marginal products, but precludes any reward being paid for purposeful research, innovation or entrepreneurial risk.

Thirdly, analysis in the Solow Model is couched in terms of 'reals', a production theoretic approach that seeks to measure the marginal physical product of capital (MPPK). The law of one price prevails and only normal profits are made. To the extent that a divergence exists between price and marginal cost, there exists super-normal profits reflecting a higher value of MPPK or higher marginal revenue product (MRP). Hence, an explosive MPK as a function of a low K/L ratio may be capturing a value component stemming from persistent super normal profits.

Fourthly, from a policy perspective the Solow Model is silent about where 'exogenous' technological progress emanates from and so provides only vague guidance as to what initiatives the policy maker should instigate to promote growth. Stimulating general research, without knowing 'how' technological progress is generated, remains only a broad growth initiative. In fact, the Solow residuals are claimed to represent total factor productivity (TFP) driven by technological progress, but other competing explanations are possible in the short to medium term, such as improvements in management, organizational and labour relations.

This book seeks to highlight the notion that TFP has a value component driven by the wide divergence between world prices and relatively low East Asian marginal costs. Thus, TFP change is not just a measurement of extra physical product but also the value of that extra product.

Several predictive weaknesses of the Solow model also exist. Firstly, poor nations enjoying a low K/L ratio should catch up, in terms of income per head, or converge on richer nations restricted by a relatively high K/L ratio (implied by the Inada conditions and diminishing returns of the model). Only 'conditional convergence,' not absolute convergence has been found by Barro (1991). Others such as Pritchett (1997) find divergence. Secondly, the model predicts rapid convergence and short transitions. If $\alpha = 1/3$, as per the national account estimates, then the speed of convergence would have to be in the order of 5 to 6% and a half life catch up of around 12.5 years.[10] The empirical evidence does not support such speed or short transition.

Thirdly, savings and investment 'appear' to cause 'growth' in a large cross section of countries, against the prediction of the model if 30 years is considered to be long term.

A major criticism of new growth theory is that it is not clearly testable and so suffers from observational equivalence, particularly at the aggregate level. Along many dimensions it is an extension of existing theory that has elucidated important microeconomic underpinnings of rational economic agent behavior.[11]

3-11 What are the Links between Growth and Trade Theory?

Several growth models have similar counterpart trade models. The innovation and product-ladder models of Grossman and Helpman (1990) are but product-cycle trade models (Vernon,1966) that focus on profit-based innovation. New products are invented in developed nations. These eventually become 'standardized' products that are shifted 'offshore' for production in developing countries, while 'non-standardized' products (high value added) are produced and exported from the developed country. Product ladders are a result of the above product cycle and represent new waves of opportunity to secure monopoly profits. Such models help explain *dynamic* comparative advantage. Trade and growth for both developed and developing countries are mutually dependent and reinforcing in these models.

The technological gap (imitation) models of growth theory (Krugman,1979; Segerstrom,1991) have their counterpart in trade theory, as in Posner (1961). In these leader-follower models, new products offer a temporary monopoly to the innovating firm in the developed nation and so stimulate both domestic sales and exports. It is assumed that the cost of innovation is considerably higher than the cost of imitation and that the speed of catch up growth diminishes as the technology gap closes. While the laggard nation may acquire 'frontier knowledge' reasonably cheaply, it has the incentive to export to mature economies as its unit costs are far lower, driven by lower labour costs.

Differences in technology (Romer,1990) and human capital (Lucas,1988) stimulate labour productivity growth, which is also the key determinant of trade in the Ricardian trade model. Ricardo was not explicit as to the forces that caused differences in labor productivity between nations but hinted at technology and climate as being key causes. New growth theory has partly filled this void. What remains is the common driving force of both trade and growth in these models.

The Solow model, with its emphasis on the K/L ratio for medium term growth, is not that dissimilar to the Hecksher- Ohlin model in trade theory, as a low K/L ratio (due to abundant labour) drives the export of labour-intensive goods. Hence, for a developing nation, the low K/L ratio is a vehement impetus to both economic growth and exports. Therefore, a small export-orientated economy, in a world of unequal income partners can exploit low unit costs in labour-intensive goods to achieve catch-up growth with OECD nations. Low unit costs are a proxy for high relative profits in the H-O-model, while a low K/L ratio is a proxy for a high MPK in the Solow model, that is rates of return under a different cape.

Dissatisfaction with the Solow model's reliance on constant returns to scale and normal profits, prompted the proliferation of growth models favoring increasing returns to scale and monopoly profits. A declining average cost curve provides incentive to the innovating firm to sell in volume and so cover initial set-up fixed costs. Helpman, Krugman and Lancaster (1979) point out that increasing returns to scale create an additional trade advantage over the pre-trade relative costs determinant employed by the H-O-model, particularly in intra-industry trade. Low unit costs hold the key for both sustainable long-term growth and trade. It should not be forgotten that Ricardo emphasized low unit costs (labor productivity differences), as does the H-O-model (factor endowment differences), as does the increasing returns models. In fact, most types of trade models, either explicitly or implicitly, emphasize low unit costs.

However, the centrality of low unit costs is sometimes lost in growth theory or at least remains in the background. The engines of growth are often referred to as the number of researchers, research and development expenditure, human capital (measured by schooling rates), technology, saving and investment. More recently, the recognition of monopoly profits protected by patents and the spreading of expensive fixed costs has signaled a reorientation to a financial perspective of growth. A growing and greater synthesis of trade with growth theory offers hope of a re-emphasis of low unit costs and super profits that will better explain modern growth phenomena. This may be as much the domain of competitive advantage as it is comparative advantage.

3-12 Growth Theory: Where From Here?

The importance of supply side factors, specifically technological progress, driving long-run sustainable growth is central to both old and new growth theory. Key engines of growth such as capital per worker (Solow,1956), human capital (Lucas,1988), monopoly profits and new knowledge (Romer,1990), product ladders and innovation (Grossman and Helpman,1991), catch-up technical efficiency (Pack and Page,1994), equipment investment (De Long and Summers,1991), respect for property rights and macroeconomic stability are all supply-side determinants.

In contrast, development theory focuses on trade (World Bank,1993), openness (Dollar,1991), hard currency (Esfahani,1991) and price differentials in a world of unequal partners. Demand stimuli are used to explain rapid development *in the medium term*. There are two price/cost levels, generating monopolistic type profits, when the developing world interfaces with the developed world via trade and capital flows. However, the divergence between price and marginal cost is not caused by the wedge of patents or secret, excludable knowledge as in the Romer Model but by product differentiation, price illusion and inertia in developed countries as well as by vast price/cost differentials caused by history.

The following Table 3-8 seeks to illustrate the theoretical growth dichotomy outlined in this chapter. The focus of this study is to explain why manufactured exports are a potent source of economic growth. In some ways existing trade and development theory is re-married to growth theory in the form of 'stages of development', product cycles, hard currency, first-mover advantage and monopolistic profits. However, a greater extension is required to marry relative prices, international allocative efficiency, low unit costs, the low level of the real exchange rate, competitive advantage and exports responding to an exogenous demand-side stimulus to growth theory.

This study highlights the importance of above 'growth theory dichotomy' and seeks to distinguish the driving forces of growth for developed countries from those of developing countries, such as those of East Asia.

Table 3-8

The Growth Theory Dichotomy

Production Theoretic		Financial Theoretic
Old Theory	New Theory	Relative Price Theory
Reals	Reals	Value
Closed Economy	Closed and Open	Open Economy
Developed Economy	Developed and Developing	Developing Ec.
One Price Level	One Price Level	Price Diffs
P=MC	P>MC	P>AC
Normal Profits	Monopoly Profits	Monopolistic P's
Con. Rets to Scale	Increasing Returns	Constant Returns
Social Returns = Private	Social Returns>Private	Soc. Rets=Private
K/L ratio	Broad Capital	P/P ratios
No externalities	Externalities	Externalities
MPK	MPK	MRP
TFP - Exogenous	TFP - Endogenous	TVP - Exog.
TFP - Tech Driven	TFP - Technology Driven	TVP - Trade
Technological Progress	Technological /Technical Progress	Allocative Eff.
Exogenous Growth	Endogenous Growth	Exogenous Growth
$S \rightarrow I \rightarrow Y \rightarrow X \rightarrow S$	$S \rightarrow I \rightarrow Y \rightarrow X \rightarrow S$	$X \rightarrow Y \rightarrow S \rightarrow I \rightarrow X$

3-13 Why Do Some Nations Miss the Shuttle Ride?

Given that manufactured exports are a short-cut to achieving rapid economic growth and acceleration in the WSM, it begs the question as to why so many developing nations have not emulated what EA has done. The Cold War explains why some nations chose not to export to the West or at least were not encouraged. However, many other developing nations failed to mount a sufficient supply-side response to match this massive demand-side opportunity. Reasons vary, but a lack of macroeconomic stability, a lack of respect for property rights and weak economic, financial and social institutions are some reasons for such a poor supply-side response. Social capability or competence were lacking, which prevented the realization of lucrative profit opportunities from trade with the West. This study acknowledges the importance of supply-side responses both ex ante and ex post, but the central focus of this study is on *why* the growth processes of those developing nations that have exported to the US have been so explosive—ex post. It is the *realization* of the demand-side opportunity via exports that is understudy not why other nations have lagged. As per the Solow model, thresholds are important – prerequisites that must be met in order for a potentially high MPK to be realized.

3-14 Conclusion

While there have been numerous attempts to explain East Asia's rapid growth experience, most have met with limited success or credibility. The technology channel has not been relevant for most of the time period under consideration, 1960-1995. East Asian nations, in general, possess relatively low levels of human capital and scientific expertise, eventhough these levels have risen in recent years. A research view lacks credibility in the light of the nature of goods produced and exported during this period. The accumulation-of-inputs view has become popular, but lacks microeconomic under pinning, other than of sweat and sacrifice. A low capital-labour ratio and the marginal efficiency of investment is a more water-tight story, but hits a credibility gap in explaining the sheer explosiveness of both rates of return and growth, beyond that of the developed world in its heyday of growth.

Given the characteristics of East Asia's growth experience (cited in Chapter One), a more plausible explanation, rests in the trade and openness view. There is a strong case for arguing the power of export growth driving economic growth, not for the traditional reasons given of knowledge flows, technology adoption and the building of human capital but for the financial reasons of super-profits, higher foreign than domestic prices, allocative efficiency, hard currency and vast impetus given to domestic savings rates. Policy initiatives and development strategies crucially depend on why exports have such an explosive impact on rates of return and the MPK. The purpose of the next chapter is to articulate a model that captures the importance of export-led growth and the financial variables identified in this chapter.

Chapter Four

Penetrating Western Markets

4-1 Introduction

In Chapter Three, the potency of exports in driving economic growth was examined from a theoretical perspective. Within the framework of the Western Shuttle Model, the rocket engines of super-profits and hard currency were identified as the catalysts propelling transitional super-growth in EA. The underlying forces or fuels so important for economic lift-off (profits) rest with vast cost and wealth differentials between EA and the USA. Hence, catch-up economic growth is driven by a super-export push to mature economy markets. This chapter ties an imperfect substitutes model of export growth to an imperfect competition model of economic growth, outlined in Chapter Three. Monopolistic type profits are exogenously driven, as world prices lay above domestic costs in EA. Although *changes* in US activity and the real exchange rate are statistically significant for EA exporters, such a methodology is fraught with danger when vast differences in cost and income levels exist. In Chapter Two, the importance of a set of international relative prices or costs overwhelming relative productivities were sighted as a major determinant of international competitiveness for developing countries. This chapter pursues the hypothesis that changes in competitiveness and US activity can only partially explain EA's export drive into the US market as vast differences in costs and incomes remain major catalysts of sustained export performance.

4-2 An Old Link Challenged

It was Arthur Lewis (1980) who claimed that trade was the *exogenous engine* of growth for developing countries – at least until the early part of this century. The fuel of growth for the developing countries, according to Lewis, was the growth of industrial production in the West. There was an almost mechanical link between industrial growth in the OECD (producing industrial goods) and trade growth in the developing world of producing primary products) of 0.87. That is, for every 1 per cent rise in industrial growth in the West there was a corresponding 0.87 per cent rise in exports of primary products. In this locomotive story, it is the volume of exports that is pulled along – as income elasticities dominate low price elasticities for those exports.

This mechanistic interdependence was challenged by Riedal (1984) who pointed to the transformation taking place in developing country exports from the 1960's onwards towards manufactured goods and the instability of the relationship for all goods. Moreover, Reidal (1988) questioned the 'price elasticity pessimism' foundation of the Lewis hypothesis; that is, the demand curve may be more elastic than suggested and as a consequence supply responses take on a dominant role in explaining sustained export success.

The battlefield of this debate appears to be whether income growth in the US (a demand-side explanation) is of greater importance than a domestic production (supply-side explanation) of export growth. Both of these models are couched in terms of elasticities and so ignore the levels of variables. According to the WSM, relative levels of cost, price and income are important for catch-up, transitional super-export growth and not just changes changes at the margin. Hence, a demand-side force generates a significant sustained response in export growth to mature economy markets so long as levels remain divergent.

4-3 Models Used to Explain Export Volumes

The literature provides basically two choices of models: a perfect substitutes or an imperfect substitutes model, to explain the determinants of export growth. The former model is based on exported goods being perfect substitutes for other goods made world-wide. In the case of developing nations exporting to developed nations, the foreign export demand curve is elastic - implying vast opportunities to sell in foreign markets without deflating world prices. This amounts to the use of a 'small country assumption' and the implication that developing country producers are price takers on world markets. Moreover, a developing nation's export supply schedule is price responsive. This is a supply-side explanation of developing country export growth.

The policy implication of this model is that a developing country may raise its competitiveness on the basis of price. This may imply lowering unit costs, suppressing inflation more effectively than trade competitors and/or lowering the nominal exchange rate.

On the other hand, the imperfect substitutes model emphasizes the importance of product differentiation and the ability to influence prices, implying that the foreign demand curve is not perfectly elastic but downward sloping. It is the supply curve that is perfectly elastic - at least by assumption. In essence, this implies that these exporters, are to some extent, price makers. What is of critical importance in this model is the rightward shift of the *foreign* demand curve that may be interpreted as an export income elasticity.

The policy implication of such a model is that the policy maker needs to monitor trends in foreign markets and the level of foreign demand. Any adverse changes in world activity may seriously impact on exports and domestic growth. Another implication is that moving up the product ladder and improving product quality raises the probability of producing highly income elastic goods. Policies toward education and on the job training assist in capturing high foreign income elasticities. Even though developing countries may appear dependent on world income *growth* there is an offset in terms of penetrating world markets on the basis of upward product ladder movement.

Both of these models explain why 'elasticity pessimism' may not be relevant to developing countries experiencing rapid export growth rates. The terms of trade may not decline as export volumes increase. Why? The perfect substitutes school of Athorakala-Reidal (AR) point to the validity of the small country assumption and so the law of one price. Small nations do not affect world prices - they are given. More importantly, export supply price elasticities are high and so export volumes are responsive to even small price changes. The imperfect substitutes school of Muscatelli,Srinavasan and Vines (MSV:1992) point to the fortuitous high income elasticities offsetting low price elasticities of demand. A nation may not be able to affect its own price competitiveness but can idulge in greater product differentation to capture high foreign income elasticities. A bouyant world economy pulls along developing country export growth.

4-4 Literature Review

An extensive survey by Reidal (1988,p140) makes him conclude that whether for developed or developing countries, or for country aggregates or individual countries, price elasticities generally lie in the range of-0.5 to -1.0 and income elasticities fall between 2 and 4. The literature finds the income term to be dominant over the price term in a consistent manner. According to the above estimates, a rise in US income of one percent could cause anywhere from a two to four percent rise in EA's exports. A change in the relative price term, known as the real exchange rate, holds less importance as it has a relatively low elasticity of around one. These latter elasticity estimates create an air of *elasticity pessimism* whereby nations seeking to grow and expand exports are inhibited from using a price competitiveness tool to suppress their own exchange rates in the hope that their exports will appear more attractive on world markets.

An alternate methodology is employed by AR to test the small country assumption. A price dependent, rather than a volume dependent, equation is employed which supports the hypothesis that price elasticities are high and income elasticities are low for Hong Kong exports. Hence, the traditional demand-side view of export success is replaced with a supply-side view of price responsiveness. Hence, elasticities matter.

The MSV camp rejects the small country assumption and the law of one price. They revisit the Hong Kong data set and the 'price equation' model used by Reidal to claim that price elastcities are low (-2.14) and income elastcities are high (3.78). They find support for long run supply elasticities of 7.2 , similar to that of Reidal of 6.05. However, they still cling to the demand equation as being a volume-adjustment equation and not a price adjustment equation as espoused by AR. Export income elasticities remain high and so foreign demand is essential for developing country export success.

4-5 A Reconciliation

What is common to the view of AR and MSV is that developing country exports do penetrate Western markets. This may not be due to *changes* in price competitiveness or *changes* in foreign income but rather to wealth accumulated in the West over 200 years. Hence the debate should not be couched in terms of the elasticity of the foreign demand curve or a shift in such a curve but its *height or position on the graph*. Neither the price nor the income elasticity is critical for EA export success but the vast income differentials between EA and the West. Export volumes respond to this vast income gap. Hence, an elasticities model may not be able to capture the determinants of export growth in a *world of unequal partners*.

As Western (1997,p62) points out, when a developed economy exports to a developed economy the export income elasticity is normal at around 2. When a developing economy exports to a developing economy the export income elasticity is around 1 to 2. Why? Because nations on *similar income levels* that trade together generate an export income elasticity that is normal. However, when a developing nation exports to a developed nation (on a higher income level) the export income elasticity is 4 or more. Vast differences in income and price levels partially determine export volumes.

This dichotomy in income elasticities between developed and developing nations has a precendent in the literature. As Marquez and McNeilly (1988,p306) noted, the export income elasticity estimates for countries exporting to the USA are dispersed over a wide range from 0.9 (for Reidal) to 4.7 (for Dornbusch). What also should be noted that there is an interesting *pattern* of elasticity estimates. It was Grossman (1982,p276) who that found it "surprising that income elasticities of demand for LDC imports were, in general, larger than those for DC imports" for certain manufactures into the US market. The simple average for LDC's was 3.07 but only 1.38 for DC's.

This brief overview of the conventional export modeling literature reveals two key features: foreign income elasticities dominate price elasticities and developing country export income elasticities dominate those of a developed country.

Even though export income elasticities appear potent and a demand-side explanation of export growth seems plausible, it was Riedal (1984) who challenged this conventional wisdom. He alleged simultaneity bias in the methodology and asked why would the same kind of machine imported from Korea rather than say, from, Germany into the US possess a vastly higher export income elasticity? Nations with high export growth rates also yield high export income elasticity estimates and vice versa. Hence, Reidal argues that the high export income elasticities are concealing important supply-side responses.

However, the mirror image of this interpretation is that a massive supply-side response is the *result* of massive differences in income and price levels. Thus, the dichotomy in the export income elasticities may not only reflect a statistical bias (as high export growth rates are correlated with high income elasticities) but may be more of a reflection of differences in incomes and costs. A massive supply-side *response* can only be realized in the face of a massive demand-side opportunity. Either high levels of foreign demand or higher foreign than domestic prices and hence export profits.[1]

In summary, what is common to both AR and MSV is that EA exporters have penetrated Western markets. The MSV view of an external demand side force driving export growth and that production differentiation is important in order to increase market shares in wealthy markets is plausible. However, this massive demand side force is a function of differences in income levels (demand side) and price levels (supply side) between EA and the West and not just elasticities. MSV maybe correct in arguing that *changes* in competitiveness count for little but overlook the importance of natural competitiveness in that the *unit cost gap* between EA and the West is wide in labour intensive goods. Price elasticities do not matter while this gap remains wide but competitiveness as such still remains important as determined by the distance of this gap. Besides product differentiation is not the only method of penetrating Western markets, as industries and product ranges in the West are displaced by cheaper counterparts. This is the product cycle model in disguise and so income elasticities may be overstated. AR are probably correct in arguing that changes in competitiveness matter *between* developing countries. This is the cross real exchange rate at work. This makes sense as there are many EA nations with cheap labour and so market shares in wealthy markets are a function of price competitiveness between themselves. Price elasticities still matter.

The overall unit cost gap between EA and the West determines the export opportunity for developing nations *collectively.* This is catch-up export growth. How such an opportunity is divided *between* developing nations is determined by price competitiveness. Both camps agree that the income elasticties appear overstated and so it is the case of an 'ommitted variable'. This study claims that such a variable is wealth or wide income differentials.

4-6 Japan: The Trodden Path

The work of Busche, Kravis and Lipsey (1986) highlights the importance of the shift in the export supply curve. They stumbled upon an important insight by finding that the export growth of Japan to the US can be largely explained by the regression constant before 1970. This constant represents a trend in export volume that is independent of the price and income variables. In fact, the US income variable and the constant compete for explanatory power. These authors estimate that the income variable may be left out completely and the equation still retain explanatory power – power which resides in the constant. In Japan's case, the constant explains a 16% export growth rate to the US by itself!

This is an important finding in that it reveals persistent trend growth in a developing country's exports to mature economy markets that may be caused by low market shares to begin with, holding domestic prices below world prices and shifting the export supply function to the right. However, Japan was a developing country itself in the 1940's and 50's with income and price levels well below that of the US and so a massive demand side opportunity existed to catch-up via export growth. Hence, the magnitude of the shift of the export supply curve was positively related to the magnitude of the difference in Japan-US costs. The massive (visible) supply-side response was but a reflection of a massive demand-side opportunity.

From the above study, it therefore follows that as Japan converged on US costs and incomes by the 1970's, there was less of a demand-side exogenous force at work driving Japan's export volumes. *Changes* in variables rather than differences in *levels* assumed importance after the mid-1970's, as changes in competitiveness at the margin became critical.

4-7 The Law of One Price

In the context of this study, there is an essential issue that needs to be addressed: it is the law of one price. What are the critical economic signals that are transmitted to the EA exporter? If the law of one price holds, then EA exporters benefit from wide profit margins delivered by world prices exceeding domestic costs. This is a *profit differential story.*[2] If the law of one price does not hold, then the EA exporter faces the prospect of segmenting markets and product lines in order to extract as much profit from these segmented markets as can be withstood. This is a *price differential story* that requires strategic planning to extract above normal profits.

Given the use of an imperfect substitutes model, the law of one price may be violated as the foreign import demand curve is not perfectly elastic. This curve can be downward sloping and prices may decline as export volumes increase, not only because of consumer preferences, brand loyalty and product differentiation but also because EA's cost and price levels are far lower than the world or US price level that creates the flexibility so necessary to 'price to market.' For persistent export growth to occur, the US foreign demand curve must reside appreciably higher than the EA's domestic demand curve for differences in price levels to send loud and clear signals for export. This nevertheless begs the question as to why the law of one (international) price for manufactured goods would not hold? Is there some type of money illusion going on? In these circumstances there are arbitragers at work seeking to buy at low prices and sell at high prices in mature economy markets. There is a price and cost convergence process in train, but it is spread across a matrix of a hundred nations all on different price levels: This is not a case of price or money illusion, as there are known and observable differences in prices. The problem is that it takes an enormous amount of time for the price levels of developing nations to rise to those of the developed world. Convergence of national price levels to an international price level takes place as investment and human capital rises in the developing world. Kydland and Prescott (1981) outline the 'time to build' problem.

In the author's view, the difference in price levels act as a catalyst for export growth, or if the law of one price holds, the differences in profit rates (driven by cost differentials) act as the same export catalyst but wearing a different cape. Even if the law of one price holds in manufactured goods, the law of one cost certainly does not. Even if the price differential story lacks credibility, the profit differential story does not. Neoclassical economists tend to ignore the power of these differentials as they claim that prices will converge in a large competitive market - if producers do not cause convergence, then arbitragers will.

EA exporters have enjoyed above-normal profits from exporting to rich mature markets, but such success brings with it feedback pains. Growth comes at a cost in terms of rising prosperity choking cost competitiveness, increased conflict over the distribution of income, tougher environmental standards and a more generous social welfare net.[3] Hence, super-export growth and the concomitant of super-economic growth is a disequilibrium and transitional phase that fades as prosperity is achieved. Only when the laws of one price, one cost and one profit hold will there be the law of one income, and that situation will constitute an international equilibrium.

4-8 Cross Sectional Evidence

From Table 4-1 it can be seen that manufactured export growth rates (Xr) are higher, the wider is the gap (Gap%) in per capita incomes between the exporting nation and the US. For example, the OECD nations registered a 12.9 per cent increase in real exports between 1965-73 while the US income gap was 43 percent but only 6.93 percent between 1984-92 when the US income gap closed to 34.3 percent. A similar trend is evident for East Asia. From Table 4-2, real export growth rates were 40.2 percent in the 1965-73 period when the US income gap

Table 4-1

Export Growth Rates and Gap on US Income (OECD)

	1965- Xr	1973 Gap%	1974- Xr	1983 Gap%	1984- Xr	1992 Gap%	Xr Ave
Australia	30.7	24.3	12.7	19.1	5.9	18.3	14.7
Austria	12.6	50.6	9.8	36.2	8.8	33.1	10.3
Belgium	6.4	42.1	2.6	29.9	3.7	30.1	4.3
Canada	16.4	25.8	4.5	13.1	9.7	8.0	9.3
Denmark	12.5	27.6	7.3	25.9	6.32	23.6	8.7
Finland	6.8	44.1	4.3	31.7	3.6	27.7	7.6
France	7.8	37.3	8.8	25.3	8.1	25.9	8.2
Germany	12.4	32.1	3.7	27.4	5.1	24.3	6.9
Greece	28.1	73.7	9.5	64.5	8.6	64.4	13.6
Iceland	23.1	46.6	18.2	38.2	14.0	26.5	15.5
Ireland	13.4	65.7	6.5	59.4	16.0	56.2	12.0
Italy	9.1	51.5	7.1	38.4	4.7	65.0	7.3
Netherlands	11.4	36.5	3.6	26.3	9.9	30.6	8.2
Norway	8.5	40.3	4.4	32.8	11.7	17.3	8.4
N.Z.	13.0	22.5	23.9	24.4	2.9	29.6	12.7
Portugal	6.1	79.3	-1.2	67.0	0.4	69.5	1.8
Spain	23.1	60.7	3.7	48.1	3.1	54.6	10.2
Sweden	8.3	19.3	8.8	16.9	4.3	18.8	8.0
Switzerland	5.7	4.3	3.8	0.0	7.3	11.0	5.3
Turkey	2.9	84.5	0.01	81.1	2.8	81.4	1.9

| U.K. | 12.6 | 34.1 | 9.8 | 33.1 | 8.8 | 32.9 | 10.3 |
| Average | 12.9 | 43.0 | 7.4 | 35.2 | 6.9 | 34.3 | 8.4 |

Source: IEDB, Canberra and Penn World Tables 5.5

Table 4.2

Export Growth Rates and Gap on US Income (East Asia)

| | 1965- | 1973 | 1974- | 1982 | 1983- | 1992 | Xr |
	Xr	Gap%	Xr	Gap%	Xr	Gap%	Ave
China	153	95.1	56.3	94.7	32.7	93.0	80.6
H.Kong	11.5	70.0	8.7	59.7	13.7	34.7	11.3
Indonesia	11.7	94.8	18.3	93.6	17.3	90.1	15.8
Japan	13.4	61.5	8.2	41.0	6.7	30.1	9.5
Korea	35.5	90.9	16.3	84.1	7.6	75.4	20.0
Malaysia	32.1	86.5	23.0	80.2	21.9	72.8	25.6
Philippines	5.5	89.3	25.3	88.7	9.7	89.7	14.1
Singapore	69.2	84.0	14.9	65.4	10.2	45.3	30.5
Taiwan	45.9	85.7	10.5	78.6	10.2	67.4	21.3
Thailand	33.8	90.0	23.6	88.3	28.6	84.9	28.5
Average	40.2	84.8	19.3	77.4	15.9	68.3	21.0

Source: Source: IEDB, Canberra and Penn World Tables 5.5

was 84.8 percent but fell to 15.94 percent during the 1984-92 when the US gap was 68.3 percent. Just as OECD export growth rates to the US slowed so too have EA export growth rates as the income gap with the US has closed. Theoretically, when the gap fully closes, EA's export growth rate will approximate the OECD export growth rate. In the meantime, a significant portion of EA's export growth is of a catch-up nature. Even though cross-sectional evidence is supportive of wide income differentials, with the US acting as magnet of export attraction, the time series evidence is more elusive. The reason for this elusiveness is that the changes in foreign income and the differences in income levels between EA and the USA are difficult to disentangle. The challenge of the next section is illustrate why the foreign income elasticity is biased upwards.

4-9 The Imperfect Substitutes Model

In accordance with the imperfect competition models espoused in Chapters 2 and 3, an imperfect substitutes model is employed to explain the forces that drive EA's export growth to the US market. The hypothesis of this chapter is that changes in competitiveness and US activity can only partially explain EA's export drive to the US market while cost and income levels provide a significant exogenous driving force.[4] Developed country exports to the US are less driven by differences in levels as they have, in general, converged close to US levels.

To test the link between developing country exports and developed country income levels, a sample is prepared and examines the export volumes of 47 nations into the US market is examined over the 28 years 1965–1992. Annual data are used and exports relate to manufactured goods. It is acknowledged that lags exist in export volumes responding to a change in variables but adjustments are assumed to take place within a one year period. This assumption is relaxed where noted.

The equation to be estimated takes the form-

$$\text{Ln } X = C + \alpha \text{ Ln } P + \beta \text{ Ln } Y$$

where

X	=	export volume
C	=	constant
P	=	real exchange rate
Y	=	US real GDP per capita

The coefficients represent elasticities. All variables are expressed in $US. Export volume data are calculated by obtaining export values (from International Data Bank, Canberra) and by dividing them by export unit values (from the International Financial Statistics). The real exchange rate and the per capita income data were obtained from the Penn World Table 5.5.

4-10 The Results: EA Exports to the USA

For developed countries the export price elasticity (Pe) is around -0.81 on average and has the correct theoretical sign – as revealed in Table 4-3. Export income elasticities are higher than literature estimates quoted earlier, around 4.57 on average. This implies that for every 1 per cent rise in US income, there is a rise in OECD exports of 4.57%. Obviously, the income term dominates the price term in explaining export volumes. Whilst most of the t statistics are plausible and R2 values are high, the Durbin Watson statistics appear low. The problem of autocorrelation will be addressed in the next section.

Table 4-3

Developed Country Exports to USA

	Con	P	Y	R2 (DW)	S
Australia	-54.8	-0.71	6.99	0.88	28
	(-9.49)	(-1.75)	(9.40)	(1.28)	
Austria	-33.8	-0.81	4.81	0.85	27
	(-8.54)	(-2.92)	(9.48)	(1.62)	
Belgium	-9.25	-0.82	2.43	0.88	28
	(-5.74)	(-7.0)	(13.5)	(1.18)	
Canada	-28.3	0.59	4.52	0.96	28
	(16.6)	(3.38)	(4.52)	(0.58)	

Denmark	-38.6	-1.09	5.47	0.95	28
	(-16.6)	(6.64)	(19.0)	(0.73)	
Finland	-29.2	-1.22	4.54	0.68	27
	(5.47)	(2.95)	(6.66)	(0.70)	
France	-36.78	-0.61	5.25	0.95	27
	(16.5)	(3.14)	(20.6)	(1.34)	
Germany	-23.8	-0.82	4.13	0.93	27
	(-12.1)	(5.38)	(17.16)	(4.13)	
Greece	-56.2	0.48	6.37	0.88	28
	(-8.52)	(0.94)	(11.73)	(0.91)	
Holland	-30.7	-0.77	4.59	0.96	28
	(17.6)	(-6.25)	(21.7)	(1.24)	
Iceland	-51.4	-2.31	7.0	0.88	28
	(-10.8)	(-6.0)	(21.7)	(1.2)	
Ireland	-48.1	-0.72	6.22	0.91	28
	(-12.6)	(-1.75)	(12.1)	(0.6)	
Italy	-25.7	-0.75	4.18	0.89	28
	(-9.55)	(-3.02)	(11.7)	(1.39)	
Norway	-32.8	-0.38	4.44	0.92	28
	(12.5)	(-1.7)	(13.1)	(0.8)	
N.Z.	-54.8	-1.47	7.12	0.91	27
	(13.4)	(3.23)	(14.7)	(1.11)	
Portugal	35.4	-0.3	-2.6	0.6	27

	(7.16)	(-0.80)	(-5.62)	(0.62)	
Spain	-68.1	-1.25	8.65	0.91	28
	(8.30)	(3.21)	(8.62)	(1.47)	
Sweden	-32.88	-1.36	5.14	0.96	28
	(-17.9)	(-8.52)	(23.7)	(1.43)	
Switzerland	-16.99	-0.05	2.81	0.78	23
	(-5.31)	(-0.81)	(8.22)	(0.36)	
U.K.	-18.1	-0.7	3.38	0.91	28
	(-10.1)	(-3.61)	(14.8)	(0.37)	
Average		-0.81		4.57	

Notes: Parentheses contain student-t values. The S means sample size.

(DW) = Durbin Watson Statistics

From Table 4-4 it can be seen that East Asian exporters face a low export price elasticity of -0.14 but an exceptionally high export income elasticity of 12.84 on average. This estimate of 12.84 is almost three times the size of the developed country estimates of 4.57. But why is there a *systematic dichotomy* in this export income elasticity? Such a dichotomy is explainable in terms of differences in income and cost levels between East Asia and the US. Hence, there should be an inverse relationship between the level of export income elasticities and the level of own income. Low income nations should generate a high income elasticity and vice versa. Results confirm a correlation of -0.53 for the 30 nations of the OECD and EA combined. For the whole sample the correlation is -0.31. Hence, there is circumstantial evidence that the income elasticity is pushed upward when low income nations export to the US.

As can be seen from Table 4-5, other low income nations exporting to the US also have a relatively high export income elasticity (6.31) compared to the OECD (4.57). However, the whole three groups reveal low Durbin Watson statistics and so suggest the problem of autocorrelation. The next section seeks to address this issue.

4-11 Addressing the Problem of Autocorrelation

Persistence in the export volumes is a reason why EA estimates may suffer from autocorrelation – a type of catch-up phenomena. Even the developed nations possessed significantly lower income levels than the US in 1965 and so experienced some type of catch-up export growth. Nevertheless, the diagnostics improve after adjusting for autocorrelation, and the export income elasticity estimates usually fall. *But the relativity between the export income elasticities remain.* Just as in the previous section, the systematic difference between developing and developed countries does not vanish. For example, from Table 4-7, the average income elasticity for EA is 11.96 whereas for the OECD it is 3.31 as can be seen from Table 4-6. The income elasticity estimate for other nations from Table 4-8 is 5.88. After correcting for autocorrelation, the correlation between income levels and income elasticities for the OECD and EA estimates at –0.26. For the whole sample it estimates at –0.39. Thus, the dichotomy between developed and developing economies in the income term remains, and so there is strong evidence that differences in income levels is the force 'behind the veil'.

Table 4-4

EA Manufactured Exports to USA

	Con	Pe	Ye	R2 (DW)	S
China	-2.56	-1.57	27.9	0.75	28
	(-2.27)	(0.40)	(2.71)	(0.83)	
H.Kong	-27.5	0.00	4.0	0.86	28
	(-8.72)	(0.01)	(11.4)	(0.26)	
Indonesia	-44.5	-1.51	6.04	0.7	28
	(4.04)	(3.13)	(5.5)	(0.57)	
Japan	-56.6	-1.05	7.72	0.96	28
	(-12.6)	(-3.88)	(13.2)	(1.88)	
Korea	-85.3	0.78	9.65	0.94	27
	(-10.5)	(9.65)	(9.24)	(0.49)	
Malaysia	-127.2	0.81	13.78	0.95	27
	(-15.3)	(1.15)	(19.9)	(1.02)	
Philippines	-79.7	0.66	8.94	0.90	26
	(9.74)	(1.00)	(12.8)	(0.57)	
Singapore	-150.7	2.03	15.8	0.93	27
	(-12.6)	(2.03)	(15.8)	(0.69)	
Taiwan	-91.3	-0.17	10.7	0.93	26
	(8.21)	(-0.16)	(6.94)	(0.32)	
Thailand	-140.0	0.89	15.1	0.97	27
	(-18.9)	(1.070	(25.1)	(1.09)	
Average		-0.14	12.8		

Table 4-5

Manufactured Exports to USA

(other nations)

	Con	RER	FY	R2 (DW)	S
Bolivia	-16.2	-1.06	2.55	0.37	28
	(-1.98)	(-2.93)	(3.11)	(0.49)	
Brazil	-16.2	-1.06	2.55	0.37	28
Colombia	-32.1	-1.50	4.70	0.89	28
	(-5.15)	(-3.72)	(8.69)	(0.68)	
Cypus	-103.8	-1.80	11.9	0.83	23
	(-8.29)	(-1.69)	(9.740	(1.52)	
India	-15.8	-0.76	2.89	0.91	28
	(-2.68)	(-2.79)	(5.50)	(0.62)	
Jamaica	3.14	1.62	-0.17	0.44	25
	(0.23)	(2.75)	(0.15)	(0.58)	
Jordan	-115.5	0.56	12.05	0.78	23
	(-7.70)	(0.82)	(8.33)	(1.93)	
Kenya	-34.3	-2.29	4.94	0.84	25
	(-3.66)	(-3.70)	(6.14)	(1.16)	
Malta	-59.16	-0.16	6.69	0.75	25
	(-6.12)	(-0.19)	(7.91)	(0.60)	
Maurit.	-140.4	4.08	13.4	0.85	28
	(5.31)	(2.59)	(4.15)	(1.25)	
Myanmar	-47.6	0.58	5.31	0.74	26

	(-6.0)	(1.91)	(7.19)	(1.24)	
Pakistan	-56.8	-0.31	6.57	0.62	23
	(-2.71)	(0.33)	(3.46)	(0.42)	
Panama	-96.8	4.51	8.67	0.71	27
	(3.91)	(1.46)	(6.16)	(0.60)	
Paraguay	-54.1	0.08	5.98	0.77	25
	(-7.97)	(0.20)	(8.76)	(1.02)	
Sri Lanka	-53.4	-2.91	7.20	0.94	28
	(-3.04)	(-4.89)	(4.38)	(0.73)	
Turkey	21.5	0.80	-2.14	0.29	28
	(3.97)	(1.14)	(-1.96)	(1.53)	
Average		-0.03	6.31		

4-12 Why Do Income Elasticities Appear High?

Krugman's (1989) explanation for such a bias is that as a developing nation devotes more resources to export production and as that export capacity grows more rapidly than world capacity then there will be an automatic increase in world demand for that country's exports. Such a growth differential generates a bias in the income elasticity. Riedal sees this bias in a similar light, as supply shifts are also captured.

According MSV (1992) there are product cycle forces at work whereby low wage, low-technology countries gain technological transfer grow faster and so obtain a growing share of world trade. Secondly, there are external effects bestowed on promising exporters in an outward orientated developing economy. Learning by watching, gaining market information and spillover effects assist in maintaining the momentum of penetration into Western markets.

Table 4-6

OECD Manufactured Good Exports to USA

	Con	RER	USY	AR	R2 (DW)
Australia	-6.13	-0.91	2.08	0.84	0.97
	(0.59)	(-3.37)	(1.93)	(20.7)	(1.76)
Austria	-32.7	-0.74	4.66	0.19	0.83
	(0.19)	(-2.24)	(7.22)	(0.89)	(1.99)
Belgium	-9.64	-0.79	2.45	0.41	0.89
	(-3.4)	(-4.75)	(7.82)	(2.11)	(1.79)
Canada	-19.1	-0.68	3.61	0.72	0.98
	(-4.04)	(-3.13)	(7.63)	(6.12)	(1.77)
Denmark	15.5	1.04	3.06	0.86	0.97
	(-1.9)	(5.13)	(3.66)	(13.0)	(2.04)
Finland	-18.3	-0.86	3.23	0.73	0.81
	(-1.46)	(-1.61)	(2.40)	(4.80)	(1.65)
France	-35.1	-0.62	5.09	0.37	0.95
	(-9.32)	(2.50)	(12.1)	(1.82)	(1.81)
Germany	-18.0	-0.65	3.45	0.60	0.95
	(-4.13)	(-3.37)	(7.38)	(3.71)	(2.03)
Greece	-48.0	-0.25	5.83	0.49	0.91
	(-4.33)	(-0.35)	(5.89)	(2.38)	(2.14)
Holland	-28.2	-0.77	4.33	0.45	0.96
	(-9.40)	(-4.46)	(12.9)	(2.34)	(2.09)
Iceland	-48.2	-1.93	6.48	0.44	0.88

	(-5.05)	(-3.64)	(6.15)	(2.07)	(2.15)
Ireland	-2.58	-0.35	2.77	0.99	0.92
	(-0.01)	(-1.03)	(2.14)	(13.2)	(2.78)
Italy	-22.2	-0.42	3.67	0.42	0.89
	(-4.33)	(-1.24)	(5.76)	(2.03)	(2.11)
Norway	49.7	-0.19	0.47	0.99	0.95
	(0.03)	(-0.63)	(0.50)	(20.1)	(2.11)
N.Z.	6.56	-0.55	0.45	0.92	0.93
	(0.35)	(-1.08)	(0.23)	(16.4)	(2.67)
Portugal	595.5	-0.19	3.65	1.00	0.85
	(0.00)	(-0.50)	(2.62)	(23.3)	(1.71)
Spain	-22.9	-0.73	3.71	0.78	0.91
	(-1.19)	(-1.37)	(1.88)	(5.35)	(2.37)
Sweden	-32.0	-1.15	4.95	0.39	0.95
	(-9.63)	(-3.96)	(12.3)	(1.48)	(1.84)
Switzealand	-20.5	-0.03	3.15	0.82	0.92
	(-2.74)	(-1.01)	(4.06)	(6.44)	(1.29)
U.K.	-17.0	-0.43	3.16	0.85	0.97
	(-3.49)	(-2.90)	(6.35)	(7.43)	(1.98)
Average		-0.66	3.31		

Table 4-7

EA Manufactured Exports to USA

	Con	RER	USY	AR	R2 (DW)
China	-209.7	-3.37	23.7	0.57	0.84
	(-1.57)	(-0.76)	(1.89)	(3.44)	(2.09)
H.Kong	-9.21	-0.38	2.28	0.82	0.97
	(-1.42)	(-1.52)	(-3.36)	(13.4)	(1.97)
Indonesia	-73.9	-0.77	8.81	0.62	0.87
	(-3.30)	(-1.15)	(0.62)	(4.73)	(1.81)
Japan	-29.6	-0.61	4.70	1.00	0.97
	(-0.09)	(-2.47)	(4.88)	(14.7)	(1.87)
Korea	-12.07	-0.29	2.62	0.89	0.89
	(-1.24)	(-0.78)	(2.58)	(42.5)	(2.07)
Malaysia	44.6	0.60	0.37	0.99	0.98
	(0.23)	(0.92)	(0.23)	(43.1)	(2.37)
Philippines	116.7	-0.10	1.41	0.99	0.97
	(0.01)	(-0.23)	(1..0)	(25.2)	(1.73)
Singapore	-31.0	0.48	4.22	0.92	0.98
	(-1.62)	(0.66)	(2.09)	(26.9)	(1.06)
Taiwan	-31.7	-0.02	4.53	0.87	0.87
	(-2.72)	(-0.06)	(3.85)	(22.7)	(1.57)
Thailand	-140	1.01	14.98	0.43	0.9
	(-12.2)	(0.94)	(15.1)	(2.23)	(1.78)
Average		-0.34	11.96		

Table 4-8

Manufactured Exports to USA

(Other Nations)

	Con	RER	FY	AR	R2(DW)
Bolivia	41.5	-0.15	-1.61	0.99	0.74
	(0.00)	(-0.24)	(-0.55)	(9.04)	(1.75)
Brazil	-27.4	-0.44	4.18	0.95	0.98
	(-1.85)	(-1.31)	(2.82)	(22.4)	(1.55)
Columbia	-38.6	-1.62	5.41	0.61	0.93
	(-3.19)	(-2.71)	(4.70)	(3.29)	(1.24)
Cypus	-107.3	-1.56	12.16	0.25	0.81
	(6.11)	(-1.19)	(6.68)	(1.03)	(1.90)
India	-29.82	-0.50	4.25	0.59	0.97
	(-4.99)	(-2.35)	(7.45)	(5.54)	(2.76)
Jamaica	22.45	1.01	-1.90	0.63	0.76
	(1.30)	(1.77)	(-1.15)	(4.33)	(2.29)
Jordan	-105.3	0.24	11.1	0.02	0.75
	(-5.68)	(0.31)	(6.31)	(0.12)	(2.00)
Kenya	-52.5	-1.10	6.36	0.57	0.87
	(-1.11)	(-1.12)	(3.66)	(2.77)	(2.03)
Malta	-66.6	-0.62	7.66	0.69	0.8
	(-3.55)	(-0.69)	(3.99)	(4.55)	(2.03)
Mauritius	-146.5	2.963	14.7	0.58	0.89
	(-3.5)	(1.76)	(3.18)	(3.36)	(1.58)

Myanmar	-46.6	0.39	5.27	0.41	0.76
	(-3.96)	(0.85)	(4.71)	(1.82)	(1.69)
Panama	-49.9	-2.89	7.02	0.67	0.89
	(-1.94)	(-0.95)	(0.67)	(5.76)	(2.07)
Pakistan	-82.5	0.93	8.99	0.64	0.88
	(-3.91)	(1.47)	(4.38)	(4.97)	(1.54)
Paraguay	-64.8	003	7.12	0.35	0.86
	(-6.43)	(0.07)	(4.38)	(4.97)	(1.54)
Sri Lanka	697.5	-1.01	-2.14	0.99	0.98
	(0.01)	(-2.42)	(-1.05)	(37.1)	(1.59)
Turkey	21.5	0.72	-2.08	0.22	0.32
	(3.31)	(0.85)	(-1.62)	(1.08)	(1.67)
Average		-0.10	5.88		

According to AR (1994) there is an econometric explanation as to why the income elasticities are biased upwards. They result from simultaneity bias in a reduced form equation and so income elasticities are correlated with export growth rates. There is also an economic interpretation that supply side influences are neglected. In their view, price normalisation is preferable to traditional volume normalisation.

This study claims that the 'ommitted variable' in the income elasticity is wealth or wide income differentials between EA and the West. Not only are export growth rates correlated with income elasticities in an imperfect substitutes model but so are income levels inversely related to income elasticities. There is a systematic bias in the income elasticity when a developing country exports manufactured goods to a developed country. This bias is absent when developed nations export to developed nations.

From Figure 4-1 using the example of Korea the difference between the Korean domestic demand curve (point a) and the US demand curve (point b) dictates the potential to expand export volumes. The realisation of this opportunity is largely dependent on the elasticity of export supply. In this case elastic, as espoused by AR. The shift of US 1 (point b) to US 2 (point c) represents an export demand elasticity. It is the *position* of the foreign demand curve that generates catch-up export growth not its elasticity.

Figure 4-1

Export Responses

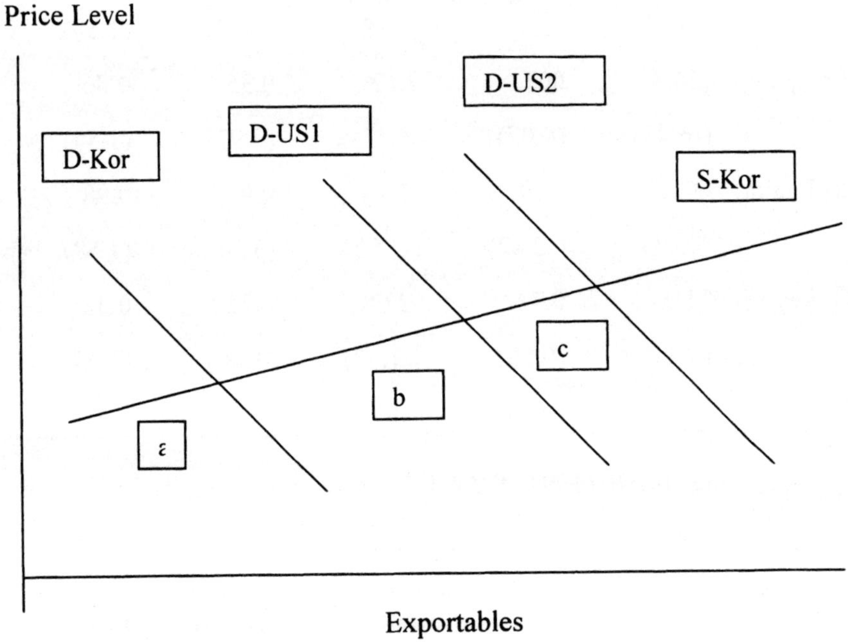

4-13 Conclusion

When Lewis (1980) used the 'locomotive – carriage' paradigm to explain how the developing world was pulled along by the *income growth* of the OECD, it only partially explained the export linkages to rich markets. The central role played by the US, according to the WSM and the results of this chapter, reveal that super-export growth is as much a function of differences in cost and income levels as it is of price or income elasticities. There is a strong case for arguing that an exogenous demand-side force attracts low income nations to export to the rich US market. Catch-up export growth drives catch-up economic growth for developing nations. Both are a function of the distance from the US income level. From a theoretical perspective, perfect or imperfect substitutes (elasticities) models, are doomed to fail in explaining export volumes in a world of unequal incomes. Foreign demand elasticities are less relevant. Nevertheless, an export supply elasticity remains important and largely determines *which* developing nations will penetrate rich foreign markets. However, as developing incomes rise and converge on US income levels, then *changes* in competitiveness and US activity assume greater importance. Given the huge export drive achieved by EA, not just to the US but to the world in general, it will be useful in the next chapter to examine the potent influence such exports have on economic growth.

Appendix 4.1
Data Set: 47 Countries

Developed:	*Asian 10:*	*Other*
Australia	China	Bolivia
Austria	Korea	Brazil
Belgium	Malaysia	Columbia
Canada	Japan	Cyprus
Denmark	Philippines	India
Finland	Hong Kong	Jamaica
France	Singapore	Jordan
Germany	Taiwan	Kenya
Greece	Thailand	Malta
Iceland	Indonesia	Mauritius
Ireland		Myanmar
Italy		Pakistan
Netherlands		Panama
Norway		Paraguay
New Zealand		Sri Lanka
Portugal		Turkey
Spain		
Sweden		
Switzerland		
UK		

Chapter Five

Rocket Engine One: Super-Profit

5-1 Introduction

Given the theoretical focus of Chapter 3 on the importance of exports in stimulating economic growth in developing nations, it is now necessary to test the potency of such a link via the use of an economic model. The work of Pack and Page (1994) draws attention to the share of manufactured exports in GDP as a statistically significant variable in explaining growth amongst a broad cross section of nations. The work of Feder (1983) concentrates on a similar 'composite' export variable that drives economic growth via economies of scale and efficiency. These authors argue that allocative efficiency is enhanced by a vibrant export sector stimulating a somewhat lethargic non-export sector. The marginal productivity of capital is far higher in the export sector and so the reshuffling of resources into that sector raises economic growth via a structural symbiosis. This 'catch-up' growth via a high MPK may represent both allocative and technical efficiency but it also may represent a high marginal revenue product (MRP) as profit opportunities in mature economy markets are far more lucrative than at home.[1] This chapter seeks to estimate the differences in the MPK between developed and developing nations.

5-2 A Trade Augmented Solow Model

A Feder-type two sector, two production function 'duality' model is employed. The major distinction is between the export and non-export sector, whereby the former sector enjoys a higher MPK than the latter sector, partially reflecting comparative advantage, economies of scale and efficiency benefits from being exposed to international competition.[2] More specifically, it is inter-sectoral allocative efficiency at work and to a lesser extent, positive spillovers to the non-export sector. The following derivation draws on Feder (1983,pp61-64, 66-69).

According to Feder (1983) the production function for the non-export sector is:-

$$N = F(K_n, L_n, X) \qquad (5\text{-}1)$$

Production function for the export sector is :-
$$X = G(K_x, L_x) \qquad (5\text{-}2)$$
where-

$$N = \text{non-exports}$$

$$X = \text{exports,}$$

$$K_n, K_x = \text{capital stocks of each sector,}$$

$$L_n, L_x = \text{labor forces in each sector,}$$

For the marginal productivities

$$(G_k/F_k) = (G_L/F_L) = 1 + \delta \qquad (5\text{-}3)$$

The ratios of the respective marginal productivities in the two sectors differ from unity by a factor of δ, and the subscripts denote partial derivatives. If $\delta = 0$, then resources are being allocated optimally. However, in the case of developing countries δ is most likely positive. Such productivity differentials are presumed not to include externalities.

Differentiate equations 5-1 and 5-2 to yield -

$$\dot{Y} = (\dot{N} + \dot{X}) = F_k \bullet I_n + F_L \bullet \dot{L}_n + F_x \bullet \dot{X} + (1 + \delta) \bullet F_k \bullet I_x + (1 + \delta) \bullet F_L \bullet \dot{L}_x$$

$$\dot{Y} = F_k \bullet (I_n + I_x) + F_L \bullet (\dot{L}_n + \dot{L}_x) + F \bullet \dot{X} + \delta(F_k \bullet I_x + F_L \bullet \dot{L}_x) \tag{5-4}$$

Equation 5-4, after manipulation, yields

$$\dot{Y} = F_k \bullet I + F_L \bullet \dot{L} + \left(\frac{\delta}{(1+\delta)} + F_x \right) \bullet \dot{X} \tag{5-5}$$

In the above equation, the F_x term represents the marginal externality effect of exports on the output of the non-export sector. A linear relationship is presumed to exist between the marginal productivity of labor in a given sector and average output per laborer in the economy.

$$F_L \quad = \quad \beta. (Y/L) \tag{5-6}$$

$$F_K \quad = \quad \alpha \tag{5-7}$$

Dividing equation (5-5) through by Y yields

$$\frac{\dot{Y}}{Y} = \alpha \left(\frac{I}{Y} \right) + \beta \left(\frac{\dot{L}}{L} \right) + \left(\frac{\delta}{(1+\delta)} + F_x \right) \bullet \left(\frac{\dot{X}}{X} \right) \bullet \left(\frac{X}{Y} \right) \tag{5-8}$$

This is a pivotal equation used in the empirical work of the next section.

It is worth noting that if the MPK's are equalized across sectors ($\delta = 0$) and if there are no inter-sectoral externalities ($F_x = 0$), then equation (5-8) reduces to a fairly standard neo-classical growth model of accumulation. The constant should pick up technological progress. However, the term $[\delta/(1 + \delta) + F_x]$ should be positive for developing countries and may be compressed into γ in equation (5-9). It also worth noting that α represents the MPK of the non-export sector and not the economy as a whole. By assumption, then,

$$\frac{\dot{Y}}{Y} = \alpha\left(\frac{I}{Y}\right) + \beta\left(\frac{\dot{L}}{L}\right) + \gamma\left(\left(\frac{\dot{X}}{X}\right) \bullet \left(\frac{X}{Y}\right)\right) \tag{5-9}$$

Decomposing the factor productivity differential γ into components:

By Feder (1983, p.67) exports can be taken to affect the production of non-exports with a constant elasticity:-

$$N \qquad = F\,(K_n,\, L_n,\, X) = X^{\theta}\, \psi\,(K_n,\, L_n) \tag{5-10}$$

where θ is a parameter. Thus

$$F_X \qquad = \partial\,N/\partial\,X = \theta\,.\,(N/X) \tag{5-11}$$

Equation (5-8) therefore may be rewritten as:-

$$\frac{\dot{Y}}{Y} = \alpha\left(\frac{I}{Y}\right) + \beta\left(\frac{\dot{L}}{L}\right) + \left[\frac{\delta}{(1+\delta)} + \theta\frac{N}{X}\right] \bullet \left(\frac{\dot{X}}{X}\right) \bullet \left(\frac{X}{Y}\right) \tag{5-12}$$

But-

$$\theta \bullet \frac{N}{X} = \theta\frac{\left(\dfrac{N}{Y}\right)}{\left(\dfrac{X}{Y}\right)} = \theta\frac{\left[1-\left(\dfrac{X}{Y}\right)\right]}{\left(\dfrac{X}{Y}\right)} = \frac{\theta}{\left(\dfrac{X}{Y}\right)} - \theta \tag{5.13}$$

making:

$$\frac{\dot{Y}}{Y} = \alpha\left(\frac{I}{Y}\right) + \beta\left(\frac{\dot{L}}{L}\right) + \left[\frac{\delta}{(1+\delta)} - \theta\right]\left(\frac{\dot{X}}{X}\right)\left(\frac{X}{Y}\right) + \theta\left(\frac{\dot{X}}{X}\right) \tag{5.14}$$

This becomes a critical equation in the empirical work. Note that if $\delta/(1 + \delta) = \theta$, the model reduces to

$$\frac{\dot{Y}}{Y} = \alpha\left(\frac{I}{Y}\right) + \beta\left(\frac{\dot{L}}{L}\right) + \theta\frac{\dot{X}}{X} \tag{5-15}$$

In this case, the productivity differentials disappear but the marginal externality effect on the non-export sector remains. Such a result may be plausible for both developed and developing countries alike.

The Objective

It was argued in Chapter 3 that a low K/L ratio possesses some explanatory power of the East Asian Growth experience as the MPK appears enormous. Open economies have a greater potential to exploit such a high MPK via exports to rich economy markets. Therefore, the total marginal product from investing in the export sector ($TMPK_x$) needs to be distinguished from a closed or domestic economy MPK. In the language of Feder (1983,p68), this $TMPK_x$ represents the social marginal productivity of capital bestowed on the economy at large. However, this interpretation is questionable in the light of open economies capturing super-normal profits from exports, maintaining a divergence between price P and average cost AC such that P>ATC; namely, monopolistic-type profits exist. This is a price and profit differential story rather than a Feder-type productivity differential story. Nevertheless, the following relationship shall be used in empirical work:

$$TMPK_x \quad = F_k \ (1 + F_x)/(1 - \gamma + F_x) \tag{5-16}$$

The above equation may be used for an aggregate γ, whereas the equation (5-17) may be used for a decomposed γ.

$$TMPK_x \quad =_k . [1 + \theta . (1 - x)/x].(1 + \delta), \tag{5-17}$$
where x is the share of exports in GDP.

It should also be noted that δ has another interpretation besides a productivity differential. This term may equally be viewed as a price mark-up or a difference in unit costs. In the paradigm of Chapter 3 and in an East Asian context, this is none other than a Hecksher-Ohlin model , whereby vast differences in labor costs drive δ.

5-3 Testing the Trade Augmented Solow Model

Samples, identified in Appendix 5-1, are drawn from countries comprising the OECD and East Asian nations. The key test is whether the $TMPK_x$ for developing nations is appreciably greater than that of developed nations. The productivity differential will be estimated separately from the externality effect where possible. Another interesting quest is to discern the difference between a traditional Solow model from that of a trade augmented model.

All Exports

The power of the interactive term $(\dot{X}/X \cdot X/Y)$ in the Feder model is quite robust as can be seen in Table 5-1, which estimates equation (5-14) and its family. Its coefficient is 1.00 and statistically significant– as per equation (5-9). The labor and investment share terms are weak and fail diagnostic tests. This interactive term in the extended Feder model [equation (5-14)] reveals an estimate of 1.32 but the rate of growth export term is not significant. The respective F statistics appear acceptable. Support for 'export-led' growth exists in these results.

Support is also found for the export-led growth hypothesis in both Tables 5-2 and 5-3, as the interactive term is 1.38 (for developing countries) and 3.01 (for East Asian countries) respectively – as per equation (5-14). For 46 developing countries, the labor growth rate and the rate of export growth do not appear to be potent whereas the investment term displays some potency. At face value, these results indicate a strong export potency that causes the productivity of both labor and capital to be more explosive in the export sector.

The next task tests the same sample with the same equations but employing total nominal GDP growth along with nominal export growth rates. As can be seen from Table 5-4 and equation 5-9, the interactive term is 1.12 and statistically significant. This coefficient is not that different from the coefficient of 1.00 found in Table 5-1. However, the results and diagnostics for developing countries (Table 5-5) are quite poor and do not resemble those found in the equivalent Table 5-2. The interactive term for EA countries (Table 5-6) is 0.62 but statistically insignificant. Nevertheless, the overall interactive term for 70 countries in Table 5-4 supports the export-led growth hypothesis.

Manufactured Exports To The World

Results for manufactured goods exports to the world are revealed in Tables 5-7 and 5-8. The interactive term for the whole sample of 47 countries, as per equation 5-9, is **0.89** and statistically significant as seen in Table 5-7. The interactive term, as per equation 5-14, is **0.94** and statistically significant. In both equations the coefficient on investment is both potent and significant. Thus, export-led growth is confirmed for the whole sample. In the case of East Asia, the interactive term, as per equation 5-14 in Table 5-8 is 0.59 and for real export growth is 0.22. Both terms are significant. The investment term remains both potent and significant.

Table 5-1

Feder Model

All Exports (Whole Sample, 67 Countries)

	Eqn 5-9	Eqn 5-14	Eqn 5-15
Con	-4.13	-5.58	0.41
	(-3.11)	(-2.74)	(0.46)
$\dot{L}/L$	0.11	0.14	0.04
	(0.57)	(0.74)	(0.22)
I/Y	0.05	0.05	0.06
	(1.77)	(1.83)	(2.09)
$\dot{X}/X$		-0.02	0.03
		(-0.94)	(0.11)
$(\dot{X}/X)_{(X/Y)}$	1.00	1.32	
	(4.3)	(3.22)	
F Stat	10.34	7.98	6.26
R2	0.33	0.34	0.23

Table 5-2

Feder Model

All Exports (Developing Nations, 46)

	Eqn 5-9	Eqn 5-14	Eqn 5-15
Con	-4.23	-5.61	0.50
	(-2.69)	(-2.43)	(0.44)
$\dot{L}/L$	-0.09	-0.07	-0.12
	(-0.34)	(-0.25)	(-0.38)
I/Y	0.07	0.08	0.09
	(2.03)	(2.12)	(2.20)
$\dot{X}/X$	-0.02	0.03	
	(-0.81)	(2.45)	
$(\dot{X}/X)_{(X/Y)}$	1.07	1.38	
	(3.92)	(2.97)	
F Stat	9.83	7.48	5.95
R2	0.41	0.42	0.29

Table 5-3

Feder Model

All Exports(East Asian Nations,10)

	Eqn 5-9	Eqn 5-14	Eqn 5-15
Con	-5.88	-17.09	-0.23
	(-1.26)	(-1.80)	(-0.04)
$\dot{L}/L$	0.14	0.64	0.70
	(0.12)	(0.54)	(0.47)
I/Y	0.12	0.16	0.12
	(1.18)	(1.74)	(1.04)
$\dot{X}/X$		-0.05	0.01
		(-1.33)	(0.55)
$(\dot{X}/X)_{(X/Y)}$	1.28	3.01	
	(1.51)	(1.98)	
F Stat	1.96	2.14	0.98
R2	0.54	0.68	0.37

Table 5-4

Feder Model

All Exports (Whole Sample, 70 Countries)

	Eqn 5-9	Eqn 5-14
Con	2.35	3.37
	(0.82)	(1.27)
$\dot{L}/L$	-1.26	-1.33
	(-3.78)	(-4.33)
I/Y	1.01	1.09
	(1.13)	(1.61)
$\dot{X}/X$		0.30
		(3.57)
$(\dot{X}/X)_{(X/Y)}$	1.12	0.18
	(2.55)	(0.38)
F Stat	12.58	14.4
R2	0.37	0.47

Table 5-5

Feder Model

All Exports (East Asian Nations, 10)

	Eqn 5-9	Eqn 5-14
Con	7.90	7.75
	(-2.69)	(2.01)
$\dot{L}/L$	-1.55	-1.57
	(-4.16)	(-4.27)
I/Y	0.94	0.93
	(1.20)	(1.21)
$\dot{X}/X$		0.17
		(1.52)
$(\dot{X}/X)_{(X/Y)}$	0.19	-0.16
	(0.31)	(-0.25)
F Stat	10.1	8.39
R2	0.41	0.44

Table 5-6

Feder Model

All Exports (East Asian Nations, 10)

	Eqn 5-9	Eqn 5-14
Con	0.47	0.63
	(0.05)	(-0.05)
$\dot{L}/L$	-0.90	-0.86
	(-2.78)	(-1.74)
I/Y	2.22	2.39
	(0.95)	(0.84)
$\dot{X}/X$		0.04
		(0.28)
$(\dot{X}/X)_{(X/Y)}$	0.62	0.63
	(1.21)	(1.11)
F Stat	4.22	2.65
R2	0.54	0.68

A similar picture to that of the previous section unfolds from Table 5-9. The interactive term, as per equation 5-9, is 0.55 and statistically significant, whereas for equation 5-14 it is 0.61. The investment in both cases is not significant. For EA, as per equation 5-14, both the interactive and the real export growth terms are significant — as seen in Table 5-10. The interactive term is 0.39 and the real export growth term is 0.18. It therefore appears that exporting to the US market yields a productivity premium above and beyond that of the non-export sector.

Table 5-7

Feder Model

Manufactured Exports to World (Whole Sample, 47)

	Eqn 5-9	Eqn 5-14
Con	-5.80	-5.71
	(-2.89)	(-2.81)
$\dot{L}/L$	0.45	0.47
	(2.31)	(2.38)
I/Y	1.22	1.13
	(2.21)	(1.97)
$\dot{X}/X$		-0.01
		(-0.67)
$(\dot{X}/X)_{(X/Y)}$	0.89	0.94
	(5.34)	(5.01)
F Stat	12.0	9.03
R2	0.46	0.46

Table 5-8

Feder Model

Manufactured Exports to World (East Asian Nations, 10)

	Eqn 5-9	Eqn 5-14
Con	4.81	-7.99
	(0.53)	(-2.58)
$\dot{L}/L$	0.00	-0.01
	(0.00)	(-0.10)
I/Y	-0.95	1.84
	(-0.40)	(2.36)
$\dot{X}/X$		0.22
		(8.02)
$(\dot{X}/X)_{(X/Y)}$	0.22	0.59
	(0.48)	(4.22)
F Stat	0.27	18.4
		(0.00)
R2	0.11	0.93

Table 5-9

Feder Model

Manufactured Exports to USA (Whole Sample, 54)

	Eqn 5-9	Eqn 5.14
Con	-0.36	0.41
	(-0.16)	(0.17)
$\dot{L}/L$	-0.07	-0.07
	(-0.34)	(-0.33)
I/Y	0.62	0.37
	(0.94)	(0.51)
$\dot{X}/X$		-0.01
		(-0.85)
$(\dot{X}/X)_{(X/Y)}$	0.55	0.61
	(3.80)	(3.72)
F Stat	5.79	4.50
R2	0.26	0.27

Table 5-10

Feder Model

Manufactured Exports to USA (East Asian Nations,10)

	Eqn 5-9	Eqn 5-14
Con	6.54	1.69
	(0.85)	(0.38)
$\dot{L}/L$	-0.15	-0.65
	(-0.47)	(-2.94)
I/Y	-1.19	-0.28
	(-0.52)	(-0.21)
$\dot{X}/X$		0.18
		(3.81)
$(\dot{X}/X)_{(X/Y)}$	0.09	0.39
	(0.33)	(2.28)
F Stat	0.22	4.18
R2	0.10	0.62

5-4 Estimates of the $TMPK_x$

From the above Feder-type model the $TMPK_x$ may be calculated. The results from Tables 5-4, 5-7 and 5-9 (whole samples) are displayed in Table 5-11. The potency of exports in generating an explosive $TMPK_x$ above the non-export sector MPK is revealed. In the case of all exports, the differential for the MPK's is around 2.5 as a multiple, for manufactured exports to the world it is 15 and for manufactured goods exports to the US the differential is 1.5.

The results for manufactured goods exports from EA (Tables 5-6 and 5-8) are also powerful, as revealed in Table 5-12. The $TMPK_x$ for all exports is 4.01 with a premium of 1.67 above the MPK_{nx}. For manufactured exports to the world, the premium is 4.0 above the MPK_{nx}. Unfortunately, the diagnostics were too poor to calculate the $TMPK_x$ for manufactured exports to the US. Even though the magnitudes of this 'productivity premium' appear large, a degree of caution should be exercised in interpretation, as they are but cross sectional estimates using aggregate data. What is more relevant than the precise number themselves is their ranking: there is the strong evidence that a substantial 'productivity premium' exists that rests well above the returns to investment in the non-export sector.

5-5 Productivity or Profitability Differentials

The above results offer a strong indication that there is indeed a significant differential force driving growth that needs to be explained or dis-entangled. The standard Solow model does not perform well in explaining the growth experience of developing countries. An export-augmented model possesses more explanatory power. However, relying on existing economic growth theory providing a dichotomy between accumulation and productivity has its failings. Productivity is a subset of profitability and not vice versa. A divergence between world prices and low domestic costs generates monopoly profits. Thus, the dichotomy may represent a profitability not a productivity differential, as manufacturing wage rates and unit costs differ widely between the developed and the developing world.[3] Table 5-14 reveals such wide disparities in manufacturing wage rates between EA and the US. For example, Korea's manufacturing wage rate was only 7% of the US rate in 1970. Modern day China, in 1990, had a wage rate of less than 3% of the US wage rate.[4] Even some European nations had wage rates of less than half that of the US rate in 1970 – in $US. To the extent that labor productivity between EA and the US is not vastly divergent in manufacturing industries, then manufacturing wage rates inversely reflect profit rates. If the law of one price holds, then such wide wage differentials spell large profits for EA Asian producers. Moreover, EA manufacturing wage rates were still less than 65% of the US rate in 1990. Tables 5-13 and 5-14 illustrate the point.

Table 5-11

Estimates of TMPKx: Whole Samples

	MPKnx	TMPKx
All Exports	1.08	2.76
Man. Exports	1.13	16.93
Man. Exports(US)	0.37	0.56

Table 5-12

Estimates of $TMPK_x$: East Asia

	MPK_{nx}	$TMPK_x$
All Exports	2.39	4.01
Man. Exports	1.84	7.34

While wide wage differentials are suggestive of super-profit rates, a more direct measure of a manufacturer's profitability is provided by capital's share in value added. Those numbers are contained in Tables 5-15 and 5-16. The OECD has an average of 49% of manufacturing value added accruing to capital and 51% to labor between 1970 and 1990. Shares for EA are considerably higher for capital – being an average of 70% to capital and 30% to labor. Such a large share of value added accruing to capital in EA is partly a function of strong authoritarian governments, weak labor unions, low environmental standards, and more importantly, high world prices relative to domestic costs. Such a profitability differential between EA and the OECD from these figures is around 1.5 and lies well within the estimates generated by equations (5-9) and (5-14).

Table 5-13

Manufacturing Wage Rates

(OECD: $US/hour)

	1965	1970	1975	1980	1985	1990
Australia	-	1.14	2.05	3.71	-	-
Austria	0.63	0.94	2.61	-	4.13	9.40
Belgium	0.89	1.30	3.92	-	4.95	-
Canada	1.96	2.58	4.47	6.35	8.62	11.44
Denmark	1.33	2.09	5.82	9.56	7.14	16.15
Finland	-	1.08	3.15	5.29	5.17	12.40
France	-	0.84	2.29	4.30	3.51	7.04
Germany	-	0.94	1.68	2.85	2.00	-
Greece	0.34	0.53	1.08	2.40	2.27	4.17
Italy	-	0.97	2.75	5.47	4.95	-
Netherlands	-	1.33	3.93	6.92	5.00	10.35
Norway	-	1.72	3.94	7.40	7.00	12.64
N Z.	-	1.28	3.10	4.52	4.57	7.56
Portugal	-	-	0.89	1.34	1.11	1.78
Sweden	-	2.61	5.72	9.36	7.26	14.75
U.K.	-	1.45	2.77	5.28	4.79	-
USA	2.61	3.36	4.83	6.69	7.27	9.54

Source: International Labor Statistics Yearbook, various issues.

Notes: These figures are estimates as results depend on exchange rates and number of hours worked per week.

Table 5-14

Manufacturing Wage Rates

(East Asia: $US/hour)

	1965	1970	1975	1980	1985	1990	1996
China	-	-	-	0.23	0.16	0.19	0.27
H.Kong	-	-	-	0.99	1.44	2.41	-
Japan	0.52	1.04	2.87	5.61	6.54	12.66	-
Korea	0.09	0.24	0.41	1.26	1.61	4.34	7.59
Malaysia	-	-	-	-	-	1.97	2.08
Philippines	-	0.19	0.24	-	0.55	0.91	1.35
Singapore	0.31	0.30	0.62	-	-	4.00	-
Taiwan	-	-	-	1.16	1.66	4.29	-
Thailand	0.18	0.18	-	0.33	0.54	0.69	1.04
USA	2.61	3.36	4.83	6.69	7.27	9.54	10.83

Source: International Labor Statistics Yearbook, various issues; Taiwan Statistical Yearbook, 1994.

Notes: These figures are estimates as results depend on exchange rates and number of hours worked per week.

Such an estimate is reinforced by statistics from the OECD, revealed in Table 5-17. Capital shares in the business sector in the OECD have been stable at around 33% between 1970 and 1990 and generated a profit rate of roughly half that (ie 17%). There appears to be a non-linear relationship between capital shares and profit rates, as can be seen from high capital share for Greece and low capital share for Ireland. The capital shares in the *manufacturing sector* for East Asia are known but the rates of return are not – in any direct sense. Using the ratio between capital shares and rates of return for the G7, 0.52 and 0.50 respectively

Table 5-15

Capital Shares in Manufacturing Sectors – OECD

(as a % of value added)

	1970	1975	1980	1985	1990	Average
Australia	47.5	44.0	47.9	51.1	55.0	49.10
Austria	52.9	43.8	41.4	44.4	46.3	45.76
Belgium	53.6	50.9	50.1	53.8	58.9	53.46
Canada	47.0	50.5	52.6	54.4	55.9	52.08
Denmark	45.6	40.9	43.2	48.2	48.9	45.36
Finland	52.9	50.5	45.9	46.7	52.6	49.72
France	-	-	31.6	33.7	37.5	34.26
Germany	53.7	50.6	49.7	58.3	58.4	54.14
Greece	68.5	64.1	61.0	57.6	60.1	62.26
Iceland	42.0	60.3	49.5	43.9	33.4	45.82
Ireland	42.0	60.3	49.5	43.9	33.4	45.82
Italy	58.6	60.3	62.5	57.6	59.1	59.62
Netehrlands	47.8	42.9	42.1	49.7	51.9	46.88
Norway	49.6	42.3	39.7	41.9	43.1	43.32
N.Z.	38.2	33.5	33.9	40.9	44.7	38.24
Portugal	66.1	39.0	56.8	60.9	64.2	57.40
Spain	49.3	40.4	55.1	60.2	61.5	53.30
Sweden	47.8	53.3	56.3	63.3	65.2	57.18
Turkey	74.1	68.0	69.3	68.9	80.8	72.22
U.K.	47.8	48.7	51.2	56.7	58.0	52.48

USA	52.7	56.9	59.1	60.3	64.4	58.68
Average						49.06

Source: World Bank Tables, various issues.

Notes: Real earnings per employee is used to calculate the residual capital share.

for the two periods, the rate of return for EA is estimated in the last row in Table 5-17. These profit rates are roughly twice that of the G7 nations.

Table 5-16

Capital Shares in Manufacturing Sector – East Asia

(as a % of value added)

	1970	1975	1980	1985	1990	Average
China	-	-	84.9	85.4	-	85.15
H.Kong	-	47.5	48.0	36.4	45.3	44.30
Indonesia	73.6	79.5	83.4	81.0	78.6	79.22
Japan	68.2	59.6	65.2	64.8	67.0	64.96
Korea	75.0	75.2	65.2	64.8	67.0	69.44
Malaysia	61.5	62.6	72.0	71.1	72.8	67.8
Philippines	79.4	85.2	78.0	77.7	76.7	79.4
Singapore	63.7	65.2	70.3	62.8	68.3	66.06
Thailand	75.5	75.3	76.8	66.4	72.1	73.22
Average						69.95

Source: World Bank Tables, various issues.

Notes: A residual capital share is calculated.

Table 5-17

Capital Shares and Rates of Return

Business Sector

	1970-1980(%)	1980-1990(%)
G7	32.5	33.4
	(16.9)	(16.8)
Ratio	0.52	0.50
Ireland	19.8	24.5
	(5.6)	(7.9)
Ratio	0.28	0.33
Greece	50.2	43.2
	(40.3)	(21.6)
Ratio	80.2	50.0
East Asia	75.0	67.7
Profit Estimates	(39.0)	(33.85)

Source: *OECD Economic Outlook* (1996).

Notes: Capital shares are in italics, rates of return in parentheses

 East Asia: Growth, Crisis and Recovery

Table 5-18

Stock Market Indexes

	1986	1989	1996	1999
Australia	1221	1509	2228	2986
Hong Kong	1758	2233	10953	11107
Japan	16670	33469	22332	16379
N.Z.	2467	1924	2090	2144
Philippines	966	1056	3170	2018
Singapore	3993	344	2267	1498
S.Korea	227	880	862	608
Taiwan	957	9297	6324	7043
Thailand	116	591	1258	366
Malaysia	2288	443	1125	508

Source: Far Eastern Economic Review (various issues)

Stock market indeces also provide rough estimates of 'rates of return,' despite the fact that capital gains and expectations are mixed in. From Table 5-18 the spectacular gains in many Asian stock markets are evident. For example, over the 1986-96 period, such gains were 623% for Hong Kong , 661% for Taiwan and 380% for Korea.

Earlier comparisons, 1974-1994, reveal rises in stock market indeces for Malaysia, Thailand and Korea to above 1600% and for Hong Kong a staggering 3,000%. Rises in developed country stock market indeces over the same period were far less impressive at around 300%. Clearly, there were vastly higher rate of return opportunities in East Asia than the West in *both* the real and the financial sectors.

5-6 Conclusion

This chapter tests a Feder-type growth model with some encouraging results. As always, the diagnostics warn of potential problems and advise caution in interpretation. For EA the capital shares are for manufacturing, not the business sector. Nevertheless, the traditional view of capital and labor accumulation being critical to economic growth in developing countries is questionable, according to the above results.

Such accumulation is a necessary but not a sufficient condition for achieving catch-up economic growth and so developed country income levels. Exports yield an additional productivity or *profitability premium* above and beyond that of input accumulation in a closed economy environment. Given wide wage rate differentials in manufacturing compared to the US, and the strong export performance of EA, it is profits that have made the MPK explosive. The exponential rises in stock market indeces partially reflected the massive profit opportunities available in the real sector of the economy. However, these profits were couched in terms of foreign currency which in turn broke many constraints on economic development. Examining the power of rocket booster two is the quest of Chapter 6.

Appendix 5.1

Data Set for Table 5-1 (67 Countries)

All 47 countries in Appendix 3.1 plus

Argentina	Guyana	S. Africa
Cameroon	Honduras	Trinidad and Tobago
Congo	Israel	Uruguay
Dominica	Madagascar	Venezuela
El Salvador	Nigeria	Zambia
Ecuador	Mexico	Zimbabwe
Egypt	Rwanda	

Data Set for Tables 5-2 and 5-5 (46 Countries)

Asian 10 plus
16 'Other Developing Countries' from Appendix 3.1
Plus 20 countries named above

Data Set for Table 5-3 (70 Countries)

Same as for Table 4.1 Plus:
Chad
Chile
Yugoslavia

Data Set for Table 5-7 (47 Countries)

Same as Appendix 4.1

Data Set for Table 5-9 (54 Countries)

Same as Appendix 4.1 plus
Eygpt
Guyana
Honduras
Israel
El Salvador
S Africa
Trinidad and Tobago

Chapter Six

Rocket Engine Two: Hard Currency

Introduction:

In Chapter Five the rocket engine of super-profits was examined in the light of export penetration into Western markets. An explosive MPK from exports was enough to offset the constraints on economic development stemming from a lack of human capital, public infrastructure and physical capital. Explosive trade profits substituted for the normal 'real factors' that drive long-run growth. However, the financial constraints of an immature financial system and a lack of foreign (hard) currency are also major bottlenecks to economic development. Financial intermediation plays an important part in the growth process as resources are released for more productive use. Additional monetary liquidity acts to ease the plight of liquidity constrained firms in an export orientated developing economy. Besides a more sophisticated financial sector, the importance of foreign exchange reserves are often overlooked in the growth process. Stocks of foreign exchange grew rapidly in EA since the early 1960's, a clear and distinctive variable associated with economic growth that contrasts with other developing nations that have acquired relatively small amounts of foreign exchange. This chapter seeks to explain the importance of hard currency (rocket booster two) in the growth process (rocket acceleration). Hence, hard currency is seen more than a 'facilitator' of growth, but an engine, in the transition phase to the international steady state.

6-2 Hard Currency: Breaking Bottlenecks

Abundant supplies of domestic currency, that are not respected in the international trade and financial arena, contain little growth energy and only raise domestic price levels to the point of destroying a nation's macroeconomic credibility[1]. There are two ways a developing nation can achieve international acceptance of its macroeconomic policy competence. Firstly, by solid domestic policies aimed at building economic fundamentals and not yielding to macroeconomic policy 'temptation' by printing money. Secondly, by gaining sizable foreign exchange reserves and so 'appropriate' the credibility of a developed nation's hard currency in terms of shoring up the reputation of its own Central Bank and its monetary policy. Any by-product of currency appreciation assists the central bank in its fight against inflation, as more imports can be used as a weapon against 'monopoly pricing' at home. Moreover, imports become cheaper in domestic currency terms. Hence, additional domestic liquidity becomes possible, without an inflationary impact, because it is foreign currency backed. In fact, both strategies are inter-linked as foreign exchange reserves support and re-enforce the acceptability of a developing nation's domestic currency and yet responsible domestic money supply growth attracts foreign capital. A welcome by-product of such an interaction is lower domestic interest rates that stimulates the growth of the capital stock and so capital per worker.

From a development perspective, a developing country with sizable foreign exchange reserves has a greater ability to tap world capital markets. Private banks seek the ability to repay in hard currency as do foreign governments. Foreign borrowing for both private and public projects is greatly enhanced. Moreover, FDI is also attracted by the 'security' of foreign exchange reserves being used to defend the domestic currency in time of attack. The credibility of a developing country's currency and central bank creates a virtuous circle of foreign capital flow and further policy credibility.

6-3 Developing Economies: Does Money Matter?

For developed countries, the notion that 'money matters' in generating growth has been hotly denied by most economists. Money does not affect growth in the long run, known as the 'monetary neutrality postulate.' Monetarists argue that money only causes inflation in the long- run even though *exogenous money* may affect real variables in the short-run. There are liquidity effects as economic agents seek to divest themselves of cash and into assets. Hence, asset prices are bid up and interest rates down. There is also a loanable funds channel whereby the central bank explodes the money base and indirectly the money supply through the banking system. However, price rises and the Fischer effect place upward pressure on interest rates over the longer term. Despite some short-run potency, monetary policy is not to be actively used as it only accentuates the business cycle and further distorts relative prices. Besides, the economy possesses 'self correcting forces' that are capable of restoring full employment equilibrium. In the monetarist's world, only real factors drive long-run growth.

Real business cycle theorists also claim that business cycle fluctuations are driven by real factors, real productivity and preference shocks. Money is neutral. Again, demand side stimuli play no role in promoting growth. Plosser (1989) points out that the real factors that drive business cycles are but the same real forces that drive long run economic growth. The central bank may appropriately respond to positive productivity shocks by expanding the money supply, implying that such a money supply response is *endogenous*. In many of these models the demand for money is transactions and activity based and so money is not regarded as a store of value. The real business cycle models of Kydland and Prescott (1982), Long and Plosser (1983) and King and Plosser (1984) completely omit monetary factors or any important financial intermediation function.

The above arguments point to the neutrality of money in the long run for a *developed economy*. But can expansionary money supply growth over a long period of time contribute to economic growth in a *developing economy*? Financial intermediation holds one key to explain why money promotes growth in a developing economy. Some of the stylised facts are as follows. Firstly, early work by Goldsmith (1969), McKinnon (1973) and Shaw (1973) emphasize the link between 'a country's financial superstructure and its economic superstructure.' Secondly,

Goldsmith (1985) points to the trend of a rising ratio of financial institutions assets to GDP for *developed countries*. Thirdly, McKinnon (1973) and Townsend (1983) point to the increases in the ratio of M2 to national income and more importantly to the rise in the ratio of private credit to GNP as one moves from low to high income countries. Fourthly, King and Levine (1993) find that financial indicators correlate positively with current growth rates and that financial sector development predicts future growth as well.[2]

Why is financial and economic development so closely linked? Firstly, as outlined by Marquis (1997), financial intermediation reduces trading frictions both intra and inter-period. The friction and mismatch between the wants of traders is reduced. The mismatch between borrowers and lenders is also reduced as search costs, risks associated with asymmetric information and the duplication of monitoring is minimised. Hence, intra-period trade is enhanced as is inter-temporal consumption. Greater activity, demand and production result. The power of intermediation rests with its allocation of funds to areas of highest valued use, a stimulus to long-term investment via higher rates of return. Galetovic (1996) stresses the importance of specialisation that follows from a more sophisticated financial sector and the need for greater access to credit. Monetary injections impact asymmetrically on credit constrained firms generating real effects on production and growth (Fuerst,1992). East Asian economies benefited from financial intermediation via an improvement in *domestic allocative efficiency*. This *endogenous* force entails more specialisation, more investment, more economic activity and so more growth. These nations, unlike other developing economies, appeared willing to pay the 'sunk costs' for a mature financial sector when incomes per head were still quite low.

Secondly, as outlined in Chapter Three, is the superior determinant of *catch-up growth* - that being *international allocative efficiency*. Profitability is very much a function of transferring resources, not only from the rural to the manufacturing sector, but also from non-traded to the traded goods sector. Exports to mature economy markets are profit-laden. Therefore, financial intermediation is very much a matter of ensuring that credit-constrained exporters are kept liquid enough to realise profitable export opportunities. East Asia's financial intermediation push was strongly associated with its export push. A virtuous circle developed in that export profits caused the financial sector to mature and vice versa. Moreover, FDI came in search of higher profits according to product cycle opportunities and so stimulated further financial intermediation. Hence, this *exogenous* force of foreign money oiled structural adjustment in the real sector of economy. Townsend (1983) emphasized the importance of the distinction between trade credit and money. The ratio of private credit to GDP rises and the ratio of currency to GDP falls with greater economic maturity. This dichotomy fits the above distinction between domestic and international allocative efficiency, as money plays a lubricating role for increased activity (productivity) in a *developed economy* but credit plays an important role for increasing foreign trade (profitability) in a *developing economy*.

Table 6-1

Money Growth/Relationships (East Asia)

	INF	M2	Y/M2	RY/M2	CPI/M2
China	12.1	27.0	0.32	0.27	0.45
H.Kong	6.81	21	0.71	0.38	0.32
Indonesia	19.2	32.3	0.22	0.19	0.60
Japan	4.9	11.9	0.86	0.78	0.41
Korea	10.5	28.4	0.81	0.67	0.37
Malaysia	3.5	14.9	0.71	0.47	0.26
Philippines	11.5	18.7	0.82	0.21	0.61
Singapore	3.2	14.2	0.89	0.60	0.23
Taiwan	3.24	17.1	-	-	0.19
Thailand	5.47	17.3	0.76	0.44	0.32

Source: IFS Yearbooks, Key Indicators (Asian Development Bank)

                          East Asia: Growth, Crisis and Recovery

Table 6-2
Money Growth/Relationships (OECD)

	INF	M2	Y/M2	RY/M2	CPI/M2
Australia	6.2	11.3	0.92	0.33	0.55
Austria	4.23	10.1	0.76	0.33	0.42
Belgium	4.57	9.9	0.78	0.29	0.46
Canada	5.02	10.8	0.81	0.28	0.47
Denmark	6.35	10.1	0.92	0.28	0.63
Finland	6.73	11.5	0.93	0.28	0.59
France	5.94	12.0	0.80	0.27	0.49
Iceland	23.0	28.5	0.10	0.14	0.81
Isreal	49.0	76.1	0.76	0.12	0.65
Italy	8.49	13.1	0.98	0.63	0.65
Holland	4.34	9.1	0.86	0.35	0.48
N.Z.	7.87	14.5	0.70	0.17	0.55
Norway	6.08	9.8	0.98	0.39	0.62
Spain	9.41	15.1	0.93	0.27	0.63
Sweden	6.41	-	-	0.30	-
Switzerland	3.73	7.32	0.88	0.30	0.51
USA	4.79	7.66	1.00	0.39	0.63

Source: World Bank (1999)

There is also a strong interaction between foreign and domestic capital to consider. The apparent explosion in TFP may be due to knowledge-laden foreign capital increasing the productivity of domestic capital as these two types of capital are imperfect substitutes (Warr,

1998). A rising ratio of foreign to domestic capital partially explains the explosion in TFP in EA in the 1990's. Not only does foreign capital assist the potency of domestic capital but foreign money assists the potency of domestic money with growth-energising consequences.

Does money matter for growth? For developing *export orientated* economies the answer is yes. Financial intermediation and even monetary injections by the central bank cause the explosive power of international allocative efficiency to be realised. It is an engine of growth in the transition phase of economic take-off (the rocket phase) but not in the steady state (the shuttle phase). From Tables 6-1 and 6-2 two stylised facts stand out. Firstly, it can be seen that a significant dichotomy in the relationship between money growth and RGDP growth over the period 1960 to 1996 between East Asia and the OECD. That is, for every 1% growth in the domestic money supply there was an associated high rate real income growth. Korea (0.67), Japan (0.78), Singapore (0.60) and Malaysia (0.47). This dichotomy is not obvious when comparing money growth with nominal GDP growth. From Table 6-2, this relationship for OECD nations is far weaker at around 0.30. Neverheless, the direction of causation is the eternal question that is raised.[3] Secondly, it appears that higher money growth in East Asia did not translate into a higher inflationary cost than the OECD. In fact, the data reveals a lower inflationary cost despite the fact that EA generated a higher economic cruise speed than the OECD.

6-4 Productivity or Profitability Shocks?

As Marquis (1997) claims, it is a legitimate response of a monetary authority in a developed economy to accommodate productivity shocks by expanding the money base and so ease liquidity constraints - when the prices are set in advance or a somewhat inflexible downwards. Firms and individuals are unable raise velocity sufficiently in the face of expanding economic activity. For a developing economy there are continual technological waves and productivity shocks occurring as the economy is well inside the PPF or world best practice. Hence, there is a continual hunger for liquidity. For the East Asia export orientated economies there is an even greater need for the central bank to accommodate with additional liquidity as higher profitability is achieved by moving up the product ladder and penetrating mature economy markets. The desire of firms to capture higher profitability via exports may be more important than continual productivity catch-up or productivity shocks in determining the demand for credit. However, authorities should respond to profitability shocks orginating from the export sector, and not those from the non-export sector, unless they are productivity driven. Just as the authorities in the West face the problem of disentangling productivity from preference shocks so do authorities in EA face the problem of disentangling profitability shocks in the export sector from foreign capital shocks (speculation) in the non-export sector. Besides, to the extent that profitability shocks are greater than productivity shocks in the export sector there is a greater liquidity response required by authorities. The insatiable desire for credit is explained by profitable export opportunities in early stages of development as per Townsend's finding.

6-5 Monetary Policy:A Fixed Exchange Rate Regime

Aside from the question of whether money affects economic growth, there is the question of whether the central bank can effectively maintain macroeconomic stability by employing a monetary policy under a fixed exchange rate regime. According to the Mundell-Fleming Model the answer is no. Therefore, a commitment to maintain a pegged currency implies the loss of control over the money supply and so a major stabilisation weapon in the hands of the policy maker[4]. A common scenario under this regime is a rise in foreign exchange reserves, a higher price level and current account deficits. Not only does foreign capital bring with it growth energy but also destabilising power in terms of a rise in the price of non-traded goods, an asset price bubble and a real appreciation of the exchange rate. Hence, international competitiveness is adversely affected.

Can the authorities sterilise large capital inflows? Probably not. By issuing more government bonds and raising interest rates there is a likelihood of more foreign capital being attracted and interest rates falling to previous levels. Therefore, sterilisation attempts may meet with failure in that the domestic money supply may continue to expand and yet higher asset prices lure more foreign capital into the economy. An independent monetary policy is forfeited for the exchange rate target. Whether such an increase in liquidity assists in capturing greater productivity and profitability in practise remains the central issue. Rising asset prices may divert liquidity into speculative activity instead. It therefore appears that both growth and inflation are exogenously determined in this regime.

6-6 The Signal Extraction Problem

The EA policy maker faces a difficult choice in whether to accommodate exogenous shocks with additional liquidity or not. As the above section outlines, this choice is compounded under a fixed exchange rate regime. This choice is further compounded by the nature of foreign capital inflows, how the foreign exchange is generated and to what 'productive use' the funds are put.

Foreign exchange generated by exports contains much growth energy and is the least de-stabilising. Likewise, foreign exchange accumulated via FDI is not inflation threatening and increases know-how and capital per worker in the short-run. Even foreign borrowed funds, if directed at the export sector, contain growth potential and a low inflationary impact as they generate more foreign exchange and raise profitability. However, foreign exchange obtained by 'hot money' and/or portfolio capital inflows contain the least amount of growth energy and the most amount of inflationary heat. Productive capacity may not increase.

How foreign exchange is generated poses a problem for the central bank as monetary accomodation and an open capital account may result in asset price inflation and only a minor restructuring of the export sector's productive potential. The rapid accumulation of foreign exchange reserves is like fire, as in the monetarist tradition, a powerful force driving of both economic activity and inflation. Screening capital flows and encouraging the channelling of funds into the export sector reduces such an inflationary threat. Hence, monetary accomodation is legitimate in a rapidly growing export orientated developing economy.

But how does the policy maker discern between preference and productivity shocks? Between export and non-export profitability shocks? This is known as the signal extraction problem. Productivity shocks are worthy of a response, even more so in the case of East Asia as both technical and allocative efficiency drive such nations toward the PPF. Continual profitability shocks are also worthy of monetary accomodation to the extent they are driven by international allocative efficiency and product ladder improvement. Why? Because these profits are in hard currency. Policy makers in EA appear to have been confused by this signal as profitability in the non-export sector, combined with productivity improvements in particular, have lured the central bank into providing abundant liquidity.

6-7 Foreign Exchange Reserves: How Large?

East Asia has not only accumulated large amounts of foreign exchange in the absolute sense but also acquired an increased percentage of world

Table 6-3

Foreign Exchange Reserves (in $US)

	1980	1985	1990	1995	1997
China	3316	13214	30209	76037	143363
H.Kong	-	-	24657	55424	92823
Indonesia	6500	5880	8520	14787	17396
Japan	21567	22328	69487	172443	207886
Korea	2956	3351	14824	32712	20404
Malaysia	4491	5002	9871	23898	20899
Philippines	3140	1116	2048	7775	8738
Singapore	6566	12847	27748	68695	71228
Taiwan	2574	23520	78064	95911	88186
Thailand	3026	3003	14273	36945	26892

Source: IFS Yearbook, 1999

foreign exchange reserves. From Table 6-3 it can be seen that China possessed $US76 billion, Hong Kong $US55 billion, Singapore $US68 billion and Taiwan $US96 billion of foreign exchange reserves in 1995. These are sizable amounts when compared to Australia ($US14b), Canada ($US18b), France ($US23b), Holland ($US24b) or Sweden ($US18b). Moreover, most East Asian nations actually increased their percentage of world foreign exchange reserves between 1960-1997. For example, Singapore's share was 1.8% in 1960 but rose to 7.6% in 1996. Korea's share rose from 0.5% to 3.2%, Taiwan from 1% to 10.8% and Japan from 6.5% to 20% in same period. Open economies tended to increase their share of world foreign exchange reserves while non-trading developing economies did not - with strong implications for growth.

Table 6-4

Foreign Exchange Reserves (% of World Total)

	1966	1972	1978	1984	1990	1996	Average
China	-	-	2.0	6.10	5.81	10.82	6.18
H.Kong	-	-	-	-	4.15	6.18	5.16
Indonesia	0.1	0.6	1.11	1.34	1.24	1.72	1.0
Japan	5.7	17.3	13.0	6.28	11.7	20.1	10.6
Korea	0.91	0.50	1.23	0.78	2.43	3.22	1.48
Malaysia	1.84	0.83	1.40	1.0	1.57	2.53	1.58
Philippines	0.47	0.47	0.78	0.16	0.15	0.96	0.56
Singapore	1.51	1.81	2.37	2.95	3.70	7.65	3.22
Taiwan	1.07	1.00	0.63	4.48	12.72	-	3.98
Thailand	3.1	0.91	0.89	0.54	2.23	3.60	1.48

Source: IFS Yearbook, 1999

Table 6-5

OECD Foreign Exchange Reserves (% of World Total)

	1966	1972	1978	1984	1990	1996
Australia	4.56	5.66	0.77	2.01	2.63	1.36
Austria	2.06	1.76	2.06	1.03	1.47	2.12
Belgium	1.78	1.15	1.18	1.03	1.88	1.49
Canada	4.70	4.56	1.15	0.50	2.62	1.75
Denmark	1.64	0.67	1.31	0.75	1.69	1.29
Finland	0.44	0.54	0.48	0.71	1.56	0.60
France	1.97	3.66	6.47	5.47	5.73	2.24
Iceland	0.20	0.07	0.06	0.04	0.07	0.04
Ireland	1.83	1.07	1.09	0.61	0.82	0.75
Isreal	2.15	1.19	1.17	0.87	1.06	1.10
Italy	7.63	2.32	4.71	5.46	10.13	4.26
Holland	1.18	1.48	1.77	2.23	2.70	2.34
N.Z.	0.69	0.75	0.16	0.51	0.69	0.56
Norway	1.81	1.16	1.11	2.47	2.41	2.45
Spain	1.17	4.41	4.40	3.01	8.32	5.41
Sweden	2.56	1.19	1.67	1.51	2.92	1.76
Switzealand	2.74	4.59	7.81	4.32	4.92	3.56
USA	5.13	0.25	0.20	0.20	0.88	0.37

Source: World Bank (1999)

Table 6-6

Foreign Exchange Reserves (% of World Total)

	1966	1972	1978	1982	1990	1996	Average
Argentina	0.51	0.31	2.06	0.36	0.73	1.72	1.08
Bolivia	0.1	0.04	0.06	0.07	0.03	0.09	0.06
Brazil	1.43	4.0	5.12	3.3	1.25	5.65	2.72
Colombia	-	0.82	1.11	1.06	1.56	1.05	1.14
Chile	1.25	0.81	1.11	1.06	1.56	1.05	1.14
Ecuador	0.24	0.15	0.33	0.21	0.17	0.25	0.23
El Sal	0.22	0.09	0.17	0.09	0.07	0.10	0.12
Mexico	1.43	0.85	0.74	0.29	1.59	1.85	0.13
Panama	0.60	0.21	0.16	0.26	0.05	0.06	0.22
Paraguay	0.05	0.04	2.02	1.94	1.13	0.09	0.88
Peru	1.06	0.92	1.74	1.32	0.90	1.63	1.26
Uruguay	0.69	0.31	0.52	0.27	0.24	0.18	0.37

Source: World Bank (1999)

From Table 6-6 it can be seen that several 'other' developing countries accumulated relatively small foreign exchange reserves as a percentage of the world total. Some in fact fell behind in the race to acquire foreign exchange. Developed countries, having reached the international steady state (the shuttle phase), are in less need for large amounts of foreign exchange as their own currencies have gained a high level of respect and credibility[5]. Many nations witnessed their world percentages fall between 1966 and 1996.

Table 6-7

Foreign Reserves-Debt Ratio

	1990	1991	1992	1993	1994	1995	1996
China	4.39	5.44	2.25	2.08	4.63	4.88	4.05
H.Kong	14.4	19.7	22.6	28.6	18.3	16.8	13.8
Indonesia	0.75	0.82	0.82	0.77	0.82	0.81	0.82
Korea	1.74	2.19	2.38	2.14	2.76	2.44	2.25
Malaysia	2.15	3.57	3.98	5.61	4.06	3.87	2.88
Philippines	0.27	1.05	1.05	0.95	1.36	1.26	1.96
Singapore	52.4	72.2	48.0	63.0	69.6	50.8	28.6
Taiwan	42.2	48.2	47.9	63.7	51.6	33.5	26.30
Thailand	2.66	2.18	3.38	3.73	3.66	4.12	3.19

Source: World Bank (1997) and International Financial Statistics
        Yearbook (1999)

Those countries with high ratios of foreign exchange reserves to immediate debt repayments (capital and plus interest) were by and large exempt from the crisis. From Table 6-7, Taiwan, China, Singapore and Hong Kong displayed ratios of 15 to a 100, while crisis riden countries of Malaysia, Indonesia, Thailand and Korea revealed low levels of coverage of around 4 or less. High levels of foreign exchange reserves and high coverage ratios are a signal to foreign creditors and speculators that there is the 'ability to pay' and defend the currency if need be. This dichotomy in foreign exchange coverage clearly distinguishes those countries affected by the crisis from those that rebounded early afterwards.

6-8 East Asia's Economic Cruise Speed

The developing nations of East Asia have enjoyed real growth rates of around 7.5%, while most OECD nations have reached 'maturity' and so have posted more modest growth rates at around 3% p.a. since the 1960's. However, such super-growth did not ignite any abnormal inflationary cost. As can be seen from Table 6-8 , East Asia achieved a lower inflationary cost for every one percent rise in real GDP (CPI/RGDP) - than the OECD. The OECD paid around 2.5% on average for every one percent rise in real GDP. East Asia paid far less at around 1.0%. Hence, East Asia grew at twice the speed of the OECD between 1960 and 1996 at half the inflationary cost. In a nutshell, this is why the 'miracle' was called a miracle.

Table 6-8

East Asia: Economic Cruise Speed

	Inflation	RGDP	INF/RGDP
China	12.1	7.5	1.61
H.Kong	6.81	7.9	0.86
Indonesia	19.2	6.3	3.04
Japan	4.92	9.3	0.53
Korea	10.5	8.1	0.53
Malaysia	3.52	7.1	0.50
Philippines	11.5	4.0	2.87
Singapore	3.22	8.5	0.38
Taiwan	3.24	-	-
Thailand	5.47	7.5	0.73

Source: World Bank (1997)

Table 6-9
OCED: Economic Cruise Speed

	Inflation	RGDP	INF/RGDP
Austria	4.23	3.3	1.28
Australia	6.2	3.7	1.67
Belgium	4.57	2.9	1.57
Canada	5.02	3.0	1.67
Denmark	6.35	2.8	2.26
Finland	6.73	3.2	2.10
France	5.94	3.2	1.85
Iceland	23.0	4.1	5.60
Ireland	7.72	4.7	1.64
Isreal	49.0		5.54
Italy	8.49	8.3	1.02
Holland	4.34	3.2	1.35
N.Z.	7.87	2.6	3.02
Norway	6.08	3.8	1.60
Spain	9.41	4.1	2.29
Sweden	6.41	2.4	2.67
Switzealand	3.73	2.2	1.69
USA	4.79	3.0	1.59

Source: World Bank (1997)

What forces oiled this non-traditional Phillips Curve relationship?
Why was East Asia partially exempt from the traditional curses
associated with rapid money supply and economic growth? How was

growth and stabilisation achieved simultaneously? The answer may rest with productivity growth ameliorating the Phillips curve trade-off by shifting it to the *left*. It may also rest with high profitability over many years and foreign money that raised capital per worker and indirectly supported productivity growth. An exogenous trade force injected profits and money into cash starved economies and so allowed higher than normal monetary growth that assisted exporters in realising further profitable opportunities. Money was non-inflationary, not only because of productivity growth, but also because of profitability growth. Both economic *and* financial bottlenecks to growth were broken. Trade profits, in hard currency, was the oil that shifted the Phillips curve to the left and so facilitated both growth *and* stability.

Even if the Phillips curve is vertical (as well as the long run aggregate supply curve) the importance of trade profits is not lost. Why? Because such profits act as a substitute for real factors in driving medium term growth, at least to one's own steady state[6]. In this environment, K/L ratio driven output per worker greatly affects the demand for labour and so wage rises are non-inflationary. As a result, the conflict over the size of the national cake takes on a lower priority.

6-9 Conclusion

Even though money, domestic or foreign, is not an engine of growth in developed economies there are reasons to suggest that hard currency is an engine of growth for *export-orientated* developing economies. Growing foreign exchange reserves not only inject much needed liquidity into a credit constrained export sector but also act as a licence for authorities to expand the domestic money supply and so achieve greater international allocative efficiency. Specialisation and structural adjustment in the real economy follow. Hence, above 'normal' money supply growth can stimulate economic growth in the medium term as a credit-hungry export economy seeks to capture profits in hard currency. More foreign exchange reserves adds credibility to the central bank and its monetary policy which in turn promotes a virtuous circle of prosperity by breaking liquidity constraints. Not only should the central bank respond to continual productivity shocks but also to widespread profitability 'shocks' from increasing globalisation and openness. East

Asia's economic cruise speed, without huge inflationary cost, is testimony to the power of trade profits and foreign capital in stimulating financial intermediation and so oil for the traditional Phillips curve trade-off. However, as noted in this chapter, the response of monetary authorities to both profitability and productivity shocks is fraught with a misperception or a signal extraction problem. Both preference shocks and foreign capital shocks in the non-export sector may tempt the policy maker to allow further liquidity and credit expansion to the detriment of asset prices and inflationary expectations. Moreover, when a nation reaches its 'own' steady state, constrained by productivity and human capital levels, then the 'long-run' monetary neutrality postulate holds. This postulate also holds in the international steady state when rocket acceleration fades and the shuttle phase begins. Chapter Seven examines the causes of the crisis in the light of past macroeconomic management and export success.

Chapter Seven

The Asian Crisis: Internal or External Causes?

7-1 Introduction

In previous chapters the causes of East Asia's development success were examined, not the least being the acquisition of super- profits and hard currency via exports to mature economy markets. Although there were several waves of economic boom, the most recent upswing of the business cycle in the early 1990's brought with it high expectations of reaching economic maturity. In short, East Asia may have fallen victim of its own success, in that accumulated wealth and high savings rates generated both a huge asset price bubble and an overheated economy. It was not just the rise in the level of asset prices that destabilized macroeconomic performance, but the distortion of relative prices, that adversely affected investment decisions and the allocation of long-term capital. A casino mentality gradually subdued rational business calculus undertaken by private investors in 'normal circumstances.'[1] The financial sector compounded the upswing of the economic boom by indulging in loose lending policies that focussed on asset backing, rather than cash flows, thus adding to liquidity effects. This chapter examines the major internal and external causes of East Asia's recent demise.

7-2 The Crisis: A Function of the Boom Years?

A key prediction of the Solow model and indeed Krugman (1994) is that East Asian growth would eventually slow-down as result of diminishing returns to factor accumulation. The emphasis is on slow-down not a sudden crash.[2] As Krugman himself admits, his prediction was not of a sudden collapse in growth. Therefore, this model is inappropriate in explaining the crisis in terms of a collapsing MPK or productivity. However, there were signs of a corporate profit slowdown in East Asia in the mid 1990's as over-investment and idle capacity squeezed profit margins. Hence, it appears more likely that EA suffered from a profitability rather than a productivity slowdown.

Another key prediction of the Solow model is that as East Asia converged on mature economy income (knowledge) so would growth rates diminish. Moreover, work-leisure choices and consumption-savings choices are expected to be affected as incomes rise. In practice, however, most EA nations are still a considerable distance from US income levels and so still enjoy 'transitional growth' opportunities from a low K/L ratio.

Given that East Asia enjoyed superlative export success, it earned and accumulated valuable foreign exchange, and so liquidity, for development goals. In a sense, it was such liquidity that fueled domestic inflation rates, asset price speculation and raised development expectations beyond current productivity constraints. Export success, also contributed indirectly to a speculative boom in assets via the provision of national 'balance sheet' credibility upon which foreign funds could be attracted.[3]

The crisis was also a function of East Asia's success in that foreign investors were lured by such an impressive track record and readiness to indulge in consumption. Although foreign investment took on many forms, much of it was short term and 'hot' in nature. Such foreign funds further fueled domestic liquidity and significantly contributed to a credit boom that in turn fueled higher asset prices and created 'false wealth' in balance sheets. This raises the whole question as to why EA borrowed so much when domestic savings rates were already high by world standards.

In summary, it was export success and the associated attraction of foreign capital (in a short time frame) that sowed the seeds of East Asia's crisis via the impact on liquidity.

7-3 The Nature of East Asia's Crisis

At face value, East Asia's crisis of the late 1990's may appear to be economic in nature. This may not be the case in that human capital, productivity levels, education, receptiveness to knowledge flows and a hard work ethic display no signs of fading. It is difficult to accept that real factors, such as capital and labor accumulation, suddenly turned sour or that diminishing returns caused economies to collapse in 1997. Moreover, economic fundamentals in general, such as inflation rates, current account deficits, size of government and budget deficits were not, by and large, at alarming levels.[4] For example, the following Table 7-1 reveals the quite modest current deficits as a percent of GDP. The exceptions, however, were Thailand and Malaysia, especially as they breached the magical eight percent of GDP – an alleged benchmark signal that concerns finance markets.

A second view is that of a currency crisis. Large depreciations of 40 percent or more were common. Such depreciations created widespread havoc in terms of foreign debt repayment, acquiring inputs denominated in $US, as well as disrupting trade and foreign investor certainty. In many cases, East Asian authorities sought to defend their currencies against overwhelming capital outflows and short-selling by drawing upon foreign exchange reserves. This was a costly defense for Korea, Thailand, Malaysia and Indonesia that failed by mid-1997. Taiwan, Hong Kong and Singapore weathered the storms of currency attack, partly due to stronger underlying fundamentals, greater commitment by authorities and sizable foreign exchange reserves.[5] But why did capital exit with such mass force and speed? External speculation was commonly blamed, as opportunities arose to slay the Asian water buffalo caught in the mud. This mud was a large percentage of short term to total debt falling due within months – and visibly so.

There was doubt as to whether domestic businesses and investors could pay off this short term debt in the face of increasing softness in asset prices, declining corporate profitability and collapsing export values. George Soros smelt blood, and so he and other speculators short-sold some EA currencies in mid 1997. However, this view is not totally 'external' in nature, as rational forward-looking agents critically assess economic, financial and government fundamentals and so are *reactive in response*.

A third view of the East Asian crisis is that of a debt crisis. Not only was there over-borrowing by the domestic private sector but also over-lending by many mutli-national and companies.[6] There were two critical mismatches. The first mismatch was the short-term nature of such foreign capital flows, and yet the long-term nature of the domestic assets held - there was always a risk that debt servicing would pose a problem. This type of strategy has to be soundly based on expected rates of return *and* cash flow being substantially greater than the cost of capital in order to compensate for any unforeseen risk. Unfortunately for EA borrowers, these risks were real and eventuated in the form of deteriorating financial fundamentals. The second mismatch was the overwhelming bias of foreign debt in $US, and yet much of the revenue driven by such debt was in local currency. Such a bias was compounded by the rise in the $US against many currencies in 1996 and 1997 creating both unrealized, but sizable, capital losses along with the difficulty in debt servicing. Moreover, devaluation and high foreign debt worked interactively in destroying corporate balance sheets and instigating a vicious circle of economic contraction.

A fourth view is that of a financial crisis, whereby the financial sectors of many EA countries were too loose in their lending policies, prudential supervision was weak, accounting and audit standards were below international standards, capital adequacy was low and an over-emphasis placed on asset backing rather than the cash flow of lenders. Excess liquidity was generated not only by the financial systems, but also by the central banks and global funds searching for higher than normal returns in East Asia.[7] The sheer flood of foreign capital, in such a short time frame, made it exceptionally difficult for profitable opportunities to be both found and realized. Price-earnings ratios hit both unprecedented and unsustainable highs. Lending officers in the financial sector were under enormous pressure to discern between good and bad credit risks, as asymmetrical information in favor of the borrower clouded prudent financial judgement. In this competitive lending environment, the financial sector undertook enormous credit risks in early 1990's for fear of losing market share and smug in the belief that implicit government backing would save major financial institutions in times of trouble. This is known as a moral hazard problem, as lending in EA was premised on the idea that 'heads, the bank wins; tails, the taxpayer loses' to quote the Krugman insight. Such a belief generated a false sense of security and caused lending policies to be reckless.

Table 7.2

Current Account Deficits (Percent of GDP)

	1991	1992	1993	1994	1995	1996	1997
China	3.27	1.33	-1.94	1.26	0.23	0.87	3.24
Indonesia	-3.65	-2.17	-1.33	-1.58	-3.18	-3.37	-2.24
Korea	-2.83	-1.28	0.30	-1.02	-1.86	-4.75	-1.85
Malaysia	-8.69	-3.74	-4.66	-6.24	-8.43	-4.89	-4.85
Philippines	-2.28	-1.89	-5.55	-4.60	-2.67	-4.77	-5.23
Singapore	11.29	11.38	7.57	16.12	16.81	15.55	15.37
Taiwan	6.94	4.03	3.06	2.70	2.10	4.05	2.72
Thailand	-7.71	-5.66	-5.08	-5.60	-8.06	-8.10	-1.90

Source: Corsetti, G., Presenti, P. and Roubini, N (p41).

Hence, EA's financial system, in general, was seen as being fragile. But this begs the question – would such a 'fragile' financial sector have been able to grow in sophistication and perform satisfactorily under less of a flood of foreign money?[8] Financial collapse may have been more of a case of too much capital, too quick, too soon and too footloose.

A fifth view is that of a liberalization crisis. Montes (1998) sees this crisis as occurring by the twin liberalization of the domestic financial sector and the capital account of the balance of payments. Such a free trade in money has its costs in terms of foreign speculators desiring high and quick returns in exchange for short-term loans oiling development aspirations. Some economists claim that such liberalization led to over-borrowing, over-investment and over-capacity as well as mis-investment. But why was financial openness such a problem for many EA nations? A major reason was the lack of appreciation by domestic investors of potential exchange rate risk – as domestic financial intermediaries 'had borrowed on their behalf' offshore. Even so, these same intermediaries lacked any fear of exchange rate risk by the unhedged nature of their foreign borrowing. Furthermore, such massive capital inflows placed great pressure on domestic companies to generate high rates of return in order to meet debt service. Skepticism was echoed by Greenspan, (1997,p2). "In retrospect, it is clear that more money flowed into these economies than could be profitably employed at modest risk." Rate of return disappointment was bound to set in eventually. Moreover, savings rates in EA appeared high by world standards in the late 1980's and 90's and so the 'need' for additional capital was questionable.

Given the suddenness of the crisis, it appears unlikely that any visible deterioration of economic fundamentals were the precipitating force. Financial rather than real factors have greater explanatory power in shedding light on the speed and fury with which the crisis broke. Moreover, the complexion of the crisis was virulently interactive, in that a vicious spiral of debt-liquidity-leverage-currency-deflation spilt over into the real sector of the economy.[9] Just as EA's economic boom possessed a financial origin, so did its economic collapse.

7-4 Origins of the Crisis

Excess Liquidity

The overwhelming precursor to East Asia's financial collapse was excess liquidity. In true monetarist tradition, it was 'too much money chasing too few assets.' Excess demand for assets was driven by the monetary authorities' failure to completely sterilise capital inflows, adequately supervise their financial systems' foreign borrowing programs, monitor the credit boom and the printing of money before the outbreak of the crisis. The sheer magnitude of capital inflows implied that complete sterilization was not a feasible option. Ambitious lending programs by the financial sector were in part spurred by deregulation and desperation to 'place funds' in a very liquid and competitive environment. A huge credit boom followed that fed on itself. As Canterbery (1993) points out, this situation is analogous to the Reagan Years in the US, whereby windfall capital gains for the US middle class created a casino mentality and a bias toward non-productive investment. Unfortunately, a complicating factor arose when some Asian economies faced adverse economic signals and the central banks yielded to macroeconomic temptation by printing money to 'buy time' for the defense of the currency, meet debt obligations and even avoid the collapse of the entire financial sector.[10]

The origins of excess liquidity rest with vibrant export sectors that reassured foreign investors that economic take-off was well underway, and so profits were available from re-exports to mature economy markets and growing domestic demand. Foreign investment complemented trade profits in creating liquidity, as did the opening of the financial sector that borrowed from abroad. The lust for economic maturity caused 'temporary blindness' amongst monetary authorities regarding monetary and credit laxity. Liquidity became the means to increase the *speed* of economic development at a pace incommensurate with the formation of human capital and productivity levels.

The Unavoidable Policy Dilemma

The case of Thailand is particularly revealing from the point of view of conducting a monetary policy in a 'fixed' exchange rate environment. The implicit guarantees outlined above attracted massive capital inflows that compromised the independence of monetary policy. There are two key and separate layers of analysis. The first layer is the *pre-crisis environment* for the conduct of monetary policy. By targeting the exchange rate, the Thai authorities lost partial control of both interest rates and the money supply. When Thai interest rates were 300-400 basis points above those of the US, there were pull factors causing Thai businesses to want to borrow abroad, as there were push factors causing foreign investors to want to invest in Thailand – at both relatively high and seemingly safe rates. Was this a marriage made in heaven or hell? It appears that it was the latter. Why? If such capital inflows went unsterilized, then a build-up of liquidity would result as the central bank issued baht in exchange for foreign currency. Such liquidity filtered throughout the whole financial sector. If capital flows were sterilized, in an effort to stabilize the baht, then domestic interest rates and the interest rate premium over US rates would widen – therefore further driving domestic investors offshore. Thus, there was a dynamic inconsistency inherent in the conduct of monetary policy pre-crisis. Higher interest rates attracted another wave of foreign capital flow which only added to excess liquidity. However, post-crisis the dynamic worked in reverse. Capital outflows triggered higher interest rates in EA which in turn compressed the MEI, depressed expectations, lowered demand and with it, asset prices. Thailand's credit crunch had two prongs: high interest rates and contracting liquidity. Such a tight monetary policy only accelerated short-term capital outflows by compounding repayment difficulties and slaughtering expected rates of return. The baht did not stabilize under this monetary strategy in the early months after the crisis - despite the theoretical appeal that it would.

Much of this monetary policy dilemma rests in the nature of the foreign funds that flowed into Thailand as well as the response of the Central Bank of Thailand to such flows. Whilst the first wave of foreign capital to invade Thailand was long term (FDI) in nature, the second wave of the 1990's was portfolio and short-term in nature.[11] This capital was debt, not equity, and was willing to leave when higher interest rates threatened to destroy asset prices and the ability to repay.

Corporate Sector Leverage

Given that EA economies were both buoyant and liquid, there was every incentive for corporations to exploit a rampant rise in economic activity via the use of high financial leverage. As Table 7-2 shows, Japan's corporations indulged in high debt-equity ratios in mid 1980's - a precursor to its huge asset price bubble. Other Asian nations applied a similar strategy a few years later, singularly rational for corporations, but collectively disastrous for the nation.

It is worth noting that Japan's debt-equity ratios fell in the aftermath of Japan's asset price bubble. Korea and Thailand's debt-equity ratios were relatively high by mature economy standards, before the crash, whereas that of Malaysia was far lower. Taiwan's debt-equity ratio actually fell before the crisis and so was less exposed to a corporate profit collapse. Both Korea and Thailand appeared exposed, according to these data, as did Japan in the late 1980's. High leverage ratios are a great servant but a tyrannical master. As corporate profits dried up, Asian companies faced the domino effects of inability to meet debt obligations, a financial credit squeeze, and a reduced cash flow that further choked corporate sector balance sheet health.

Internal Speculation

In an environment of excess liquidity, there was plenty of fuel for speculation on asset prices. Easy access to credit combined with aggressive financial sector lending policies caused price-earnings ratios to skyrocket along with real estate prices. Internal speculation would trigger interest rate rises eventually, as the central bank would react to preserve its own reputation. Canterbery (1999,p29) provides insight and warning on the self-fulfilling nature of a speculative bubble "pure speculation takes over whereby players buy for resale rather than income." It is the belief that asset prices will rise that spurs even the ordinary working-class citizen to purchase assets irrespective of expected income flows. Such 'irrational exuberance' flies in the face of the rational expectations view of economic fundamentals driving asset prices. As Canterbery (1999,p6) points out" if the rate of price increases of an asset equals (or exceeds) the rate of interest, then the share of the value of all assets accounted for this asset would grow without bound, a condition inconsistent with long run (fundamentals) equilibrium." A rise in the interest rate or even an expected rise may be enough to cause the bubble to collapse. There is some evidence of rising interest rates in Asia (even before the crash) generating fear and anxiety among asset holders. Moreover, the interaction between the (more liberalized) financial sector and the casino mentality of 'investors' proved to be a very potent mixture in driving asset prices to unsustainable limits in terms of cash flow and realistic rates of return (profits). In short, asset bubbles are inherently unsustainable but also may be pricked by government-led interest rate rises.

Policy Errors

Given the success of Japan and the respect for the 'Japanese Model,' many EA nations favored active government intervention in order to accelerate economic development. Three implicit government guarantees were employed, in the hope of accentuating development. The first involved pegging the exchange rate to the $US. There were no doubt very good reasons why some Asian nations pegged their exchange rate to the $US. Benefits included the appropriation of 'US Federal Reserve credibility,' stability for decision-making on trade and investment and most importantly the attraction of capital inflows for very large and ambitious development plans. There was an implicit guarantee to the foreign investor, by government, that exchange risk would be absorbed by the Central Bank and domestic citizens. Foreign investors interpreted such a guarantee as the host government's commitment to sound economic management, and 'promise to pay' in $US, in time of crisis. Such an open check was drawn upon in 1997.

Table 7-3

Debt- Equity Percentages

	1986	1988	1990	1992	1994	1995	Average
Japan	69.2	60.8	56.1	56.1	52.8	50.4	57.
Korea	73.8	64.5	65.2	71.9	67.9	67.1	67.
Malaysia	25.4	28.7	25.6	27.0	30.4	36.1	29.5
Taiwan	40.5	37.0	31.9	33.1	30.2	28.2	33.1
Thailand	45.1	35.7	28.9	46.8	47.4	52.1	42.5

Source: Alles, et al (1998).

A second type of implicit guarantee given by government was for large development projects, both public and private. Foreign capital required re-assurance that such projects met with government commitment and legitimacy. From hindsight, the 'close relationship' between government and business backfired in that 'crony capitalism' eventually failed to satisfy foreign investor demands for openness and transparency in decision making.

A third type of implicit guarantee involved closeness of governments to the financial sector via shareholdings by government officials, government deposits and the lender of last resort facility available from the central bank. Depositors seemed reassured by government association.

From the point of view of macro-economic stabilization, several mistakes and failures were evident. Firstly, financial sectors were fragile and most governments failed to adequately supervise such an important sector of economy in terms of money creation, foreign borrowing, domestic lending polices and bank capitalization.[12] Secondly, there was a significant delay in raising interest rates and tightening liquidity when it was blatantly obvious that asset price inflation was escalating. Such an asset price bubble was ballooning in the very early 1990's (even though goods inflation was modest) and yet most Asian central banks were reluctant to cool off an already over-heated property market. Thirdly, when it became obvious that the whole financial sector was at risk in 1997, by way of increasing non-performing loans, deteriorating balance sheets and softening asset prices, the central bank increased domestic liquidity via money creation. Such a rescue effort was knowingly undertaken despite all of the ill side-effects of increased domestic liquidity (eg, Thailand, Indonesia). However, such an excess liquidity response to a collapsing financial system should be seen in the light of a choice of two evils – an exchange rate collapse or a collapse of the whole financial sector.

Managing the structural transformation of the economy also met with challenges. According to 'sequencing theory' (Edwards,1988), there are procedural steps in opening up an economy. Firstly, stabilize the domestic inflation rate and remove onerous government distortions on relative prices. Secondly, open up the current account and reduce tariff barriers to foster greater domestic efficiency and to allow the economy to re-orientate itself toward its natural comparative advantage in response to a set of international relative prices. Thirdly, after the domestic economy has reacted to the new set of relative prices, the capital account may be opened. Such a sequence encourages foreign capital to flow into areas of highest-valued use. Unfortunately, Asia did not follow such a sequence, as the capital account was opened 'too early' in the sequence.[13]

There is also a second theoretical sequence requirement for opening up the financial sector of an economy. Internal liberalization precedes external liberalization, in that credit controls are removed, competition within the sector is increased, bill and bond markets are introduced and strengthened prudential supervision. Even then, external capital flows are liberalized on the current account before the capital account. EA did not adhere to this sequence either.

Financial Fragility

It was not only the corporate sector that employed a high leverage strategy to secure high profitability, but the financial sector did the same as well. Heavy reliance on banks and finance companies, rather than bond markets, was a distinct characteristic of Asian financial markets. Such a structure created a bias in favor of short, rather than, long-term borrowing. A mismatch arose when financial institutions borrowed short offshore in $US and lent long in domestic currency (eg, Thailand). The corporate sector in Indonesia followed a similar strategy. To make matters worse, when the crisis broke, a lack of clear, enforceable bankruptcy procedures complicated the effective collection of debt.

Table 7-4

Nonperforming Loan Ratios and Fiscal Costs of Restructuring

	Official estimate End of 1998	Official estimate Sept 1999	Unofficial estimate, peak level	Fiscal costs of restruc. as share of GDP
Indonesia	-	-	60-85	58
Korea	7.6	6.6	20-30	16
Malaysia	18.9	17.8	20-30	16
Philippines	11.0	13.4	15-25	-
Thailand	45.0	44.7	50-70	32

Source: Asian Development Bank, (2000)

The size of the non-performing loans problem became apparent in 1998 and as Table 7-4 reveals there was no significant improvement in official estimates ny september, 1999. Perhaps this was because the unofficial size of this non-performing loans problem was far higher than official estimates. In terms of the fiscal costs of restructuring, the estimates for Indonesia and Thailand appear to be the highest.

Loss of Competitiveness

Several East Asian nations witnessed their competitiveness erode in the 1990's. Several forces were at work. Firstly, by pegging to the $US, several Asian currencies rose on the back of a rising $US and so became 'over-valued' in comparison to other trade competitors. Secondly, large capital inflows placed upward pressure on non-traded goods prices and so the 'internal' real exchange rate became overvalued. Thirdly, inflation and wage costs in particular, in many Asian countries displayed an upward trend above those of trading partners. Fourthly, China with its low level of the real exchange rate and wage levels in particular posed a competitive threat to the South East Asian region. Fifthly, the appreciation of the US$ and the depreciation of the Yen in the mid-1990's caused much consternation and currency re-alignment in the region. Increased competition from Japan posed a threat, as did the shrinkage of capital flows from Japan to the rest of Asia. Thus, Asian currencies were placed under downward pressure.

Given a decline in competitiveness, there should have been no surprise that several Asian nations experienced an export collapse in 1996, at least in growth terms. The following Table 7-6 illustrates the export growth slowdown story. That is of note is the severity with which Thailand's exports crashed and the rapid export recovery of both China and the Philippines.

External Forces

Many Asian policy makers have voiced their views on foreign currency speculators. In the early days of the crisis, much of the blame was placed at the feet of *foreign speculators* that sought to extract large profits from the forward sale of some Asian currencies. Quick profits were no doubt the objective. But the question remains as to whether such external speculation triggered the crisis or whether it signaled the deterioration of a deeper set of economic and financial fundamentals.[14] Forward looking, rational economic agents obviously were perturbed by national policies, declining corporate profitability, an export collapse and unsustainable asset prices. It appears that the foreign currency speculators sought the exit door before other (more long-term investors) made their way to the same exit. Blame, therefore, is in the eye of the beholder.

Worldwide fund managers could also share some of the blame. In the early 1990's when rates of return were low in Europe, and extremely low in Japan, there was a push of funds to the Asian region with a kind of self-fulfilling optimism. Developing Asian markets seemed ripe for the picking, and with vast amounts of world liquidity there was ample room for fund managers to diversify their portfolios. As more Asian nations liberalized their financial sectors and economies in general, so did foreign fund managers increase their portfolio investment. What also should be noted is that the international financial system is in need of an improved architecture, as international capital flows have become extremely volatile. The continual search for higher rates of return combined with increased international capital mobility has increased the vulnerability of developing Asia to an international financial business cycle.

Table 7-6

Export Growth Rates (%) for East Asian Countries

	1994	1995	1996	1997
China	25	19	2	21
H.Kong	11	13	4	4
Indonesia	8	12	9	7
Korea	14	23	4	5
Malaysia	20	21	6	1
Philippines	17	24	14	21
Singapore	24	18	5	-1
Taiwan	9	17	4	4
Thailand	19	20	-1	3

Source: World Bank (1998)

It is also possible to allocate blame toward the *US Federal Reserve* and its 'pre-emptive strike' against "inflation" in the US in 1994. The US Federal Reserve raised US interest rates which caused industrial activity to decline and created a worldwide economic slowdown, with a lag, in

1995. Other factors affecting demand included the possibility of market saturation, rising protectionism and depressed demand from Japan. Such downward pressure on aggregate demand further compounded Asia's export slowdown – as can be seen from Table 7-6. Moreover, upward pressure on Asian interest rates further squeezed profit margins in the region.

Pre-crisis contagion effects were still being felt, as the ongoing recession in Japan only exacerbated Asia's export slowdown as intra-regional links amplified Japan's economic and financial contraction. Conversely, China's expansion and growing share of world exports sent warning signals to policy makers and investors alike around Asia that competition in labor-intensive exports was not a temporary phenomenon.

In summary, there is some credibility to the view that Asia's crisis was partially externally driven, as international forces were at work in destabilizing the region.

7-5 The Asian Crisis: In Search of a Theory

Many economists were puzzled by the suddenness, speed and lack of warning that was associated with the Asian crisis. The economics profession did what it does best - it looked backwards toward theory - with a degree of disappointment. First generation models by Krugman (1979) and Flood and Garber (1984) focused on the crisis as being a by-product of fiscal laxity. Cumulative and persistent budget deficits needed to be financed, and governments were tempted to use seignorage as a weapon. A fixed exchange rate could not endure under such circumstances, as foreign investors withdrew funds and diminished the host nation's foreign exchange reserves.

Moreover, rational economic agents would foresee the host nation's foreign exchange reserves declining to a critical level, and so via a speculative attack, *cause* this level to be struck. As noted above, fiscal laxity (*in any visible form*) was not observable in these Asian nations in the 1990's and so these models appear to lack applicability to the Asian crisis.

Second generation models by Obstfeld (1994) viewed a crisis as being the result of a conflict between maintaining a fixed exchange rate and either the pursuit of domestic expansion or monetary laxity. These

Table 7-7

Developed Country Import Demand (Percentage Changes)

	1991	1992	1993	1994	1995	1996	1997
USA							
From							
Ind.Nations	-1.7	6.7	9.7	12.4	9.2	3.3	7.8
	(58.6)	(52.7)	(58.3)	(57.0)	(55.6)	(54.3)	(53.2)
Asia	4.2	16.1	6.8	21.9	15.8	5.0	10.5
	(21.3)	(22.8)	(22.4)	(23.8)	(24.7)	(24.4)	(24.5)
Japan							
From							
Ind.Nations	-2.4	-2.4	2.5	13.5	21.1	1.9	-5.1
	(48.7)	(48.2)	(47.2)	(47.6)	(47.0)	(46.1)	(45.1)
Asia	9.5	2.1	10.0	17.1	26.5	6.2	-4.1
	(31.5)	(32.7)	(34.7)	(35.8)	(36.9)	(37.7)	(37.2)
Germany							
From							
Ind.Nations	12.2	4.9	-22.7	12.3	18.8	0.4	-2.9
	(78.7)	(79.9)	(75.4)	(75.1)	(74.7)	(74.9)	(74.1)
From							
Asia	24.2	2.6	4.4	11.3	16.9	-0.8	-0.4
	(7.6)	(7.5)	(9.6)	(9.5)	(9.3)	(9.2)	(9.3)

Source: Direction of Trade Statistics (1999)

Notes: Percentages in parentheses represent import shares of importing countries total import bill from respective country groups.

models have a 'macroeconomic temptation' foundation whereby the government may choose employment creation over exchange rate stability. While this view does not strictly fit the EA experience, in that money creation was not a prime motive, there is enough evidence to state that EA was awash with money – due to capital inflows and so there was a special type of monetary laxity, partly of an external origin. There was also a strong pro-growth rather than pro-stabilization bias that was bound to eventually pressure the exchange rate.

Third generation models concentrate on moral hazard via implicit government guarantees to the financial sector that 'underwrites' a lending and investment boom. Krugman (1998) claims, in Asia's case, this was a 'hidden investment subsidy' and Corsetti, Presenti and Roubini (1998) claim that it represented a 'hidden government budget deficit' as banks possessed unfunded liabilities. Beneath the surface it was governments that underwrote a huge lending boom - to the private sector.

The financial sector (and investors) felt comforted by the thought that governments would bail them out if the investment boom faltered and non-performing loans became troublesome.[15]

A variation of this implicit guarantee view is that of Canterbery's 'casino economy' view whereby governments grant privilege to the rich in society via tax breaks and investment incentives. In the case of the US, the Reagan supply-side initiatives were in essence a huge wealth stimulus to the American rich. As Canterbery (1993,p169) states, "During the Reagan years the entrepeneur's share of national income declined drastically even as the rentier's (unearned) income share has soared. All of the increase in disposable income during the 1980's is more than accounted for by the rise in the share of interest income, while the shares of labor and other income sources declined." Hence, real capital formation took a back-seat while enormous speculative profits were made – America moved away from making goods to making fast money. It was the lop-sided distribution of income that compounded the speculative craze and so contributed to the speculative bubble that burst in 1987. The relevance of this 'speculative bias' in the US for EA is that the desire to make fast money transcends national boundaries - with dire consequences for the real economy - sooner or later. The granting of privilege, by government, to the small wealthy business class of EA acted as a funnel that caused a diversion from productive activities.

Another strand of the third generation models is based on financial fragility and Diamond-Dybvig (1983) view bank runs. In these models there can be a sudden exit of funds from the financial sector resulting from a herd mentality and panic. Investors may panic because they fear other investors are panicking and withdrawing funds. This self-fulfilling prophesy scenario is capable of explaining the speed and suddenness of the Asian crisis. There is a clear distinction between liquidity and solvency of a financial system and indeed a nation. In these models, the financial system is somewhat exposed and vulnerable to a funds withdrawal as it borrows short and lends long. Any panic that demands immediate payment causes long-term investments to be liquidated at fire-sale prices. There is no doubt that with the onset of collapsing asset prices around Asia in 1997, there was enormous pressure placed on the liquidity of the financial system.

There is a growing movement toward the creation of fourth generation models led by Krugman (1998). This embryonic model is based on the health of private or corporate balance sheets that is adversely affected by a currency depreciation. Amidst a contractionary or deflationary period, it is declining sales, higher interest costs and a depreciating currency that squeeze a firm's profitability but more importantly suffocate its balance sheet.[16] The firm's ability to lend is drastically reduced, even if its willingness remains. In short, it is capital inflows that inflate the health of a firm's balance sheet, and capital outflows have the opposite effect. Such capital inflows combined with high corporate sector leverage create a potent investment boom that interacts positively with a firm's balance sheet. However, this expansion strategy is high-risk in nature, as panic and capital outflows can impose cumulative deflationary effects on the private economy and the financial sector.

Of all of the generation models, the most promising in explaining Asia's crisis is the fourth generation profitability variety. A key reason for such optimism is that this generation is mainly financial and not economic in nature. It also embraces the concept of an open and not a closed economy. Nevertheless, fragments of other generation models also have some plausibility. The theoretical search continues for an explanation that adequately comes to grips with the suddenness of the crisis, the ferocity of impact on the real sector of the economy and the lack of anticipation of its occurrence.

7-6 Conclusion

The vagaries, and sometimes ferocity, of the business cycle is accepted in the West as being part of the growth experience. East Asia has learnt that an extended boom is more than likely to sow the seeds of a severe downturn. Super-profits from exports, a flood of foreign capital, excessive foreign borrowing, high corporate leverage and monetary accomodation for asset speculation all combined to generate an asset bubble that was unsustainable. As per the WSM, a loss of international competitiveness was the crucial link in the growth chain that broke pre 1997. Foreign speculators seized on an export downturn in the region, a rising current account deficits and the inevitability of rising interest rates to 'protect' the exchange rate and raise domestic savings levels. Asset prices were bound to tumble and a stampede for the foreign exchange gate result. Even though domestic causes of the crisis were many there was a flood of foreign capital that caused fragile financial systems to become excessively liquid. External reasons for the crisis of 1997 should not be underestimated. Amisdt the crisis there was a great deal of panic both within the government and private sectors as to how to respond to crashing currencies and huge capital flight. Banks were facing insolvency. Some EA nations called in the IMF. The next chapter examines how and how well the IMF assisted these nations through the dark months of the crisis.

Chapter Eight

IMF Intervention: Boon or Bane?

8-1 Introduction

The nature of East Asia's crisis differed from many previous crises (eg Mexico, Chile). Firstly, it was a financial not an economic crisis. Secondly, it was a banking sector and not just a currency crisis. Thirdly, debt was accumulated by the private not the public sector. Fourthly, current account deficits were the result of 'optimal' choices of private sector capital flows rather than wasteful public sector spending or old-fashioned consumption binges. Fifthly, exchange rates and even real exchange rates, did not appear to be overvalued according to several measures. These five features distinguished East Asia's crisis from many 'typical' developing country crises of recent years. Hence, the IMF faced a testing challenge of formulating a rescue package design of East Asia. This chapter explains the major strategy of the IMF in promoting 'sustainable growth' along with the objective for immediate stabilisation. The key features of policy design are examined. Criticisms of the IMF strategy and rescue packages are discussed, as well as the philosophic battle between the IMF and the World Bank as how to best engineer a financial and economic recovery in East Asia.

8-2 Why Call in the IMF?

When several Asian nations appeared close to exhausting their foreign exchange reserves, when capital outflows reached flood proportions and when defaults were imminent on short-term debt repayments, they called in the IMF 'doctor.' The *benefits* of an IMF rescue package were perceived mainly in terms of loans in valuable foreign exchange, assistance in debt restructuring and the provision of valuable liquidity for the cash-drained financial systems. The *costs* of such intervention by the IMF were the loss of national sovereignty by way of macro policy-making, the speed and timing of structural reforms and the possibility of national asset sales to foreigners. Moreover, these conditions set by the IMF for the transfer of promised funds were formidable constraints.[1] At face value, the short-term benefits of IMF 'help' outweighed the perceived long-term costs. Perhaps there was no real choice other than national bankruptcy, eternal shame and serious civil unrest.

When the crisis first broke, the IMF faced fierce international criticism for its policy rescue package. It was deemed too austere, too irrelevant to the needs of this Asian-style crisis and too uniform in nature - 'one size fits all.' The IMF was also blamed for the way and manner in which it hastily waved a flag to the international business community that some nations were near bankruptcy and required enormous assistance. Such haste, from hindsight, may have accentuated the panic and withdrawal of funds from Asia.

8-3 The Initial IMF Strategy

Of necessity, the IMF had to act quickly in mid-1997 to promise liquidity to the foreign-reserve drained Asian economies. In fact, the early IMF packages contained several objectives, the first being to extend lines of credit and provide liquidity for the purposes of debt repayment and to fight off speculators that sought to drag currencies lower. Secondly, by providing back-up and liquidity support, the IMF was targeting the stabilization of the exchange rate and so providing a circuit-breaker for the vicious circle of devaluation-debt-disintermediation.[2] Thirdly, by intervening, the IMF claimed that it was 'restoring confidence' to governments and citizens of the region, as well as the foreign investor, thus encouraging capital flows to return. Fourthly, the overwhelming objective was immediate stabilization– not growth – in the early IMF packages. By reducing inflation, lending, consumption and import demand, these economies would regain 'balance'. Although the short-term costs of a crunch in activity existed, the long-term benefits of a stable currency would reinvigorate capital inflows and so boost economic activity.[3]

The IMF methods recommended to achieve the above objectives include the running of fiscal surpluses via increased taxes (vat) and decreased government spending, raising interest rates to exceptionally high levels, restructuring the financial sector and policies aimed at increasing competition, trade reform and privatization.[4] These austerity measures have met with severe criticism. Radelet and Sachs (1998) query the rationale for most of these objectives. For example, why would the waving of the 'crisis flag' by the IMF be seen as 'restoring confidence.' Would not panic increase and foreign investors withdraw funds because of fear of the 'unknown'? Market confidence was not restored in the latter months of 1997. Moreover, requesting a stiff lid on the inflation rate amidst a severe devaluation (that places upward pressure on the domestic price level) only added to domestic discipline and social misery.

8-4 The Modified IMF Strategy

After conceding some deficiencies with the initial packages, the IMF instigated a modified set of packages in 1998. Objectives and methods were changed. For example, instead of seeking to provide lines of credit and so singular dependency, renegotiations of repayment between creditor and debtors were encouraged. Rolling over 'expired' debt to a medium time frame would assist in preserving foreign exchange reserves and would provide time for debtors to 'trade their way out.' Another change of heart included the allowance of fiscal deficits (partly for reasons of social welfare) and less emphasis on the closure of banks. As Radelet and Sachs (1998) point out, there was more emphasis on long-term restructuring and capitalisation of the financial sector. No longer was stabilisation the sole objective of the IMF rescue, as some aspiration for growth was now a distinct possibility. Monetary and fiscal austerity could be (slowly) relaxed in line with currency stabilisation. On one objective the IMF did not relent, and that was on *structural reform* of the real economy via increased competition, openness and efficiency of the financial sector in terms of functions, demarcations, mergers and transparency. Structural adjustments *now* would improve the quality of growth in the *future*.

8-5 Criticisms of IMF Strategies

Economists such as Sachs (1998) reminded the IMF that Thailand was a hailed as a flagship and a model of development in following IMF guidelines of openness and liberalisation. Why then did the IMF then claim the Thailand's economic fundamentals were in such poor shape only months later? Sachs (1997) also criticised the IMF for a policy of 'overkill'. More sarcastically, he questioned the IMF's commitment to *its own transparency* in policy making.

The IMF was severely criticised for the innappropriateness and harshness of its policy recommendations. Why would the closing of banks amidst a crisis restore market confidence? Why would the removal of government guarantees, of all kinds, restore market confidence? Would not a credit contraction and high interest rates choke trade credit and possibly send viable companies into bankruptcy? Would not fiscal contraction disproportionately hurt the poor that never enjoyed the fruits of the boom? Besides, aggregate demand had already collapsed. Why accentuate the recession when there already existed severe constraints on spending; that is, investment, consumption and public spending were shrinking with only the export life-line offering some hope of economic revival?

On the question of reversing capital flight, and indeed restoring medium term capital inflows, there is a criticism that the IMF has only *one arrow in its pouch* - the return of the foreign investor. At face value, such a narrowly based strategy is high risk in itself. By handcuffing Asian policy makers in terms of tight monetary and fiscal policies, by demanding greater liberalisation and less protectionism, the IMF has reduced Asia's economic revival to a dependence on the restoration of the macroeconomic stability and the return of the foreign investor. This is but the neoclassical policy prescription of lazzez faire in disguise.

Unfettered markets produce optimal results and therefore policy intervention in peace or in crisis is unacceptable. Nationalism then raises its head in the form of foreign ownership resentment, as foreigners buy Asian assets at fire sale prices. Moreover, waiting for self-correcting forces of the market to work tests the patience levels of those facing bankruptcy.

More heat and animosity is generated by the accelerated quest for more openness and access to domestic markets. Structural reform agendas appear very long and detailed, raising anxiety amongst Asian officials concerning their timeliness (amidst recession) and speed, as human capital formation takes time to build. Grenville (1998) makes the following analogy - when the emergency room is full of train crash victims it seems more appropriate to attend to those in mortal danger and leave those with only minor abrasions till later. Priorities in structural reforms is therefore essential in maintaining credibility and stability during the process. Other criticisms were more sinister, claiming the IMF to be a puppet of the USA and so implementing reform packages mainly for the benefit of US companies and interests. Calls for greater openness, competition and less onerous foreign ownership laws could only favor US interests.[5] Moreover, the IMF may have exceeded its mandate in prescribing widespread policy initiatives upon which there was no consensus in the economics profession. Therefore, strict conditionalities and policy advice of the IMF on reforming the EA economies are seen in the light of US self-interest.

Whether the IMF prescribed the appropriate medicine for Asia's crisis is still a matter of debate. But the IMF has learnt some valuable lessons itself during this crisis. Firstly, the idea that 'one size fits all' is no longer accepted. The Asian crisis was not similar to that of Mexico or Argentina, in that much foreign debt was private, not public, and the 'epicentre' of an overvalued exchange rate also did not apply. Secondly, the trade-off between growth and stabilisation is a delicate one, much more so under wild swings of the business cycle, due to the shrinkage of flows (profits) and the shrinkage of stocks (balance sheets). Standard austerity prescriptions are questionable in the light of such massive corporate and national balance sheet destruction. Keynes would have questioned the preference for *balance* in poverty over *imbalance* in prosperity. Thirdly, the IMF has learnt the importance of using players in the market to resolve their disputes rather than having governments, domestic or foreign provide even more guarantees as lender of last resort. Fourthly, the problem of moral hazard arises in relation to IMF intervention, as market participants 'recklessly' invest on the basis that world institutions will not stand by and watch countries go bankrupt. To the extent that market participants believe that the IMF will save a country in crisis there is every incentive for the private sector to 'over-lend'.

8-6 Low versus High Interest Rate Response

The advantages of a low interest rate strategy are many. Short-term benefits include the stimulus to aggregate demand and the restoration of consumer and investor confidence. By reviving spending, rates of return are stimulated and so asset prices are supported indirectly. Bank confidence, and their willingness and ability to lend, is stimulated and so credit flows revive and break the downward spiral of contraction. By implication, this strategy is Keynesian in nature that seeks to offset collapsing aggregate demand with expansionary monetary and fiscal policy. This strategy has merit *after* asset prices have fallen and deflation set in. Hence, this strategy focuses squarely on the asset and financial markets as the major sources of contractionary vibrations and *not* the goods and labour markets. Non-performing assets generate adverse wealth effects and so reduce big-ticket spending. Non-performing loans accumulate in the financial market as a result. It is balance sheet destruction, not solely a lack of profit flow, that has suffocated economic activity in East Asia. It also highlights the distinction between solvency and liquidity. This strategy focuses on stocks, levels, balance sheets, wealth and capital flight in contrast to the IMF strategy outlined below.

The central issue of capital flight deserves greater theoretical attention. The above strategy recognises that capital flight is a central cause of concern but seeks to reduce such a flow by restoring asset prices not destroying them. When Thai asset holders were intimidated by threats of higher interest rates and the prospect of an exchange rate fall they panicked into disposing of real estate and shares. Such a panic pressured the Baht lower. It was not just the debt-devaluation interaction causing chaos in the foreign exchange market but the interaction of high interest rate-asset price deflation pushing the Baht lower. In fact, the additional supply of Baht on the foreign exchange market became a flood when Thai asset holders realised that domestic asset markets had collapsed. Given large short-term foreign debt obligations, Thai businesses faced liquidation sales of all kinds of assets to meet imminent debt obligations - with all sellers moving together to 'get out'. Therefore, there is some merit in lowering interest rates in order to prevent capital flight. Not only by reducing the supply of domestic currency onto the foreign exchange market but also by attracting long-term foreign purchasers back into a stabilised asset market as the MPK rests above the interest rate.

So how is the IMF's high interest rate strategy to be justified? Given the huge collapse in asset prices, lending and aggregate demand the obvious question arises as to why a policy maker would wish to oversee a further decline in demand and activity by raising interest rates? Why accentuate an already vicious circle of contraction? *The IMF considered other vicious circles of contraction to be greater evils*. For example, a free-falling exchange rate creates the risk of a moratorium on foreign-debt payment. The valuation effects are so burdensome that domestic residents have little hope of paying in hard $US. The question of national reputation raises its heads as future capital flows are placed in jeopardy. Secondly, capital flight had become so virulent that the IMF targeted the slowing of this flow as quickly as possible. Although some type of capital (hot and portfolio) was exiting crisis stricken countries, the idea was to attract other types of capital flow (FDI and Bonds). High interest rates on financial assets were meant to be the attraction but also asset deflation caused asset prices to fall to bargain basement levels in terms of $US. No doubt higher interest rates contributed to asset price softness. Thirdly, another channel of reducing foreign indebtedness and increasing the accumulation of foreign reserves was via domestic demand contraction that would turn the current account deficit into a surplus. Fourthly, the cash drained banking systems would benefit as depositers were attracted by the promise of high returns on savings. These are all sound justifications as to why the IMF requested a standard neo-classical prescription to the Asian crisis. Such a strategy was based on attacking flows, imbalances, intermediate macroeconomic variables and capital flight. There is a query on whether capital flight was curbed by the IMF strategy. Not just in response to bank closures and depositor uncertainty but in relation to the notion that higher interest rates were destroying asset prices at a rapid rate. Hence, the increasing *supply* of domestic currency may outweigh the increasing foreign *demand* for such currency causing further collapse in the short-term.

Table 8-1

Exchange Rates - Post Crisis

| | 1997 | 1998 | | | | 1999 | | |
	IV	I	II	III	IV	I	II	III
China	8.28	8.28	8.28	8.28	8.28	8.28	8.28	8.28
H.Kong	7.74	7.75	7.75	7.75	7.75	7.75	7.76	7.77
Indonesia	14900	10700	7025	8685	6726	8386	8685	6805
Japan	130	132	141	135	116	120	121	107
Korea	1695	1383	1373	1391	1204	1227	1157	1216
Malaysia	3.89	3.65	4.17	3.80	3.80	3.80	3.80	3.80
Singapore	1.67	1.61	1.71	1.69	1.66	1.73	1.70	1.70
Taiwan	32.96	32.76	33.86	32.76	32.14	33.10	32.34	31.7
Thailand	47.20	38.80	42.30	39.30	36.70	37.60	36.90	41.00

Source: IFS, February, 2000
Note: Exchange rates against the $US

From a theoretical perspective there is a J curve effect of raising interest rates in order to stabilise the exchange rate. From Table 8-1 it becomes obvious that nominal exchange rates collapsed 1997 and then stabilised on a plateau from the end of 1998 onwards. The exceptions were Hong Kong (a fixed rate), China (capital account not open), and Taiwan (large foreign exchange reserves) that suffered less from contagion.

In the short-run there is asset price deflation, adverse wealth effects and panic that all pressure the exchange rate lower while in the long-run there are positive effects from increased saving, a current account surplus and a replenishment of foreign exchange reserves. The composition of foreign capital inflow is crucial to the ex-post response of the exchange rate to interest rate rises. For example, the bias of composition toward foreign borrowings and portfolio investment over FDI creates an unstable dynamic when rising interest rates smash asset prices. The supply of domestic currency may appear infinitely elastic in the short-run. After the supply side panic has subsided the foreign demand for domestic currency rises as the percieved exchange rate and asset price risk stabilize. Once asset prices have settled on a floor, as higher domestic interest rates cool off activity and so domestic residents respond with higher saving so can the exchange rate find its new equilibrium.

The World Bank points to the near term accentuation of exchange rate collapse via increased supply of domestic currency while the IMF points to the increased foreign demand for domestic currency restoring currency stability. Kregel (1998:58) sheds light on the matter by arguing that the typical high interest rate strategy favoured by Camdessus (1998) was but an example of *defending* a fixed exchange rate not a sign of policy success *after* a devaluation had taken place.

8-7 The IMF-World Bank Clash Over Policy Strategy

Ideological clashes in economics are far from dead. The old debates of whether there is a role for government in stimulating economic growth and whether a nation should employ expansionary or contractionary policies in response to a severe recession or crisis are alive in well in an Asian setting. The clash between the IMF and the World Bank on the 'appropriateness' of the rescue package for East Asia has been virulent. A vehement critic of the IMF's strategy and response to the EA crisis has been Joesph Stiglitz (a senior Vice President at the World Bank). He also casts doubt on the relevance of the neo-classical model for policy prescription for EA policy makers in the current environment. His major arguments are that both political economy and the role of financial markets need to be integrated into an economic model in order to understand reality. By using a debt-deflation model he points to the redistribution effects associated with devaluation and interest rate increases. A lack of appropriate indexing in contracts causes debtors to pay back more in real terms to creditors and causes companies to cut back on spending and so affect the real economy. Even though there are winners and losers in this fluctuating sea of fortune there are asymmetries evident in that winning firms fail to offset the collapse in spending by the losing firms. This non-linear relationship creates adverse supply-side effects because of the severe dent to corporate net worth.

Moreover, there are more cumulative adverse factors at work. Namely, bankruptcies destroy informational capital, and as corporate and household balance sheets are damaged so is the whole financial sector weakened. Credit lines shrink and businesses are starved of capital that further contracts the economy into a vicious circle of poverty. Real wealth effects cannot be ignored. It is the sheer destruction of net worth that not only causes domestic demand to collapse but also mutes the potential export response – as banks are wary of lower asset values and the ability to repay. If such firms possessed heavy short-term debt and were highly leveraged then rises in interest rates drastically increase the size of non-performing loans. The banking system further loses its confidence and so credit is further restricted. These are supply-side effects that cause the supply curve to shift leftward.

Stiglitz (1999) also stresses the failing demand-side of the equation, as falling stock and real estate values restrict spending, cause uncertainty regarding 'true net worth' and again slow the flow of credit. This demand-supply-side interaction is partly clothed in financial forces, that causes the neo-classical model to be somewhat impotent in policy prescription. Why? Because wealth, balance sheets, stocks and levels override the importance of income, profits, flows and marginal changes in determining economic activity post crisis.

It should not come as any surprise that Stiglitz is a critic of the IMF's strategy for solving the East Asian crisis. Why should a 'beggar thyself' policy be preferred by EA – that involves enormous domestic contraction – a policy of domestic balance by restricting imports. The risks of such a strategy should be seen in the light of a world contraction – current account surpluses of other nations must fall. Stiglitz claims that the fear of 'competitive devaluations' is overstated and is probably a legacy of the great depression era. In some circumstances, a devaluation is preferable to a rise in tariffs, and besides, the dynamic reactions in the world economy may actually raise world income. Likewise, the fear of contagion is overstated in that global output does not necessarily have to fall as 'other nations,' particularly the US, may be forced to lower interest rates in order to orchestrate a fall in its currency.

In essence, there is a query on the motive of the IMF's strategy. Surely, lower Asian currency values raise the risk of default and the possibility that some large (US) corporations may not be paid; therefore the above devaluation strategy is not preferred by the IMF and its vested interests. Again, sending the domestic economy into recession and preventing 'capital flight' in an anti-contagion manner benefits the foreign investor by minimising the falls in currencies throughout the region. Regardless of the IMF's motive in policy prescription, there is the whole question of how a prolonged recession in EA could benefit anyone?

In summary, the view of the World Bank appears to appreciate the importance of damaged asset markets, financial disintermediation and timely expansionary policies aimed at raising aggregate demand. By contrast, the IMF view has favoured contractionary policies *initially* and so austerity to balance and stabilise Asian economies. To a large extent, the dynamic workings of the asset market are ignored in this view that concentrates on flows rather than levels of economic variables.

8-8 Conclusion

From a theoretical perspective, the IMF position of immediate stabilisation over immediate economic recovery via high interest rates aimed at shoring up the exchange rate appears justifiable. The devaluation-debt-disintermediation interaction threatened a major wave of bankruptcies and prolonged recession - analogous to that of Japan in the 1990's. The risk of further exchange rate induced recession appeared high. However, as discussed, there is no clear theoretical justification that higher interest rates stabilise the exchange rate in the near term. There is a J curve effect. Moreover, the prudence of the IMF strategy in terms of delivery, execution and medium term-cost is questionable. The severity of policy measures and severe decline in output and employment raised questions of whether these measures were 'too austere.' As to the effectiveness of the IMF approach, the current economic recovery of East Asia is at least partial testimony to the success of such an approach. Moreover, the motives of the IMF in demanding economic and financial reforms, and indeed more open economies, raises the question of who benefits the most from such measures? Scepticism aside, the IMF's objective was to stabilise the regions' currencies and financial markets in the hope that a recovery in the real sector would eventuate, and it has by the year 2000. More importantly, the IMF has sought to accelerate structural reform in order to raise efficiency and productivity levels that are commensurate with greater integration with the global village. Not only are the there lessons to be learnt from the IMF's policy intervention strategy but also from Japan's financial crisis of the 1990's. These lessons are examined in the next chapter.

Chapter Nine

Lessons From Japan's Financial Crisis

Introduction 9-1

Just as Great Britain experienced its depression in the 1920's, before the rest of the world experienced the great depression, so did Japan experience a recession before the rest of Asia experienced the great recession of 1997. Common seeds of crisis between Japan and Asia were rampant speculation in assets, excess liquidity and high financial leverage ratios. It was the asset and money markets that later caused so much suffering in the labour and goods markets. A loss of confidence and capital in the financial sector spread much contraction throughout the real economy. Japan's policy response was first one of wait and delay, then astonishment as 'flagship' bankruptcies mounted, and then intermittently the application of traditional monetary and fiscal initiatives to offset a collapse in aggregate demand. Such *traditional* strategies failed. Relying on the old strategy of the US locomotive pulling Japan out of recession via export-led growth no longer proved to be effective. This chapter outlines the root causes of Japan's prolonged recession and why policy responses were bound to fail. There are lessons for the rest of Asia.

9-2 Lessons from Japan's Financial Crisis

Much of Japan's economic misery in the 1990's can be traced back to the asset price bubble of the 1980's and to the macroeconomic mismanagement that followed. An asset price hangover and a debt hangover were the two dark clouds that dwelt over Japan for much of the 1990's. Collapsed asset prices spelt massive deflation and damaged corporate-sector balance sheets that translated into economic stagnation in the real sector. Although the origins of Japan's excess liquidity were somewhat different from those of EA, the consequences of excess liquidity were, and are, basically the same: asset prices boomed and eventually burst, causing major reverberations in all sectors of the economy. Of key interest to the rest of Asia is how Japan's financial sector reacted to prolonged asset price deflation in terms of managing non-performing loans and extending further credit in a high risk corporate environment. Secondly, how the Japanese government sought to assist the bewildered financial sector suffering damaged balance sheets and a loss of confidence. Thirdly, how effective Japan's traditional policy strikes were in reviving spending flows against a backdrop of spiralling deflation. Asia can learn 'what not to do' from Japan's financial nightmare.

9-3 The Origins of Japan's Stagnation: The Asset Price Bubble

Japan experienced a huge rise in asset prices in the 1980's due to reasons of high debt-equity ratios, cross-ownership of financial and real assets by Japanese companies, accumulated trade surpluses, money supply creation by the Bank of Japan, speculation in stocks and real estate and a financial system that over-lent for private sector speculation. Persistent current account surpluses for over 30 years also generated a huge pool of liquidity - a build-up that assisted the fuelling of the 1980's asset price boom. Japan failed miserably in crawling out of recession and in dealing with the root causes of its own economic problems. Two central problems suffocated any potential economic recovery: the debt overhang (non-performing loans) experienced by many Japanese companies and the asset price overhang (non-performing assets) experienced by investors in general. The Tokyo stock market has languished for years – between 13,000 and 22,000 points after reaching 39,000 in the late 1980's – as can be seen from Figure 9-1. Commercial real estate prices in 1997 have returned to their 1985 levels. Such adverse wealth effects have severely dented consumer and business expenditure, depressing sales, income and employment.[1]

Investment and money multipliers have worked in reverse, *accentuating* contraction throughout the entire economy. Hence, gross disequilibrium in the asset market sent shocks waves throughout the economy for many years after the visible epicenter of 1990. However, the asset market were *pumped* by both the money market (abundant liquidity) and the financial sector (loose lending). Hence, the origins of Japan's bubble were attributable to the interaction of these three markets.

9-4 Financial, Not Economic in Origin

At face value, Japan has an economic crisis, but stagnating economic indicators are the symptoms of more deep-seated problems. Japan has lost its financial pulse and heartbeat, akin to blood circulating the body faces declining profits, a high percentage of non-performing loans, damaged balance sheets and a gross unwillingness to undertake risk.
More importantly, declining and so facilitating activity. A lack of oxygen is suffocating the real sector. Financial *disintermediation* is taking place as the financial sector

Interest rates instigated by the Bank of Japan (BOJ) have furnished the financial sector with windfall gains via bond holdings – gains that have taken priority over extending credit in what is still a deflationary environment in the late 1990's. Hayakawa and Maeda (1999) highlight this point, "... An unpredictable phoenomenon has occurred within the interbank market: while the Bank of Japan has adopted the exceptional zero interest rate policy', funds supplied by the Bank are not maintained as bank reserves, but are being accumulated as on-hand funds of tanshi compnaies (money market broker-cum-dealers)." As a result, the monetary transmission mechanism has been damaged or lost its signal; in short, Japan has fallen into a Keynesian-type liquidity trap.

Table 9-1
Financial Indicators in Japan (%)

	Banking Lending	Credit to Enterprises
1985	12.4	23.4
1986	13.0	25.3
1987	12.0	29.5
1988	10.8	30.0
1989	10.7	25.0
1990	9.1	10.0
1991	4.8	1.6
1992	3.0	3.0
1993	0.0	5.2
1994	-0.8	9.6
1995	0.5	12.0
1996	0.0	8.0

Source: OECD Economic Outlook (June, 1999)

Figure 9-1
Japan's Asset Prices

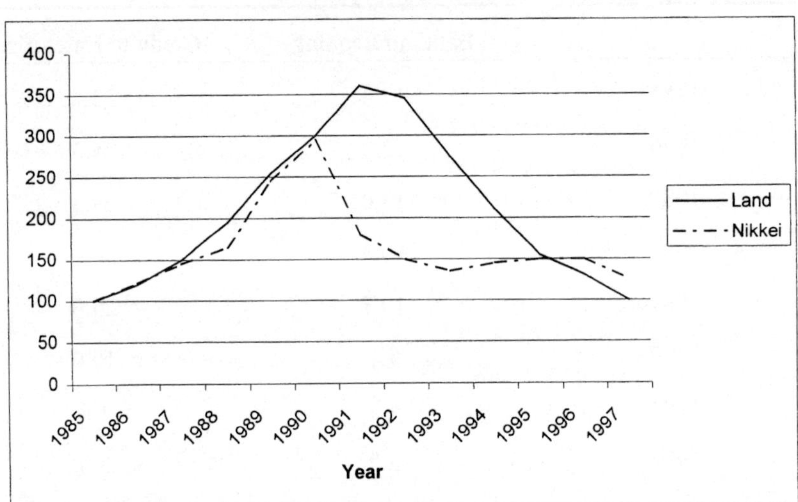

There are three constraints to any significant *supply-side restoration* of bank lending in Japan. Firstly, the banks are encouraged by government to use operating profits to write off bad debts and so reduce the abnormally high levels of non-performing loans. However, this strategy has the damaging side effect of reducing lending in the near term, creating further doubt over outstanding loans as spending and asset prices remain soft. Secondly, raising low levels of capitalisation may be addressed by operating profits. Here again, government attention to address inadequate capitalisation levels is at loggerheads with its desire for banks to undertake more lending. Thirdly, while risks in lending to corporate Japan are still perceived to be high, there is great reluctance by the banks to risk exposure to higher levels of non-performing loans. This dilemma is in fact a stalemate.

9-5 Causes of Japan's Asset Price Bubble

A monetarist interpretation of this bubble revolves around the excess liquidity that built up in the Japanese economy in the mid 1980's. According to Meltzer (1995), the BOJ deliberately pumped up the money supply in order to lower the value of the Yen against the $US, an agreement that was reached at the Plaza Accord in 1985. This *excess liquidity* in the Japanese system drove asset prices higher across the board – a case of too much money chasing too few assets. A second interpretation is the vast build-up of *export related wealth* in Japan that was looking for an investment home. Many Japanese investors shied away from overseas investment partly because of exchange rate risk and partly because of unfamiliarity with overseas investment opportunities. Japanese banks were amongst the biggest in the world by the 1980's and Japan gained the nickname of super creditor. A third interpretation is the *loose lending policy* view, which points to inadequate risk management and an over-reliance on asset backing rather than cash flow by Japanese banks. A lack of surveillance of high financial gearing ratios employed by the private sector accentuated the boom in asset prices. The cross-holdings of shares between companies (ziabatsu) also clouded prudential judgement. A fourth interpretation of Japan's bubble is that of *poor prudential supervision* whereby moral hazard and over-ambitious lending policies were partly government backed via a government safety net that 'secured all.' Government regulation and protection from competition, mergers, takeovers and bankruptcy cocooned the whole banking system from market discipline. A 'convoy approach' was employed, whereby healthy banks would cross subsidize or pull along weaker and even non-viable banks.[2]

Regardless of the interpretation as to why the bubble expanded to such a size, vast amounts of credit were used for speculative purposes that pushed up asset prices to heights that could not possibly yield long-run, or even normal rates of return. In other words, price earnings ratios reached heights that were unsustainable. What was not foreseen amidst the hype of the bubble was not only the size of the implosion to come, but also the extent to which Japan would suffocate itself from the devastation of asset price deflation. Japan entered unchartered waters in the 1990's, a test of the skill and finesse of the BOJ and MOF as well as Japan Inc, in responding to a crisis embracing a new set of challenges.

9-6 The Export Led Growth Strategy

The primary policy strategy, relied upon in past recessions, has been to wait for the locomotive of US recovery to pull Japan out of economic stagnation via export expansion. During the 1990's, Japan export growth was around 3 percent annually, but not enough to cover or offset the severe damage done by the debt and asset price overhangs on domestic spending in Japan. Current account surpluses, as a percentage of GDP, have averaged more than 2.5% in the 1990's.

Even such a powerful export response was not enough to pull a deflationary Japan out of a prolonged recession. Why? Firstly, the sheer size of wealth destruction in the aftermath of the bubble would require many years of liquidity injection via export growth to offset. Secondly, this one-pronged strategy was bound to be inadequate with only mild support from monetary and fiscal stimuli for most of the 1990's.

9-7 Japan's 'Nominal' Monetary Initiative

How did the Japanese government seek to reflate its flagging economy in the 1990's? An 'expansionary' monetary policy was part of the recovery strategy, that included lowering interest rates, to exceptionally low levels of around 0.25 per cent in 1998 from a decade high of 7 per cent in 1990. However, the deterioration of the economy in 1998/99 caused the BOJ to commit to a 'zero interest policy'.

However, on the demand side of the fence, business and consumer confidence was low, rates of return from business enterprises under severe downward pressure and so the demand for credit remained weak. Bank lending grew at a rate of 11 percent from 1985 to 1989, and credit to enterprises grew at around 25% in the same period. Still, there was a collapse of both rates to around 1.5% and 6% respectively from 1990 to 1997. As can be seen from Table 9-1the massive and decisive decline in credit and lending in 1990 can largely explain the equally sharp decline in asset prices (with lags) in the early 1990's (from Figure 9-1). What also should be noted is the slow of money supply growth between 1991-1994 of around 1.5% and 3.3% from 1995-1997, that exerted a contractionary influence on demand. Hence, an apparent monetary 'expansion' via a low interest rate policy was not enough to offset the deflationary effects of sluggish money supply growth. This failure was particularly evident in 1997-99 as Hayakawa and Maeda (1999) state "the relationship between the growth in money and the economy in the past two years looks different from what orthodox economic theory tells us." That is, money growth accelerated in 1998 while the economy was in recession and yet money growth decelerated in 1999 as the economy picked up." Traditional empirical relationships seem to have gone astray.

9-8 Which Monetary Transmission Mechanism?

There is not one, but many channels, through which the monetary transmission mechanism (MTM) may operate. The elasticities approach emphasizes the *interest rate and the exchange rate channel*. The former channel focuses on a change in the interest rate affecting investment and consumer durables whereas the latter points to a change in the exchange rate affecting exports. Japan has witnessed a strong responsiveness in the latter channel but not the former. From a demand perspective, while the cost of capital 'appeared' cheap by historical standards, rates of return were even lower and so there was little incentive for new investment, that is, the MEI<r. Real interest rates also 'appeared' cheap and even negative, but with fear of a capital loss and with little prospect for any significant asset price inflation there was no great rush for portfolio adjustment toward long-term assets and no great demand for credit.[3]

The monetarist view of the MTM focuses more on the *quantity of money and cash balance effects*. A broader monetary transmission mechanism is evident as economic agents adjust their portfolios according to changes in relative prices and marginal utilities. Excess liquidity in the 1980's drove all asset prices higher in Japan.

A third view of the MTM is the credit channel. One focus is on the *bank-lending channel* whereby the central bank conducts a policy change that affects the deposits of banks and credit creation. However, in Japan's case, the lower interest rate strategy of the BOJ has provided windfall gains for the bank holdings of bonds and a risk-free rate of return. This has curtailed the extension of bank credit so exposure to more risk could be avoided.

Another focus is on the *bank balance sheet channel*, as bank 'health' affects confidence and its own lending policies. Given the massive need to re-capitalize Japan's banks and the squeeze on bank profitability, there was a move toward a credit crunch, partly as a result of risk aversion and continued asset price deflation. Given the size of non-performing loans in Japan (15 percent of GDP) and the questionable quality of assets supporting these loans, it is difficult to discern credit worthy from non-credit worthy customers, due to aysmmetric information. Moreover, capital adequacy ratios have taken a hit from weak and falling equity values, as unrealized profits could normally be counted as bank capital. This crucial link with equity prices has proved troublesome for the vitality of Japan's banking sector, as a *Nikkei* below 15,000 points has generally been regarded as a critical danger level for the whole of Japan's financial sector. Another debilitating influence of the banking sector's behaviour on the real economy is its desire to rebuild and repair its own balance sheet by exploiting the privilege it has with the Japanese authorities. Official cuts in prime interest rates benefit banks in that lending margins can be maintained or widened and so operating profits can be increased, allowing write-offs of further bad debts. Banks could also invest in safe government securities and so reap a profitable margin without taking lending risks and thus insulate themselves from exposure to possible company bankruptcies. The legacy of such bank behaviour is that the volume of bank lending may not increase, the real economy may not be given a boost. Short-term interest rates fell from 7% in 1990 to 0.5% in 1997 and yet bank lending grew by only 1.5% a year during this period. Cautious and low risk lending policies by banks may have assisted in repairing bank balance sheets but not in re-stimulating aggregate demand or asset prices. Herein lies the dilemma: weak asset prices generate more non-performing loans, which in turn weaken bank balance sheets which further reduce lending confidence. Income growth collapses, further depressing asset prices. This is financial disintermediation at its worst, whereby the MTM works in reverse and actually contracts the economy due to rational bank behaviour.[4]

Damage to household balance sheets creates the same kind of contraction in aggregate demand. Fear of high transaction costs in retreating out of assets, and general illiquidity, cause consumers and savers to favour cash. Debt service costs also imply balance sheet repair. What is often forgotten in explaining the potency of the MTM is the damage done to private sector balance sheets. Adverse wealth effects, debt servicing amidst sluggish sales and balance sheet repair impact on expectations and spending. The demand for credit contracts in response.

Japan displays all of the hallmarks of a break-down in the credit channel of the MTM, which more than offsets any theoretical benefits from the elasticity or interest rate channel. In short, the collapse of rates of return, caused in part by asset price deflation, is faster than the collapse in the price of credit. Hence, the MEI shrinks to a point that both demand and supply of credit contract to almost stagnation between borrower and lender.

9-9 Japan's 'Nominal' Fiscal Initiative

Fiscal policy was another major alternative to stimulate economic recovery, attempting numerous public work programs and increasing government expenditure to boost aggregate demand. There were a series of attempted piecemeal fiscal rejuvenations in the 1990's culminating in a $US120 billion package in mid 1998. While such a fiscal impetus was theoretically well founded, the end results were disappointing. Why? Because many projects had little long run economic value, multipliers were weak, tax cuts were presumed to be temporary, private sector balance sheets were still damaged and many economic agents feared there was worse to come in terms of asset price deflation. Japan's demographics point to an aging population (mindful of retirement) and with security under threat and unemployment rising there was a definite drag on the willingness to spend.[5] Continual downward pressure on asset prices, further weakened the balance sheets of banks and in turn compromised lending for productive investment. Despite the fact that interest rates are still extremely low in 1999, the rates of return from real estate, business and stocks are also very low and fragile.

There was also a policy mistake made in the mid-1990's, a premature attempt to employ a fiscal contraction (raising taxes) in the belief that a sustainable recovery was underway. From hindsight this policy initiative was unwarranted and only delayed any potential recovery. In fact, there is some evidence to suggest that Japan's underlying structural budget 'deficits' were in fact budget 'surpluses' for the early part of the 1990's.

As Figure 9-2 reveals, the average cyclically adjusted budget deficit as a percentage of GDP in the 1990's was less than 2 percent, in effect, a very weak contribution to aggregate demand stimulus.[6]

Japan's Economic Policy:Handcuffed?

There are good reasons to believe that Japan's policy-led expansions are reaching their limits. From a monetary policy perspective, interest rates are at historical lows, even negative in real terms and so there appears little room left for policy impetus. A constraint exits in that the BOJ can only force the overnight rate to near zero - not below. Driving real interest rates lower entails raising the inflation rate - a difficult task amongst asset price deflation, industry and financial sector restructuring and the fear of job loss. Hence, suppressing the nominal or the real interest rate lower appears remote in the immediate term. Besides, any BOJ move to improve liquidity is soaked up by the *financial sectors' liquidity trap*. Balance sheet repair, combined with risk aversion, remain the financial sector's primary objective. Monetary initiatives, via the expansion of the *money base*, have failed because the financial sector has obstructed the expansion of the *money supply*.

With regards to the effectiveness of Japan's monetary policy it has become obvious that financial sector disintermediation has further depressed asset prices, ballooned non-performing loans and caused consumption and investment spending to be weak. On the demand side, economic agents cannot be forced to borrow and so monetary policy can be likened to pushing on a string. Given that real rates of return have been either soft or declining for most of the decade why would potential investors wish to borrow? Banks defend their cautious lending policies by claiming that the demand for credit has collapsed whereas potential investors claim they are credit worthy customers refused funds for productive investment. There is a stalemate, with declining asset prices driving a wedge between borrower and lender.

The ability of low real interest rates to stimulate consumption is also questionable. Research undertaken by Nagagawa and Oshima (2000) suggest that Japanese consumer/savers are more influenced by the income than the substitution effect of low interest rates. Why? Because the percentage of safety assets (liquid assets) in their portfolios is over 60 percent and the dependence on credit is low. Japan's aging population is inclined to save harder under this scenario. The opposite is true for the

UK and the USA, whereby the percentage of safety assets is low and willingness to use credit far higher than in Japan. Hence, the substitution effect dominates the income effect and so lower real interest rates stiumulate consumption.

Figure 9-2
Japans Budget Stance

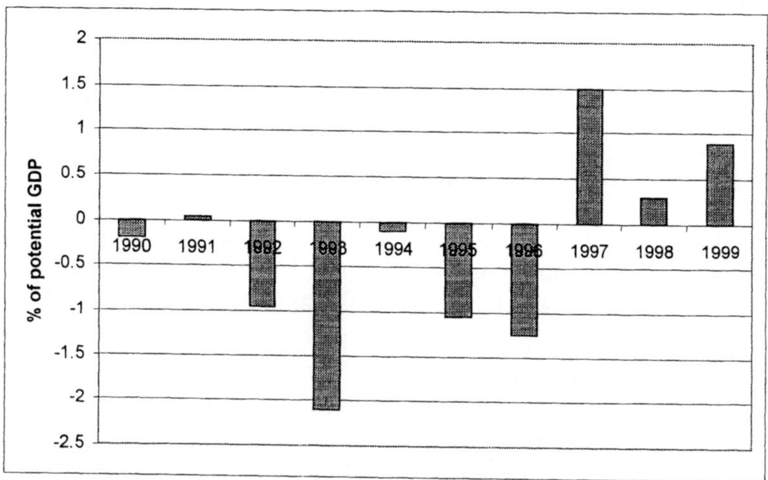

Source: OECD Economic Outlook (June,1999)

The use of an expansionary fiscal policy also has its limits, as Japan's public debt as a percentage of GDP is 200% (Dornbusch,1998,p.52) – high by world standards. Conservatism and balanced budget philosophies act as a constraint on a series of budget deficits being employed as they contribute to further long-term indebtedness and future tax rises. What has become evident in the money market, is the rise in interest rates at the long end of the yield curve in response to the cumulative effects of Japan's budget deficits on the national debt in the 1990's. Japan's demographics also interact with the budget deficit and the national debt. Japan's aging population generates a long-term liability for government that will impinge on the government budget over the medium term.

With regards to the effectiveness of Japan's fiscal policy, there is the question of whether tax cuts are potent in raising private consumption. Consumer-savers must believe that tax cuts are permanent, raising permanent income. It may be that future productivity gains from structural reforms may persuade consumers to lift consumption levels. Nevertheless, consumption responses from tax cuts to date have been muted.

Export-led growth also has its limits as large surpluses with the USA incur Congressional concern and retaliatory measures. There will be some point in time when the USA's current account deficit as a percentage of GDP is considered to be 'excessive' and market censure will lower the $US and raise the Yen.[7]

9-10 Krugman's Panacea

Given that Japan is in a liquidity trap, Krugman (1998) argues for a massive printing of money in order to push economic agents out of cash and into assets for fear of 'missing out' as asset prices rise. Not only should current monetary policy be expansionary, but future monetary policy as well, for the BOJ needs to credibly commit to sustained (asset price) inflation well into the future. It is raising inflationary expectations that is the key to Japan's economic recovery, not a cut in the cost of capital via lower interest rates. Excess liquidity rather than cheap money should be the major objective of monetary policy. By driving real interest rates negative, there should be less incentive to save and more to invest. Krugman (1998) appreciates that the 'cost' of such negative real interest rates will probably cause the Yen to depreciate further, but in his view this would place upward pressure on inflation and inflationary expectations. Production, exports and asset prices should benefit from such depreciation. However, there is considerable fear in the Asian region that such Yen depreciation will cause China to devalue its own currency and trigger a round of competitive devaluations around the region. Any prospect of other Asian nations dragging themselves out of the current crisis via an 'export-led recovery' would diminish. Therefore, Krugman's panacea of printing money in Japan does contain an element of risk, not from a rapid rise in inflation but from regional instability.

But does Krugman's recommendation address the root cause(s) of the crisis? Yes, in that Japan has a demand-side, not a supply-side problem, and because investor and consumer confidence has sunk very low. In many ways Japan 'over-saved' in the 1970's, and early 1980's, 'over-invested' in the late 1980's and then 'over-saved' in the 1990's to compensate for lost wealth and poor investment decisions – albeit at lower levels of income and amidst sluggish growth. Yet the answer to Krugman maybe no, as this is no ordinary deflationary spiral in the Keynesian tradition, but a downward asset price spiral that debilitates corporate and financial sector balance sheets and not just income and spending flows. The Krugman recommendation has merit in that any boost to aggregate demand that raises rates of return to business activity must raise asset prices. Whilst this is an *indirect* and possibly slow method of recovery, a more *direct* method of asset price support may be required.

9-11 Japan's Policy Response : Why So Ineffective?

Asset price deflation affects all sectors of the economy and cannot be confined to asset markets alone. The appropriate response, at some point, is to reflate asset prices and re-stimulate the virtuous circle of income flow. Japan's first mistake was not to arrest the viciousness of non-performing assets souring non-performing loans, as weak asset markets placed stress on an already weak financial sector. Japan's mistake was to address wounds in the financial sector rather than wounds in the asset market.[8]

The second mistake was to allow the economy to lose its dynamism. An economy that grinds to a halt and loses its confidence requires enormous energy to restart. Central to any recovery strategy is to engineer a 'jump start' for the economy in order to restore lost dynamism. Policy reactions were left 'too long,' imposing severe costs in terms of foregone income flow and allowing asset price deflation to destroy balance sheets to the point of illiquid firms becoming insolvent.

A third mistake was an incremental, piecemeal approach to refloat the Japanese economy. Government spending initiatives, combined with low multipliers were not enough to kick start the economy. Many stimulus packages were announced and yet the impact on economic activity was low. Given the massive decline in wealth and asset prices, a more aggressive and comprehensive policy stimulus is required - a big bang approach to restart the economy is required by the BOJ.

A fourth mistake was the strategy of over-reliance on cheap money, a low interest rate monetary policy to jump-start the economy once it had stalled. This strategy met with blatant failure. Other channels of the MTM, money supply growth and liquidity are crucial to economic revival, a lesson that Japan is only beginning to learn. Post financial crisis, the objective is to raise asset prices via monetary creation and credit expansion.

A fifth mistake was to rely on a supply-side strategy to overcome an excess supply-side problem. Fiscal stimuli were aimed at public works spending and a public sector revival. The objective of raising productive capacity was ill-founded and mis-directed as many of these projects contained little short-run productive value.

9-12 A Multi-Pronged Approach to Recovery

Given the complexity of Japan's problems, there is a need for a simultaneous and comprehensive policy effort to stimulate economic activity. Whilst supply-side reforms are necessary, there is an even greater need to revitalize domestic demand. Firstly, raising consumption and durable good demand impacts on rates of return. Raising profitability via an income stimulus is preferable to depressing an already minuscule cost of capital as a higher MEI will provoke more investment. Hence, the multiplier-accelerator interaction may be invigorated by an aggregate demand side stimulus. In this strategy, a bias should exist toward permanent tax cuts, rather than government spending, aimed at restoring private consumption.

Secondly, the BOJ needs to become more aggressive with a big bang philosophy toward money supply creation. Extra liquidity holds the key for raising both asset prices and rates of return. Economic agents need to be simultaneously pushed out of cash via the threat of *future* inflation and the threat of a lower Yen.

Thirdly, priority needs to be given to the restoration of private sector balance sheets over financial institution balance sheets. Raising asset prices will indirectly reduce the severity of non-performing loan problem suffocating financial sector vitality.

Fourthly, government policy attention must focus on the excess supply of real estate with the objective of either supporting real estate prices or clearing excess stock or both. Failure to arrest asset price deflation will drag the financial sector into a deeper malaise and the stock market with it. Stimulus to residential housing construction holds the key to raising consumption demand.

Fifthly, public confidence in the financial sector must be maintained. Therefore, public funds must be made available for deposit insurance and for the re-capitalisation of the financial sector.

Sixthly, measures aimed at improving financial sector efficiency are likely to yield long-term results. There is no doubt that foreign competition and take-over bids will make Japan's financial sector more efficient and generate lower costs. However, this supply-side initiative may generate adverse effects on capitalisation and lending that pose significant short-term transitional problems.

9-13 Implications for East Asia's Recovery

To the extent that the Krugmanite solution is appropriate, if implemented, the Asian region may be blessed by several benefits. Firstly, a lower Yen may stimulate domestic demand in Japan and exports abroad, reviving Japan's income growth. Expected inflation becomes the motivating force to spend. Such a revival in income growth should encourage more imports from the rest of Asia. Secondly, the Asian component of the financial sector's non-performing loan problem should become less of a problem under a lower Yen. Thirdly, the prospect of a lower Yen should also push Japanese investors offshore into 'cheap' Asian assets. This could result in the second wave of FDI flowing to Asia based on a strong current Yen but an expected weaker forward rate. Fourthly, excess liquidity may cause Japan to export lower interest rates around the world via a stronger US bond market. Downward pressure on the Yen may assist in the current export of capital and purchase of US bonds. Buoyant world activity is a pre-requisite for an early Asian recovery.

However, there are negatives of a lower Yen. Competitive pressure is placed on various Asian exporters, together with adverse valuation effects on $US denominated foreign debt. A devaluation by China may trigger further devaluations by SE Asian exporters of labour intensive goods. To the extent that a lower Yen implies a stronger $US, there is pressure on Asia's foreign debt to rise.

An Appropriate Policy Response

Even though Japan's economy is languishing under two heavy debt and asset price overhangs, there is still a real opportunity to reflate economic activity by aggressive demand-side stimuli. Recent supply-side initiatives have failed to solve what is basically an excess supply- side problem. A Big Bang approach is required, not so much in the financial sector, but in the real sector, boosting aggregate demand. Such a package should have several prongs and be implemented simultaneously, maximising cumulative momentum. However, the Japanese policy maker must be mindful of raising deflated asset prices, directly, if possible.

Hence, a vibrant expansionary Japan may raise demand for EA goods and cause FDI around Asia to rebound and a recessed, yet liquid, Japan may cause US and European recoveries to be sustained via lower world interest rates.

9-14 What Lessons Can East Asia Learn From Japan's Stagnation?

A key lesson from Japan's experience is the destructive power of asset price deflation that may hound an economy for years after the initial collapse. Damaged corporate and financial sector balance sheets cause spending flows to shrink as debt repayment retains priority over new spending on consumer durables and investment. Adverse wealth effects send contractionary propagation waves through the economic system for years. Therefore, a demand-side stimulus to offset private sector strangulation is required to avoid the two poisonous debt and asset price overhangs.

Indecision by policy makers is also costly in terms of greater balance sheet damage and its spreading effects to the rest of the economy via reverse multipliers. Waiting for the natural 'self correcting forces' of the market may be a fruitless wait in that changes in inflation rates, wage rates and profit rates may not be enough in terms of *flows* to offset the massive damage inflicted on the *stock* of wealth. A fifty percent fall in asset prices cannot be healed by an incremental yearly decline in prices and wages – unless a wait of 10 years is acceptable. East Asian policy makers need to respond quickly and decisively in terms of restoring asset values- albeit not to former levels.

Restoring financial sector health is a major priority as lending flows hold the key to increased economic activity post crisis, and indeed the indirect key to supporting sagging asset values. However, the financial sector should be prevented from repairing its own balance sheets at the expense of the corporate sector and the community in general. Bank stockholders should bear some of the burden of recovery.

9-15 Conclusion

It should come as no surprise that a mercantilistic Japan fell victim of its own success. Accumulating wealth has its costs in terms of asset price inflation and underwriting speculative fever. Unlike previous recessions that were inventory and over-capacity related, this great recession of the 1990's stemmed from Japan's over-heated asset market. Expenditure *flows* contracted in response to collapsing asset price *levels*. Financial sector disintermediation compounded the softness in aggregate spending by constricting lending flows. A vicious circle of debt-deflation suffocated corporate, household and financial sector balance sheets. Such a virulent interaction posed an enormous policy dilemma for Japan's policy makers. That is, how to kick-start the economy once dynamism was lost. A lethargic and sick economy plagued Japan for most of the 1990's. East Asia could learn well from Japan's corporate sector and policy mistakes. Chapter 10 examines how East Asia can turn a crisis into an opportunity by learning from Japan's financial sector malaise and its own governance mistakes.

Chapter Ten

Policy Challenges, Dilemmas and Tradeoffs

10-1 Introduction

A key theme of this book has been the notion that EA has taken a different flight path to economic development than any of the OECD nations or indeed any other set of developing countries. According to the WSM, the very nature of *catch-up growth* is based on international competitiveness and strong links with rich, mature economy markets. Foreign investment and liquidity also played a role in capturing lucrative export opportunities. The reason for EA's demise was outlined in Chapter Seven, as being predominantly internal in complexion but compounded by a set of external factors related to the growing integration of the global village. For any policy prescription to be successful it must be based on the understanding of the root causes of EA's ascent to prosperity and so a 'return to basics' based on past success. This does not necessarily imply a return to the 'Asian Model of Development,' inferring strong state intervention, but it does imply a return to profitability via export-led growth and foreign investment. To the extent that EA's financial fire-storm was fuelled by foreign interests and unstable global markets, safeguards must be found as a defence against such international instability.[1] More importantly, any policy recovery package must repair financial, as well as economic, fundamentals. Valuable policy lessons from Japan's collapse and recovery were outlined in Chapter Nine.

10-2 The Philosophical Battleground

Using the language of the WSM, the control center 'has a problem'. Rocket acceleration has faded, and there is a need for an economic recovery - but how and through what channels is fiercely contested by control center personnel. The philosophic battleground of how best to stimulate economic development has always been full of noise, blood and shrapnel. In the aftermath of the crisis, the ferocity of the contest between neo-marxists and neo-liberals has not abated. Neo-marxists point to the excesses of the private sector in terms of unbridled foreign lending, 'reckless investment,' greedy foreign capitalists and speculators seeking quick-fire profits, and market failure on a broad scale. Their view of EA's flight recovery path includes government regulation, industrial steerage, capital controls, currency boards, stronger foreign ownership laws, preserving economic institutions and easier credit policies.[2] In short, the neo-marxists favor a government-led and institutionalist recovery that focuses little on market directions.

On the other hand, the neo-liberals point to government failure, crony capitalism, corruption, closeness of state and business, excessive government guarantees, inefficiencies in most sectors of the economy, a lack of human capital, and runaway asset price inflation as being major reasons for EA's crisis. In their view, for EA to achieve economic recovery there needs to be reform in terms of greater domestic competition and private sector efficiency, more market-driven allocation of resources and more openness in terms of capital, trade and knowledge flows. There needs to be considerable reform of the financial sector in terms of accounting and transparency standards and greater exposure of government policy- making procedures. By raising human capital levels there is a greater likelihood of achieving stable growth in the future.

The battlelines are clearly drawn: EA collapsed because of a lack of respect for market rules versus a collapse caused by market excesses and greed by owners of capital. On one side, government only needs to create the environment in which the private sector can flourish, whereas on the other side, the government needs to regulate, restrain and indeed direct the private sector in its quest for wealth creation. Philosophical hatred has been rekindled by the EA crisis and the old debate of 'markets work' versus 'markets fail.' Policy prescriptions should be seen in such a light.[3]

10-3 Facing the Economic Challenges

As discussed in Chapter Seven the twin liberalisations of the financial sector and capital flows posed enormous strains on macroeconomic management strategies of these EA economies. A direct result of degregulation was the creation of an asset price bubble and subsequently asset price deflation. A major economic challenge is how to deal with the negative effect of the *devaluation-debt* force interacting to damage corporate balance sheets and so corporate ability to borrow.

Many EA Asian policy makers fear the worst in the aftermath of the recent financial crisis – an economic recovery that is both sluggish and painful. Firstly, the task of preventing the recent financial tidal waves from sending the real economy into a tailspin, generating greater unemployment and social distress that in turn becomes politically unmanageable. Why should the working class poor be asked to pay for a rich man's crisis? Economic austerity must be a means to an end, not an end in itself. Secondly, there is a need to face up to fact that the growth-stabilization tradeoff is ever-binding and therefore needs to be respected. Although EA's economic cruise speed was exceptional by world standards, the tradeoff was still binding albeit at a higher growth plateau than the OECD's.[4] Amidst the crisis there was a strong case for giving priority to stabilization over any quest for growth. Immediate priorities focused on the devaluation-debt nexus that threatened to cause both financial and economic collapse. However, by late 1998 the huge pro-stabilization bias was allowed to fade, and greater focus was placed on positive growth targets. Thirdly, there is a need to minimize the damage inflicted on productive capacity and the medium-term development potential of the real economy. Many viable Asian companies have been adversely affected by the collapse of the financial sector via a contraction of domestic credit and the recalling of loans. Many private and public sector infrastructure projects have been shelved. The contraction of investment and consumption spending must not continue to the point that solvent but illiquid Asian companies collapse and so delay recovery on the (future) supply side of the real economy. Of particular interest to the policy maker is how many firms in potentially sunrise export industries have gone or will go bankrupt. Fourthly, on the export front there is not a calm sea. Several EA nations have collapsed together, and all seek an export-led recovery in the medium term.[5] Strong competition amongst EA nations and China may still trigger competitive devaluations. Hence, the cross real exchange rate between EA nations assumes greater importance. Moreover, many other developing nations simultaneously seek the benefits of export-led growth and current account surpluses.

10-4 Facing the Financial Challenges

Just as Japan experienced a debt-overhang, so does Asia have to cope with a similar interactive force. That is, how to moderate the negative interactive *deflation-disintermediation force* that causes spending to shrink via less bank lending. Governments face the challenge of raising asset prices or raising lending levels or both.

Just as liquidity played a key role in facilitating thriving economic activity during the boom years, so too has a lack of liquidity (foreign capital outflows) caused economic activity to languish since 1997. Such a lack of liquidity, in part, caused interest rates to rise dramatically in 1997 and 1998. The challenge is to attract foreign capital of a long-term variety into the traded goods sector, to assist continued export expansion and the long-run growth potential of the real economy. Relaxation of foreign investment, foreign ownership and alien laws play a part in both restoring liquidity and lowering interest rates. Assisting and promoting mergers amongst financial institutions augurs well for future efficiency.

A second major financial challenge is to restore financial sector confidence and lending flows. That is, reinvigorate the role of financial intermediation and thus indirectly support asset prices. By so doing, the percentage of non-performing loans as a percentage of outstanding loans should diminish. Asset price deflation, if prolonged, imposes enormous strain on the financial sector, as poor private-sector balance sheet health is reflected in the balance sheets of the financial sector. A major danger is that of the financial sector indulging in disintermediation, playing a reverse role in the liquidity process by calling in loans, refusing to grant new loans and generally repairing its own balance sheet by extreme caution in lending. A continued credit crunch, above and beyond that required for stabilisation, only destroys business confidence and causes the real economy to lose its dynamism. Lessons from Japan should be well understood.

As a third major challenge, the life-line of trade credit must be maintained to solvent export companies in order to seize the nominal benefits of exchange rate falls. Any significant export response is premised on the notion that export companies can gain access to trade credit amidst a general, economy-wide credit squeeze.

Fourthly, there is both Satan and Lucifer to contend with; that is, the asset price overhang that has trapped many an investor into assets that halved in value and show no sign of being sold or rented. There is also a debt overhang that is linked to collapsed asset prices in that many business people cannot service their bank loans or in some cases even meet interest payments. These *twin overhangs* have suffocated EA's real economy and so have retarded the recovery.

Many of the economic challenges facing EA since 1997 are similar to those facing Japan in the early 1990's. Indeed, Japan experienced its asset price bubble in the mid 1980's and suffered a collapse in asset prices by 1990. Hence, there are major similarities between Japan's financial crisis and EA's later financial crisis in 1997. Such issues were examined in Chapter 9.

10-5 Circuit Breakers for EA's Economic and Financial Tradeoffs

Amidst the crisis, the potency of the interactive devaluation-debt force threatened to place EA into a contractionary tailspin. Autonomy over monetary policy was lost as domestic interest rates had to rise in order to protect the exchange rate. Crunching economic activity, across the board, was the painful by-product of such a strategy. Policy makers responded in different ways to breaking or immobilizing the interest rate-exchange rate nexus. Prime Minister Mahatir responded by setting a fixed exchange rate once again and restricting capital flows by regulation to that rate. The IMF was not called in. Other EA nations did call in the IMF in order to restore liquidity into their economic systems and not default on international debt service.

What is needed to combat the vicious circle of debt-devaluation are circuit breakers that will overcome any short-circuit in the economic and financial system. Putting in place capital controls is one method of regaining control over domestic monetary policy and so avoid the destructive force of sustained high interest rates on the real economy. The negative side of such a strategy is the long-term damage inflicted on foreign investor attitudes to capital losses, risks of appropriation of assets by default and the non-credibility of the Central Bank and government economic management of the economy. Such a strategy may have short-term benefits in breaking the stranglehold of a credit crunch but may cost more in terms of lost reputation and future capital flows.

A second circuit breaker is increasing liquidity via IMF funding that takes pressure off the exchange rate and so the interactive force. Moreover, a signal is sent to foreign creditors that debt default is not an option and to potential investors that the exchange rate has indeed stabilized and capital flows have been encouraged. Extra liquidity also eases the immediate credit crunch and allows for interest rate declines and an eventual credit expansion.

A third circuit breaker involves the use of orderly debt workouts, debt rollovers and private arrangements between debtors and creditors that takes pressure off immediate debt servicing and reduces the demand for $US. This method involves buying time for debt-burdened corporations to sell assets in an 'orderly market' and to generate short-term cash flow.

A fourth circuit breaker, espoused by Tobin (1978) is for a tax to be placed on capital flows via foreign exchange spot transactions. The objective is to discourage the flows of hot, short-termism money that has the potential to destabilize developing economies. Given that the value of foreign exchange transactions was 67 times the value of international trade in 1995 it is not difficult to appreciate the speculative nature of capital flows.[6]

A fifth circuit breaker, is that of a currency board that 'fixes' the exchange rate in terms of the $US. The rate is determined by tying units of local currency in circulation to the amount of foreign exchange reserves. This implies that every local currency unit is 'backed' by an amount of foreign exchange reserves at a set exchange rate. This creates an image of monetary responsibility by the central bank. However, this circuit breaker is more suitable to *future* monetary responsibility than soaking up an already excess money supply and weak demand for local currency.

A sixth circuit breaker is the creation of an Asian Monetary Union whereby trade and capital flow transactions are denominated in Asian currencies, a basket or in Yen. Such a union avoids the necessity of demanding and using $US for transaction purposes and so protects countries from any future contraction caused by collapsing currencies or a rising $US. To the extent that capital and trade flows are strongly intra-regional, this strategy may be useful in breaking the devaluation-debt nexus.[7] However, this is very insular strategy that smells of isolationism fraught with all of the dangers of an 'Eastern European style union'. Asian currency values may be lower in the long-run despite the perceived benefits of short-term stability.

Whatever circuit breaker is employed, the ultimate objective is to avoid the destruction of an excessive debt burden and a credit crunch that brings an economy to its knees, which may in turn may damage its long term productive potential. In short, circuit breakers allow the achievement of growth *with* balance. Hence, the launching pad for the recovery is laid.

10-6 Long Term Development Constraints

It appears that the 'Asian Development Model' of strong state invention in allocating resources, close relationships between government and business leaders, implicit government guarantees for private projects and investments and government regulation of competition and trade is no longer a viable option for EA policy makers. The transition from a heavy-handed state approach to a more open economy with less government interference poses a formidable adjustment problem for EA policy makers themselves. There is the question of how open a transition economy should be. As Prime Minister Mahatir said in response to Vice President Al Gore's demand for more openness, "Openness for whom?" implying, is this openness for the benefit of US multinationals? It suggests the question, "Closed for whom?"[8]

There are three major constraints on the productivity of physical capital. Many EA economies are still in economic transition in human capital levels, sophisticated institutions and public infrastructures, compared to developed country standards. There is a lack of complementarity between physical and human capital in an EA context; a collision of forces and a significant imbalance, that contributed to EA's inevitable economic slowdown. Human capital accumulation accrues quite slowly in comparison to the accumulation of physical capital. As Barro (1994,p11) noted, "Machines and buildings can be assembled quickly, but people cannot be educated rapidly without encountering a sharp drop-off in the rate of return to investment." This mismatch lowered the MPK beneath its potential.

A second complementarity was also lacking, as the maturity of economic institutions lagged in sophistication behind the large increase in physical capital. Long-term rates of return are very dependent on political, social and economic institutions building and sustaining the economic incentives so necessary for balanced growth. Respect for property rights and legal contracts together with openness and transparency, as key business principles, augment the realisation of productive physical investment.

A third lack of complementarity between the accumulation of private sector physical capital and public infrastructure in terms of efficient transport, water, sewerage, health and relevant education systems acted as a constraint on the productivity and undermined the effectiveness of physical capital in EA. A lack of respect for environmental standards also imposes long term costs on a nation's productive capacity. Hence, an imbalance can arise between private and public investment that causes the MPK to collapse or lose its effectiveness.

It follows that any policy package aimed at restoring economic recovery in EA must address the above constraints and make them less binding. Accumulating physical capital and attracting foreign capital are commendable short-term objectives but need to be augmented by raising human capital levels, public infrastructure and institutional maturity. Otherwise a potentially large MPK will not be realised due to these offsetting forces.

10-7 Immediate Policy Initiatives

At the heart of the post-crisis recovery package must be the restoration or achievement of a broad set of economic, financial and government fundamentals. Firstly, *macroeconomic policy* must be implemented with courage and not only with wisdom. Credibility, in particular, lies at the heart of restoring government fundamentals. EA governments must be credible in terms of maintaining a 'set of rules' or a 'set of economic incentives' that encourages a commitment to both long-term human and physical investment. Stabilisation policies must be credible in terms of interest rates, inflation and government taxes being within bounds accepted by finance markets, bond holders and foreign investors. Rules, rather than discretion, by policy makers may remove problems of dynamic inconsistency and temptation. Regardless of how EA governments restore credibility, finance markets in general will act and react to government decision making as costs and profits are affected. However, as the crisis has revealed, over-commitment as well as under-commitment has its costs. Implicit government guarantees caused a flood of foreign capital to EA and so the bubble economy. Nevertheless, consistent and clear government policies aid the growth of real economic factors generating economic growth.

Secondly, it is imperative that resources flow from the non-export sector to the export sector, and so it is essential for the 'necessary condition' of internal real exchange rate be conducive to such economic incentives. Once this necessary condition is met, it is then important that the external real exchange rate be conducive to stimulate export growth. Hence, the policy maker needs to pay special attention to asset price inflation, as well as to goods price inflation. Resources flowing back into the non-export sector led to the crisis. Competitiveness still holds the key to second-stage take-off and so there is a vacuum for *trade policy* to have an impact on export growth. As Brulhart and Thorpe (2000) point out, as the composition of Asian trade evolves and more dependence on intra industry trade takes place there are lower pressures and costs associated with labour market adjustment.

Thirdly, capital flows may need monitoring in the future. An open capital account is a commendable long term objective but needs to be achieved in line with sequencing criteria. Moreover, long-term FDI is preferable to short-term destabilising portfolio investment; a balance is needed. An aggressive *foreign investment policy* is particularly useful in laying the foundations for attracting FDI into key sectors of the economy that have spill-over benefits to the rest of the economy.

Fourthly, moving from the first growth plateau (labour intensive exports) to the second growth plateau (sophisticated manufactured goods) is essential in order to break the shackles of diminishing returns. This requires a coherent government *education policy* that seeks to raise technical efficiency levels via formal and informal education. Subsidies are warranted.

Fifthly, the reforming of the financial sector and bringing it into line with international standards remains a high priority. And yet, at the heart of any EA recovery must be the revitalisation of the financial sector, as it represents the heartbeat of the economy. Financial fundamentals must be restored in terms of emphasis on cash flow not just asset backing, thorough examination of credit risk, lower financial leverage ratios and the re-capitalisation of the financial sector.[9] The ultimate objective of financial restoration is to cease the destructive power of disintermediation, cause a revival in lending flows and to lower interest rates in order to resuscitate the real economy. Trade credit must be targeted. But as credit expansion resumes there is an urgent necessity to impose accounting, auditing and disclosure standards that will strengthen the financial sector's long-term credibility.

Given that huge capital inflows assisted in ballooning EA economies and then large capital outflows helped in deflating EA economies, the basic policy response should be to restore capital flows. Just as blood is vital for the operation of the human body, so is monetary liquidity vital for facilitating growth in a transitional economy. Foreign capital is essential for any economic recovery in EA, and so ways must be found to reassure foreign investors that economic, financial and government fundamentals are currently being restored. The non-mutually exclusive alternative is to re-discover the power of export-led growth.

10-8 Harnessing Positive Interactive Forces of Growth

The are four important interactive forces. Firstly, the knowledge laden power of foreign capital augmenting that of domestic capital. A lower foreign capital/domestic capital ratio (Kf/Kd) generates an explosive MPK and a high rate of TFP growth. As the ratio rises so does the MPK lose its potency. Hence, Asian governments need to assess the level of this Kf/Kd ratio in order to alter foreign investment laws and so attract foreign capital. Raising domestic capital formation without a strong foreign component may not be enough to kick-start economies that aspire to move higher up product ladders.

Secondly, as discussed in Chapter Three the cumulative interaction of exports and human capital generates growth. Technological transfer, ideas and learning by doing occurs through export orientation which in turn supports further export growth. Increasing product quality and variety maintains lucrative profit rates. Such profits assist in funding general education and providing the manufacturing sector with a skilled, literate work-force.

Thirdly, as Garnaut (1998) points to the strong link between FDI and exports as the hallmark of the Asian growth experience. Both FDI and exports have mutually reinforced each other. The product cycle model explains why FDI is mobile, why it chose low wage rates in EA and why it leaves higher productivity levels in its trail. Such investment was *recycled* into exports to western markets. Therefore, governments need to create a tax and cost environment conducive to attracting foreign investment in the traded good sector.

Fourthly, as per the WSM, the ratio of exports to non-exports (X/NX) drives allocative efficiency and corporate profitability by exploiting wide cost differentials between East and West. The cumulative interaction stems from profits being ploughed back into the export drive and further export diversification raising profitability.

All of these interactive forces impinge on productivity but the X/NX force places more emphasis on profitability. Exports also play a central catalyst role in most terms. Given that the crisis contained several *negative* interactive forces, the policy maker has a role to play in harnessing several *positive* interactive forces to offset the cumulative downward momentum.

10-9 Longer Term Policy Initiatives

In the language of the WSM, the causes of long-term steady state growth are productivity and technological progress. The fuels driving these shuttle engines are human capital, research and innovation – in short 'new knowledge.' Therefore, EA is well-advised to promote both general and tertiary education in order to build human capital so necessary to generate new ideas. To the extent that Krugman is correct and EA has hit the wall of diminishing returns, then EA must devote more resources to education, formal and informal training in order to raise productivity levels.

Moreover, the education thrust needs to produce specific, scientific skills so necessary to rise from first-stage export-led growth (labour intensive goods) to second-stage export-led growth (sophisticated manufactured goods). Moving up product and quality ladders also requires that diminishing returns to the first-stage export thrust be broken. The acquisition of up-to-date knowledge is an essential complement to the acquisition of physical capital. Thailand, for example, has embarked on an aggressive vocational training program in order to raise work-place skills. In short, acquiring knowledge now is a major defence against a future economic or financial crisis.

As per the WSM, the role of allocative and technical efficiency is to provide fuels for the rocket engines of super-profits and hard currency. Hence, capital formation and technology transfer still remain sound medium term objectives in order to modernize economies and so provide the foundation for additional knowledge acquisition. Exports remain a medium term growth force because cost differentials still remain wide between EA and the West as of the year 2000.

10-10 Conclusion

Undeniable macroeconomic trade-offs have been revealed by EA's financial and economic collapse. The EA policy maker faces painful choices between stabilising the economy, with all of the associated costs of high interest rates, higher unemployment and social distress, and yet pursuing growth with all of the associated risks of currency depreciation and debt blow-outs. However, as greater stability is achieved and risks subside, a pro-growth bias is purchased. From 1999 onwards East Asia has been in a position to undertake policy initiatives to expand output and employment.

Designing circuit breakers assumes importance when the devaluation-debt nexus threatens to retard the economic recovery. Likewise, the deflation-disintermediation nexus needs to be moderated in order for lending flows to stimulate asset and final good demand. In short, the twin overhangs of deflation and debt need to be confronted. While dealing with financial problems, the medium term objective of restoring balance can be achieved. Moreover, devoting more attention to the growth of human capital, institutions and public infrastructure that will assist both capital formation and exports constitutes a set of wise medium-term objectives. The next chapter examines the recovery under-way in East Asia as of the year 2000.

Chapter Eleven

Economic Recovery 2000 and Beyond

11-1 Introduction

This book identifies the key variables of East Asia's growth and recovery experience. East Asia should witness a revival of financial variables before a revival of economic variables, given that the crisis was of a financial nature. Even so, the crisis did spill over into the real sector as output and employment were severely squeezed in the financial year of 1997/98. According to the WSM there are several channels of short-term recovery. Lost altitude and rocket acceleration can be rectified by reparing the twin rocket engines of super-profits and hard currency. It is stage two of economic take-off that relies heavily on improving technical and allocative efficiency so necessary to offset the second wave of diminishing returns. Besides seizing higher product ladder opportunities, there is a need to restore foreign capital flows, monetary liquidity and trade credit; all important fuels for economic recovery.

11-2 Major Channels of Recovery

According to the WSM, the very nature of Asia's economic growth is of a catch-up nature, driven mainly by an exogenous force. Hence, foreign markets, foreign capital and foreign know-how still hold the key for realising catch-up growth and indeed the current recovery. Domestic determinants of growth will have to play a secondary role, as they have in the past[1]. Furthermore, for the *recovery* to be immediate, the channels must embody short-term energy and not just be of a structural and reformist nature that only impinge on long-term growth. Policy recommendations for the resumption of a more sustainable long-term growth path were outlined in Section 10-7. They included the closer monitoring of the internal real exchange rate, the capital account and the efficiency of the entire financial sector. Policy initiatives directed at increasing international competitiveness and moving up product and quality ladders were also isolated. However, these policy initiatives will impact on growth over the *longer term*.

An economic rebound first requires a financial rebound, and it is here that growing liquidity will assist in revitalizing export growth, restore asset prices and attract the next wave of foreign investment.[2] What is also essential from the evidence of previous chapters is the need for the US, and OECD in general, to remain buoyant – an exogenous stimulus to growth.

There is no doubt that supply-side initiatives and structural reforms are essential for EA to move up the product-quality ladder and converge on OECD productivity levels. Nevertheless, the demand-side force of catch-up growth is still available as the wealth of the OECD remains high and so profitability via exports acts as a short-term substitute for raising productivity levels.

Recovery in East Asia rests with the short-term forces of growth. The first channel of economic recovery rests with exports to mature economies. Given that Japan is still weaving its way out of its financial hole, the US and Europe remain the major targets for an export attack. Retrieving super-profits (rocket engine one) and regaining hard currency (rocket engine two) constitute major channels of economic lift-off mark II. However, price elasticities and the large devaluations of the real exchange rate will determine the degree of export success in the short-term. From Chapter 4, the hope of high price elasticities generating an export boom, even to mature economy markets, remains slim as most estimates are around 1. More to the bone, hope rests with high export income elasticities to mature economy markets, as estimates from Chapter 4 are around 3 to 4. If these estimates are reasonably plausible, then buoyant US and OECD economic growth over the next few years holds the key to an export and GDP revival in Asia. However, there is a twist to this analysis, explained in Chapter 3, in that elasticities (or responsiveness to changes) do not hold the only key to an export revival, as vast differences in cost and income levels act as an exogenous force on Asian export growth rates. Hence, there is an air of long-term, permanent optimism as differences in levels remain, assuring a near-term recovery. In the short term, import price elasticities of East Asian nations are high and so imports from mature economy markets should contract as exhange rates tumble. Hence, the replenishment of foreign exchange reserves can be achieved by registering a trade account surplus.

Table 11-1 creates the impression that export responses in most Asian countries were negative in 1998 but robustly positive in 1999. Imports contracted ferociously in 1998 as a result of the collapsing exchange rates. However, as stability and confidence returned so did imports rebound strongly in 1999. According to the ADB, the outlook for export and import growth in the near future appears positive.

Given the above responses, it comes as no surprise that many Asian nations have registered current account surpluses. As Table 11-2 reveals, the rebounds in 1998 for Indonesia, Korea, Malaysia, Taiwan and Thailand were quite miraculous. However, superior export responses by Korea, Malaysia and Taiwan over Thailand and Indonesia promise a more enduring recovery. Curtailing imports, however drastically, constitutes only a short-term, stop gap initiative.

Table 11-1

Mechandise Export and Import Growth (%)

	1997	1998	1999	2000	2001
China	21.0	0.5	6.0	5.0	5.0
	(2.5)	(-1.5)	(18.2)	(10.0)	(8.0)
H.Kong	4.0	-7.5	-0.1	9.1	10.0
	(5.1)	(-11.6)	(-2.7)	(10.7)	(11.0)
Indonesia	12.2	-10.5	-7.4	8.1	9.0
	(4.5)	(-30.9)	(10.8)	(7.5)	(14.0)
Korea	6.7	-4.7	10.1	10.0	7.4
	(-2.2)	(-36.2)	(29.0)	(23.1)	(14.3)
Malaysia	1.2	-7.5	10.1	8.0	8.0
	(1.4)	(-26.5)	(10.0)	(12.6)	(13.0)
Philippines	22.8	16.9	18.8	14.0	14.0
	(14.0)	(18.8)	(4.1)	(14.0)	(16.0)
Singapore	-0.2	-12.2	2.6	3.5	5.3
	(0.7)	(-23.2)	(6.8)	(7.9)	(8.8)
Taiwan	5.4	-9.5	6.8	12.5	11.5
	(10.1)	(-7.4)	(2.8)	(15.8)	(13.4)
Thailand	3.8	-6.8	7.4	7.0	8.0
	(-13.4)	(-33.8)	(17.7)	(16.5)	(17.0)

Source: Asian Development Bank (2000); estimates last 2 years

Notes: Exports are outside parentheses and imports inside

Table 11-2

Current Account Balance (% of GDP)

	1997	1998	1999	2000	2001
China	3.3	3.1	1.2	-0.4	-0.9
H.Kong	-2.3	4.1	3.5	2.2	0.5
Indonesia	-1.7	12.8	6.1	2.4	0.8
Korea	-1.7	12.8	6.1	2.4	0.8
Malaysia	-5.0	12.9	14.0	11.3	8.1
Philippines	-5.3	1.7	9.1	6.3	5.6
Singapore	15.8	20.9	18.5	17.8	16.0
Taiwan	2.4	1.3	3.0	1.8	1.5
Thailand	-2.1	12.7	9.1	5.5	1.9

Source: Asian Development Bank (2000); estimates last 2 years

The second channel of economic recovery is that of the return of foreign capital. Preferably that of a long-term, knowledge-laden nature. However, given recent capital starvation any short-term borrowed funds are welcome, as exchange rate stability remains a priority. The benefits of such capital inflows are best seen in the light of building up foreign exchange reserves, providing funds for recapitalising the banks, offsetting domestic capital flight and restoring confidence to the financial system.

The third channel of economic recovery is that of restoring domestic liquidity and credit creation. Reforms of the financial sector and initiatives from the central bank are important. As discussed, the prime dehabilitating evil of a collapsed financial system is the parasitic role it plays in contracting credit and destroying economic activity. This curse is called disintermediation and involves reverse multipliers that constricts asset prices and profits in the private sector. Therefore, the re-capitalisation of the banks and the regeneration of bank lending are major domestic channels of financial and so economic recovery. Trade credit should also benefit. From Table 11-3 it can be seen that money supply growth has picked up in most countries, and according to the ADB, will continue into 2001. The main exceptions are Indonesia and Thailand. Both countries are still soaking up excess liquidity from the boom years and suffering from asset price and debt hangovers.

Table 11-3
Money Supply Growth (%)

	1997	1998	1999	2000	2001
China	17.3	15.3	14.7	16.0	16.0
H.Kong	8.3	11.8	8.1	12.0	15.0
Indonesia	23.2	62.3	11.9	13.0	17.0
Korea	14.1	27.0	27.3	24.8	21.5
Malaysia	18.5	2.7	8.3	12.0	14.5
Philippines	20.9	7.4	19.3	17.0	18.0
Singapore	10.3	30.2	8.5	11.6	11.8
Taiwan	8.0	8.6	9.2	9.3	9.0
Thailand	16.4	9.5	2.1	8.0	12.0

Source: Asian Development Bank (2000); estimates last 2 years

11-3 The Regional Engine: Japan

Just as the Flying Geese paradigm of Asian development suggests, Japan has played a key role in stimulating capital, trade and technology flows within the region. But the big push into Asia of the 1980's was premised on a strong Yen and the prospect of hitting the lucrative US market from third bases. However, with the Yen weakening in the 1990's some of this impetus was lost, and combined with the crisis, there was a great deal of anxiety amongst Japanese banks concerning exposure to the region's downturn. The crisis created more uncertainty by disturbing relative unit cost levels in the region via exchange rate instability[3]. According to the

Flying Geese model, relative productivities and costs are important in determining investment patterns. Capital flight further accentuated the complexity of this business calculus.

In return for allowing greater foreign investment and openness, Asian countries sought to penetrate the rich Japanese market with exports. However, as discussed in Chapter 9, consumption and aggregate demand in Japan have been weak and so import growth from Asia has weakened in the late 1990's. Asia has suffered from a twin-shock; Japanese investment in the region softened from the heady days of the 1980's and Japan's languishing economy has offered little opportunity for export growth.

For Japan to contribute to regional recovery it must achieve a *broad based* economic recovery for itself and not rely only on exogenous demand and export growth to the US. Consumption and investment must rise in Japan to alleviate the over reliance on export success and government deficit spending. Even though structural adjustment will stimulate long-run growth, it has its costs on short-run growth by adversely affecting profitability, bankruptcy, lending confidence and employment in old industries. The policy maker faces a delicate trade-off between structural reform and macroeconomic stimulus. If the latter is overgenerous, the urgency of structural reform in the non-traded good and financial sectors may dissipate.

Evidence to date from Table 11-4 illustrates how East Asian exports to Japan increased far more slowly than to the USA. For example, in 1998 exports to the USA soared by 51% for Malaysia but only by 10% to Japan. Korea's overall export performance was less impressive than both Malaysia and Thailand but still revealed a biased response to the US over Japan.

Table 11-4

Total Exports to USA and Japan ($US millions)

| | USA | | | JAPAN | | |
	1997	1998	1999	1997	1998	1999
Mal.	10822	16349	18524	7232	7957	9813
		(51%)	(13%)		(10%)	(23%)
Thai	9288	13118	12557	7093	8079	8169
		(41%)	(-4%)		(14%)	(1%)
Korea	21625	22805	29474	14771	12237	15862
		(5%)	(29%)		(-17%)	(29%)

Source: Bank Negara Malaysia, Central Bank of Thailand and Bank of

Korea

Note: Percentage increases are in parentheses

11-4 The US Boom : A Case of Fortuitous Circumstances?

The US economy has flourished in recent years. Several significant geo-political changes occurred in the late 1980's that laid the foundation for a sustained US recovery. Firstly, the end of the Cold War promised a 'peace dividend' as more resources would flow toward consumption and peace-time activities. The technological lead of the US in many high-tech goods and services could be more fully exploited in a world desiring a more consumption-based lifestyle. Secondly, GATT agreements sought to reduce protectionism worldwide and so stimulate greater trade flows and thus economic activity. Lower tariffs spelt more export opportunities for US companies. Thirdly, other global institutions such as the World Bank and the IMF intensified their push for greater openness of the world economy in terms of trade, capital and knowledge flows. The US economy itself became far more open from the early 1980's onwards. US multinational companies embraced the prospect of globalisation with both hands and sought to aggressively seize market share across a broad spectrum of countries. In short, it was corporate America that was well situated to penetrate world markets more forcefully in the 1990's.

Besides these favourable changes on the world stage, there were other favourable domestic occurrences that boosted America's profitability in the 1990's. Even though real wages rose, by and large, unit costs did not. Labour productivity growth was strong enough to offset increased wage costs. No doubt strong capital equipment expenditure improved the quality of the capital stock which in turn stimulated labour productivity. Falling prices for computer equipment and related technology partially provided the impetus for increased capital spending. This key industry provided spill-over benefits to the whole economy and so made a major contribution to stable US costs and productivity growth. Even though the labour market has been tight for most of the decade, workers did fear job loss at times and increased competition in product markets made it less acceptable for employers to 'give in' to wage demands. Moreover, a reformed social welfare net encouraged workers to accept low pay jobs. Import prices were also soft, given the state of global demand and so assisted in dampening both the US price and wage level.

Given respectable productivity growth and stable unit costs, business profits were given a boost. Improved corporate profitability caused the US stock markets to surge for many years. Some economists have called this a 'real bubble,' in contrast to a speculative bubble, that is driven by a vibrant lift in productivity growth. To the extent that productivity growth is a permanent rather than a cyclical phenomena, the US growth experience is sustainable and the level of US stock prices justifiable.[4] However, to extent that liquidity and wealth effects are supporting exceptionally high price-earnings ratios there is fertile ground for a correction in US stock prices. After all, a rising market bouyed by ample liquidity, easy credit and margin lending may create the appearance of a 'one-way street' but beneath the tranquility are speculative motives that are more concerned with fast entry and exit than with long-term fundamentals.

At first glance, the Asian meltdown of 1997/98 appeared to undermine the vitality of the US economy and US stock prices but in reality the US bond market enjoyed a flood of support by fearful Asian investors indulging in capital flight out of unsafe assets and currencies. As bond yields fell in the US in late 1997, support came for stocks, albeit with a lag. As foreign investors demanded US assets so did the US$ gain further support. Hence, US assets and the $US benefited from Asia's demise - at least in the short term. An already liquid US economy received yet more liquidity.

On a general note, the strong $US from 1995 onwards only assisted the expansionary plans of US companies in terms of strategic foreign investment, importing goods made abroad under a US label, maintaining profits at home via low interest rates and keeping credit both accessible and cheap as the US bond market enjoyed strong foreign support. Dollar strength only added more liquidity and profitability to the US economy. Therefore, a degree of caution is warranted before the 'robust' US expansion is declared productivity or efficiency driven. Abundant liquidity, easy access to credit by the consumer and the stock's holder, together with solid foreign support for US financial assets has underwritten an unprecedented expansion in the US economy. Disentangling these two effects on US stock prices remains a challenge for US policy maker and the US Federal Reserve.

It is robust growth without inflation that places the US Fed in unchartered waters as old empirical relationships fail to hold. In fact, the threat of deflation is just as likely as is the threat of inflation. The information technology revolution may have smashed costs so far that normal inflation measures maybe unreliable indicators. As Canterbery (2000: 4) points out, this combined with the old Fed mandate against *goods price inflation* rather than *asset price inflation* causes a grievious dilemma for Greenspan. His concern over 'irrational exuberance' in US stock markets tempts him to prick the asset price bubble on the basis that it was mainly driven by liquidity and abundant stored wealth.

11-5 The US Expansion: What are the Weaknesses?

Given the massive amounts of wealth housed in US stock markets and the associated 'unrealised gains,' any shock that dislodges US stock market levels will have severe consequences for household balance sheets. A danger exists if households have incorporated unrealised profits into their balance sheets and have 'counted' such gains as permanent income then past spending levels are but a reflection of illusory wealth. Adverse wealth effects could drastically alter US consumption patterns in a short time frame, particularly if other asset prices are dragged down by a sudden, unanticipated correction on Wall Street. US stock levels are finely tuned, everything must fall into place for current valuations to be justified, and so any domestic or global shock could trigger a sell-off in stocks.

Even though the monetary policy stance of the Fed has been cautious before 1999, and contractionary thereafter, there is always the possibility of the Fed becoming concerned about asset price inflation (a lesson from Japan), of inflationary expectations rising at home, leading economic indicators revealing excess heat or just general anxiety that the US economy needs to be cooled as *precautionary measure* against expected inflation. A policy induced sell-off in stocks is a possibility. Under this scenario, corporate profits are squeezed by both higher future and current borrowing costs. There is also the opportunity cost argument that US companies and fund managers may at some point switch from stocks to bonds as respective yields swap over or are not wide enough to compensate for perceived risk in stocks. That is, it may not be the *push factor* out of stocks that drives this switch but the *pull factor* of US bond yields appearing too attractive to be missed. Even a re-evaluation of risk may trigger the shift.

A common fear amongst economists and financial analysts is that the US economic 'recovery' is past maturity and due for a cooling off period if not a downturn. After all, the US economy is its 9th year of consecutive growth and perhaps the seeds of the next downturn have already been sown? What then are these possible seeds? The fear of inflation has always permeated the minds of the US Federal Reserve. However, the Fed's mandate is targeted more toward 'goods price inflation' and not asset price inflation (Canterbery, 2000: 4). Despite fears of wage and price inflation in the US in the 1990's - there was little evidence that this terrible beast had raised its head. In fact, Fed Chairman Alan Greenspan went chasing this imaginary phantom in 1994 by raising bond yields and so dampening economic activity, only to return in disappointment that this phantom actually failed to arrive. He called this a pre-emptive strike against the inflationary phantom despite the fact that it was not a 'clear and present' danger. This was not Greenspan's finest hour. Why?

Because an old paradigm may have died and the Fed was trapped in using traditional strategies against an old but dead foe. The new foes are goods price *deflation* and asset price *inflation*; a combination that requires a new finesse.

Domestic triggers may come from a tight labour market that has enjoyed real wage rises and workers may seek to press home the advantage in a boom economy. Other labour costs may also squeeze profit margins. On the demand side, credit-laden households may seek to restore some stability to their household balance sheets by reducing debt levels and market saturation in some consumer goods, in some income categories, may cause consumption spending to moderate. In turn, highly competitive product markets may restrict the seller's ability to pass on price rises in a rising cost environment and amidst soft final good demand. In short, the US stock markets may face *profit disappointment* as America's corporations cope with a profit squeeze. Sensitivity to poor earnings results may be higher than anticipated and so cause an accentuated sharp sell-off in stocks.

Other exogenous factors may trigger a major correction in US stock markets. The price of oil rose dramatically in late 1999 and early 2000 causing upward pressure on the world inflation rate. Currency shocks are also very destabilising for world financial markets, as evidenced by Asia's recent turmoil. Contagion via debt, investment and export linkages cause investor heartburn. Developing country debt default can also cause financial institutions in the US to incur significant losses. Any of these shocks have the potency to erode the bouyancy of US financial markets.

Hence, the risks of a significant US stock market correction rest with Fed policy, profit dissappointment, a change in sentiment over perceived risk and external shocks or any combination thereof.

11-6 The Achilles Heal of the Robust US Expansion

The US has accrued a vast amount of wealth over the last 300 years. As Canterbery (2000:35) points out, much of this wealth is held by the very rich in the US. It is this rich bond-holding class of people that wield much power and control over public policy, and monetary policy in particular. America paid for the Vietnam war and much of its social expenditures for over 40 years by spreading an inflation tax around the world and by running up huge budget deficits and national debt. The bond-holding class gained by receiving interest payments on US bonds and gained yet more via its avoidance of paying taxes to finance such deficits. This is not to mention the *real prize* of capturing capital gains by holding bonds. Canterbery (2000:104) succintly paints Reagan's economic strategy of the early 1980's as that of marrying the Laffer idea of 'low taxation' with Friedman's idea that inflation must be held in check via 'tight money'. Such a strategic combination caused much bullion to flow into the hands of the already rich. Tax cuts for the rich provided more funds for the accumulation of more bonds - at gilt edged high interest rates. Thus, a rich class of bondholders possesses much power over the conduct of monetary policy.

It is this class that desires a 'Goldilock's economy' that must not be 'too hot' or 'too cold', but 'just right'. Why? Because an economy that is too hot causes interest rates to soar and demolish the much cherished capital gains in the bond market. An economy that is too cold is also to be avoided as yields on bonds become 'too low.' Hence, the US bond holding class always seems dissatisfied as the temperature of the economy is not quite right. As Canterbery (2000:19) states, they are known as the 'good news bears,' as a potentially robust economy spoils their fun.

With vast amounts of wealth accumulated by the bond-holding class there is always the threat of a 'capital strike' or a provocation of the Fed to give US bond market what it wants. The great fear of the bond holding class is higher *expected* inflation that provokes the Fed to raise interest rates *now*. Such a pre-emptive strike against inflation causes bond-holders to suffer capital losses. According to Canterbery (2000:89) the 'bond market strategy' employed by the Fed is a result of the symbiotic relationship it has with Wall Street and Treasury. Mutual interests aim to keep the economy moderately cool or luke warm in order that capital gains may be realised in both bond and stock markets. Therefore, the expectations of bond holders concerning the expectations of the Fed concerning the expected inflation rate results in a dangerous game of second guessing.

What then is the Achilles heel of the current US recovery? It is the combination of highly concentrated wealth in the hands of a small elite with high sensitivity to changes in inflationary expectations. A sudden or prolonged shock to long-term bond yields will in turn shock the stock market. Large capital losses, interacting with margin calls, could stir panic selling. Over exposure in US markets by foreign interests also complicates the sell off scenario. Therefore, this game-theoretic interaction by the Fed and the bond-holding class is a delicate fight that needs to be managed skillfully in order that a rapid financial meltdown does not occur. Perhaps Greenspan's objective is to engineer a soft landing with regard to asset prices.

11-7 The US Business Cycle: Past Maturity?

The centrepiece for an ongoing Asian recovery is a continuation of a robust US economy. Asian exporters are still dependent on the US market for volumes and prices. As discussed earlier, high export volume responses were swamped by low values in 1998 - an adverse terms of trade problem. Strong US domestic demand supports commodity prices and indirectly world export growth and demand. Given the lack of business cycle synchronisation between the US, Europe and Japan in the recent times there has been a disproportionate burden placed on a continuing cyclical upswing in the US. Secondly, a return of US foreign investors and fund managers to Asia is an integral part of any financial recovery for the region. Liquidity has been identified an important fuel for rocket engine two; enhancing activity, exports and re-capitalising Asian banks for their important intermediation task. Thirdly, a robust US economy indirectly underwrites stock prices and financial markets in general. Confidence in the bond market and the $US has assisted US growth. Such confidence spills over into world financial markets and indirectly assists credit expansion and economic growth.

11-8 Evidence: The Recovery

In searching for signs of economic recovery the leading indicators of exchange rates, interest rates and stock market indeces require examination. Also a more stable or declining inflation rate assists in the return of economic growth. These are pre-requisites for the recovery of real variables such as GDP growth and employment.

From Table 11-5 it can be seen that exchange rates have not only stabilised, but in the main, have achieved major appreciations from low levels. Even though the Thai Baht, the Indonesian Rupiah and the Korean Won have not returned to early 1997 levels they have displayed far less volatility. Besides, current levels are probably more in line with true economic fundamentals than the boom years and provide a greater opportunity for the restoration of export-led growth.

Table 11-5

Exchange Rates (per USD)

	1997		1998			1999		
	II	IV	II	III	IV	II	III	IV
China	8.28	8.28	8.28	8.28	8.28	8.28	8.28	8.28
H.K.	7.74	7.75	7.25	7.75	7.75	7.76	7.77	7.77
Indon	2.4	5.4	11.5	10.8	7.5	7.3	8.3	7.0
Japan	113	130	141	133	120	120	106	102
Korea	881	1420	1403	1388	1217	1171	1202	1133
Malay	2.52	3.91	3.40	3.80	3.79	3.80	3.80	3.80
S'pore.	1.43	1.68	1.71	1.73	1.66	1.71	1.70	1.67
Twn	27.9	32.7	34.7	34.5	32.3	32.4	31.6	31.7
Thai	25.8	46.2	43.6	40.8	35.9	36.9	40.0	38.1

Source:International Financial Statistics (Feb., 2000)

Note: Indonesian Currency in thousands

Despite the huge credit crunch of 1997/98 and shortage of liquidity in the financial sector there has also been a dramatic fall in interest rates since the peak of 1998 as revealed in Table 11-6. No doubt policy initiatives have assisted such falls but also softer economies and a reduced demand for credit have contributed to lower rates. Nevertheless, a lower cost of capital and relief from excessive debt repayment will assist interest rate sensitive expenditures. As the Asian Development Bank (2000) points out, there has been a dramatic return of consumer confidence and consumption spending in Korea and Singapore.

Table 11-6

Interest Rates - Short Term

	1997	1998				1999		
	IV	I	II	III	IV	I	II	III
China	8.64	7.92	7.92	6.93	6.39	6.39	5.85	5.85
H.Kong	9.5	10.0	10.0	10.0	9.00	8.75	8.25	8.50
Indonesia	26.2	26.3	32.1	34.9	35.2	34.1	30.3	24.5
Japan	2.38	2.37	2.34	2.31	2.27	2.24	2.17	2.16
Korea	13.1	17.3	16.9	14.8	12.1	10.7	9.4	8.9
Malaysia	10.0	11.1	12.2	10.9	8.2	8.0	7.4	6.9
Singapore	6.51	7.7	7.7	7.7	6.5	5.8	5.8	5.8
Thailand	14.9	15.2	15.2	14.8	12.3	10.2	8.9	8.6

Source: International Financial Statistics (Feb., 2000)

Notes: These are bank lending rates

Of particular interest is the energetic revival of several Asian stock markets. As can be seen from Table 11-7, Hong Kong and Singapore have rebounded to former pre-crisis levels. Malaysia, Thailand, Indonesia and Taiwan have bounced well but still remain under the high levels of early 1997. Nevertheless, confidence in stock values reflect investor beliefs that profitability has and will return in near future. Currency stability has encouraged the return of foreign buyers and the desire to seize merger opportunities while Asian governments are receptive to greater foreign ownership in key sectors of the economy. Stock market revivals have been nothing short of miraculous with the exceptions of Thailand and the Philippines. As wealth effects permeate the balance sheets of corporations and households, once again so too will consumption expenditure rise.

Table 11-7

Stock Market Indeces

	1997		1998		1999		
	II	IV	III	IV	II	III	IV
H.Kong	14307	10346	7661	10428	13007	13472	16212
Indonesia	705	256	321	399	679	543	646
Japan	20594	15985	14227	14723	17188	17575	18175
Korea	792	404	314	515	822	934	967
Malaysia	1077	544	393	515	783	710	788
Philippines	2798	1801	1101	1834	2391	2106	967
Singapore	2004	1562	878	1377	2058	2123	2370
Taiwan	8679	8194	6860	7303	7974	7972	7782
Thailand	497	370	211	338	515	434	451

Source: Far Eastern Economic Review (various issues)

As currencies collapsed, there were pressures on domestic inflation rates to rise as imports cost more in $US, inputs into the production cost more and consumers were keen to avoid shortages by 'buying now.' Table 11-8 reveals a major achievement by authorities in reducing inflation and wrenching high inflationary expectations out of the economic system. In the near term, there should not be an expectation that domestic investment would pick up but the trade balance should improve and to a lesser extent domestic consumption. Although Indonesia is still under inflationary threat, some Asian nations have not only reduced inflation significantly but generated deflation. Lower inflation interacts with lower interest rates and so takes stress off contactionary monetary policy.

Table 11-8

Inflation Rate (%)

	1997	1998				1999		
	IV	I	II	III	IV	I	II	III
China	0.4	-0.1	-0.1	-1.1	-1.1	-1.0	-2.2	-1.3
H.K	5.0	4.8	4.2	0.4	-0.8	-1.2	-3.0	-5.0
Indon	13.2	29.7	29.7	.....	-5.3	30.8	30.8	2.8
Japan	2.1	1.8	1.0	-0.2	0.3	0.0	-0.7	-0.2
Korea	6.6	8.9	8.2	7.0	6.0	0.7	0.4	0.6
Malay	2.9	3.6	5.0	5.5	5.3	4.7	2.9	2.3
Sing.	2.4	0.9	-1.2	-1.5	-1.5	-0.5	0.1	0.9
Twn	-0.1	0.5	1.6	0.5	2.1	0.7	-0.1	0.7
Thai	7.9	8.4	10.0	5.9	4.2	3.6	-0.5	-1.0

Source: International Financial Statistics (Feb., 2000)

Notes: Annualised Rates

What the above economic indicators reveal is a degree of optimism with regard to the recovery of GDP growth and employment. As can be seen from Table 11-9 there has been a contaction of GDP in most Asian economies for most quarters up until the end of 1999. However, future prospects appear positive for the debt ridden countries of Korea, Thailand and Malaysia. Therefore, this economic dowturn was short-lived, contrary to the view of many economic policy makers in mid 1997. Why? Because financial rather than economic variables went sour and so dragged the real economy with them. Once exchange rates, interest rates and monetary liquidity stabilised then a rational business calculus could be performed by investors and consumers could release their purse strings.

Table 11-9

GDP Growth (%)

	1997	1998				1999		
	IV	I	II	III	IV	I	II	III
China	11.0	9.0	8.2	7.6	7.8	8.2	8.2	8.2
H.Kong	5.5	4.0	-2.0	-4.6	-5.5	-0.5	-1.0	-1.0
Indon	8.0	-1.5	-15.0	-15.0	-15.0	-3.4	-1.8	-1.7
Japan	1.9	1.9	0.3	0.3	-2.1	-0.7	-0.7	0.9
Korea	5.5	…	-7.0	-7.0	-5.9	2.7	5.0	7.0
Malay	8.0	4.5	-2.1	-5.8	-7.0	2.0	2.0	3.0
S'pore	7.0	6.0	2.0	-2.0	1.3	1.7	2.5	4.0
Twn	6.0	6.4	6.0	4.7	4.9	4.5	4.5	4.5
Thai	6.6	0.5	-8.0	-8.0	-7.0	-0.5	-0.5	1.5

Source: International Financial Statistics (Feb., 2000)

Notes: Annualised rates

Table 11-10

Scenario of GDP Growth (%)

	1997	1998	1999	2000	2001
China	8.8	7.8	7.1	6.5	6.0
H.Kong	5.0	-5.1	2.9	5.0	5.5
Indon	4.7	-13.2	0.2	4.0	5.0
Korea	5.0	-6.7	10.7	7.5	6.0
Malay	7.5	-7.5	5.4	6.0	6.1
Philip.	5.2	-0.5	3.2	3.8	4.3
S'pore	8.0	1.5	5.4	5.9	6.2
Taiwan	6.7	4.6	5.7	6.3	6.2
Thai	-1.8	-10.4	4.1	4.5	4.6

Source: Asian Development Bank (2000)

11-9 Conclusion

The major theme of this book is the central importance of financial and monetary factors in both the growth and crisis experience. An export orientated East Asia has built an economic super structure on an immature, but growing, financial super structure that have combined together to deliver super-growth up until 1997. Economic fundamentals suffered minor collapses despite the fact that financial fundamentals deteriorated significantly during the 1997-98 period. Hence, the economic recovery required a financial rebound of a type, before output and employment growth could resume their upward trend. This financial revival took the form of more stable exchanges, interest rates and stock markets - beyond the wildest of expectations. Not only did capital outflows subside but so did foreign capital return, in search of asset bargains. As per the WSM, profitability returned via an export revival and foreign injected liquidity (hard currency). This is not to deny the role of policy initiatives or the rebound in domestic consumption and investment but these growth energy forces reacted to the re-strengthening of external linkages.

The continued economic revival of East Asia depends on how well the fuels of catch-up growth, technical and allocative efficiency, can be realised. While wide price and cost differentials remain between East Asia and the West there is every reason to believe that the economic recovery will continue and in fact constitute the second stage of economic lift-off. There have been valuable lessons learnt from this recent 'pruning process' as structural reform and greater efficiency in key sectors of the economy will doubtless build a more viable and sustainable economic recovery over the medium term.

Chapter Twelve

Common Forces of Acsent and Demise

12-1 Introduction

For many years the economics profession pondered over the causes of the development success of East Asia, without much clarity, credibility or conviction. Whilst economists played theoretical catch-up, along came the Asian crisis. Such a quick-fire calamity caused economists to re-think their position on the East Asian miracle, some downgrading it to a mirage and others to just rapid accumulation in fortuitous circumstances. Explanations of the crisis are far more plausible, from a theoretical perspective, than those of the growth miracle. A by-product of the crisis has been a greater illumination of the driving forces of economic growth than ever before, as economists have ventured away from the traditional long-term real factors of growth and toward financial, short-term factors.

12-2 Common Forces of Ascent and Demise

This book has both identified and married the driving forces of economic growth with those driving the crisis. From Chapter 2, the Western Shuttle Model of economic take-off identified the importance of international competitiveness for aspiring developing nations as the key to achieving sustainable development success. A loss of international competitiveness, pre-crisis, was instrumental in causing a decline in the rate of growth of exports and export revenue, so vital for the financing of national development. The likely causes of this decline are the emergence of China as a major world competitor, the saturation of OECD markets and the exhaustion of the first-stage export thrust in labor intensive goods. This latter view of diminishing returns hitting labor intensive export industries is a major cause of some East Asian nations hitting the first growth plateau and so showing warning signs of economic slowdown. In a sense, Krugman is right, diminishing returns do matter and are relevant, but not for reasons of exhausted accumulation or a mature economy K/L ratio being achieved. Rather, it is the difficult leap to the second stage of export led growth in higher, more sophisticated product ladder goods that break the immediate shackles of diminishing returns from first stage export thrust. As stated in Chapter 2, international competitiveness for developing economies is crucial for growth *with* stabilization.

A second common factor of both boom and bust was the under- and then over- valuation of the exchange rate of these East Asian nations. In the 1950's and 60's many of these nations enjoyed both very low nominal and real exchange rates for reasons of low integration into world markets, relatively low wage costs to the OECD and suppression of the nominal rate by governments in order to 'artificially' stimulate export growth. The low level of the real exchange rate was examined in Chapter 4 as a key determinant of East Asia's super export growth. Vast differences in price and income levels between East Asia and the OECD acted as an exogenous catalyst of export growth. However, as prosperity in East Asia rose, so did wage rates and costs in general rise, causing the real exchange rate to rise off a low base. Moreover, governments were being warned by the USA and others that the deliberate under-valuation of the nominal exchange rate was unacceptable and its market-determined equilibrium level should be found. Hence, natural cost competitiveness was being eroded with each year of additional prosperity - an income-competitiveness trade-off. Not only was the external real exchange rate appreciating for these nations, but more importantly the *internal* real exchange rate skyrocketed. The price of non-traded goods (assets in particular) increased dramatically in the late 1980's to mid 1990's in most of these nations. Hence, the economic incentives to invest in export industries became unfavorably biased, it became far more profitable to invest in the highly speculative, but extremely profitable, non-traded goods sector. Thus, international competitiveness was eroded far more on the supply-side of the export drive as economic incentives diminished to shift resources into the traded good sector. Nevertheless, pegged exchange rates had their costs, in that a rising $US placed enormous pressure on the cross exchange rates against China and Japan in particular. Even the *external* real exchange rate became overvalued in some cases.

A third common factor of both East Asian growth and crisis is the central role played by profits. Whilst increasing, rather than diminishing returns are important for growth in an East Asian context, it is the high *level* of returns that is central to growth. East Asia was blessed with the advantages of backwardness, in that labor costs in early years were very low compared to the OECD. Given the law of one world price, profit margins to East Asian exporters were exceptionally high indeed. Romer's emphasis on unit costs and monopoly profits was well founded, for in his model the engine of growth was the invention of a new good that involved the spreading of unit costs over a large production run. However, in East Asia the level of unit costs was already low, driven by cheap labor, and so it was not a matter of smashing them lower or even capturing economies of scale in order to create larger profits. Such monopoly profits existed in a world of unequal partners, economies of scale or not. Thus, it is not a case of a downward sloping LRAC, but its low position, that is relevant for EA. When East Asian exporters were able to exploit super-profits, even in the first stage of export-led growth, super-economic growth resulted. This same force, of declining profitability, was a major cause of East Asia's demise in the mid 1990's. Reduced profit margins were partly the result of both world and domestic factors. World prices for semi conductors collapsed in 1996 but also some East Asian nations failed miserably in building up their human capital during their early boom years. Failure to move up the product and quality ladders lay at the background of the crisis. Diminishing returns in the form of diminishing profits spelt the beginning of the crisis for East Asia.

A fourth common factor, and a corollary of the third, is the enormous liquidity that built up in East Asia for over 30 years of profitable export growth. During the first stage of export-led growth (labor intensive goods) such abundant liquidity was the vital lifeblood for the invigoration of a sustained export drive. Export profits were ploughed back into the export drive as high wage rates, higher costs and thinner profit margins had not yet suffocated the vitality of first stage export industries. Abundant liquidity was not a problem in this environment as it did not ignite inflation or inflationary expectations– as the acquisition of super-profits was still a realizable option facilitated by monetary creation.

Friedman was right: Money creation is both a powerful and dangerous force that is not to be played with. Well, maybe. In the long run, money is neutral. However, in the short run there is potency, especially for a developing export economy facing a wide, profitable opportunity set. The monetary transmission mechanism, in an East Asian context, operated more through the liquidity effects, balance sheet and credit channels rather than through the interest rate channel. Returns from exporting were so high that credit was rationed in most East Asian nations in the 1960's and 70's. In many circumstances it was directed by government. Hence, the availability of money rather than its cost, was the critical constraint in realizing export potential. Export profits, FDI and mobile foreign capital caused balance sheets to balloon, of both the corporate and financial sectors. Healthy balance sheets made trade credit easy to attain. Unfortunately, it also made credit for asset and non-traded goods sector speculation easy to obtain. In short, 'money matters', it is non-neutral for developing economies in the transition phase of development.

However, as diminishing returns to the first export stage set in and as profitability in the non-traded goods sector now looked more attractive (easier to attain) than achieving second-stage export led growth so did 'excess liquidity' cause more inflation, distort relative prices and in turn misallocate national resources. The end result was an asset price bubble that absorbed resources away from productive manufacturing and export based investment. Hence, the seeds of the crisis were sown in the heat of the boom, in that lucrative profitability generated very liquid economies that lacked the sophistication and maturity to deal with such new-found wealth. It must be acknowledged that money supply growth was not all a function of export profitability but also the associated foreign capital flows in the form of direct investment in the early years of growth. But even this investment was attracted by the lucrative export profits available based on comparative advantage, and so indirectly, abundant liquidity was driven by export performance.

A fifth common factor was the corporate and financial sector love of high financial gearing. With high expected profits, ex ante, it was rational for economic agents to borrow heavily in this 'one way street'. Exceptionally high debt-equity ratios were partly a result of potent export success in early years but more the result (cause) of the asset price bubble in latter years. Excess liquidity in the financial sector was very much a function of foreign borrowing post liberalization. There is no doubt that highly leveraged corporations in Asia, for much of the 1960-1996 period benefited greatly from such a strategy. Returns were explosive in this environment. But so too were losses, when this 'two edged sword' cut inward in 1997.

12-3 Growth and Development Theory Challenged

This book questions the relevance of existing East Asian development models. The Japanese model embraces worker loyalty, on the job training, commitment to productivity and structural adjustment by workers. Corporations commit to investment, productive efficiency and up-to-date management techniques. However, this production theoretic framework is not capable of explaining long-run super-profits in a closed economy, nor can it explain the current malaise of the Japanese economy or even the onset of the Asian crisis. This model has fallen from grace in the 1990's.

The Locomotive- Carriage model focuses on the USA as being the prime mover (locomotive) of world growth. An increase in activity and demand in the USA drags the rest of the world along with it via export and import linkages. According to Lewis (1980), developing economies' exports are particularly dependent on US economic activity. However, this model does not explain why the carriages have accelerated faster than the locomotive, nor why the Asian crisis arose while the USA was experiencing one of the most vibrant growth phases in its history.

The Flying Geese model explains East Asian development in terms of complementarity of economic tasks (comparative advantage) and the quest of moving to higher value added products (tiers). Asian nations depend on Japan for access to a rich market, capital and technology flows and of the possibility of moving up the product ladder. In exchange, Japan enjoys monopoly profits from its technological leadership, cheaper unit costs from spreading its production around Asia and lower import prices. The weaknesses of this model stem from the fragile nature of complementarity and the common quest to move up the value added ladder (competition). China is the big bird that scatters the flock. Moreover, Japan lacks the will to act as flock leader. Also, Japan in the early years, lacked the wealth and the wide price differentials to support a sustained regional export drive.

Some of the above deficiencies in development models are rectified in the Western Shuttle Model, discussed more below in a growth theory context.

This book also challenges the traditional pillars of economic growth theory. There is not one singular flight path to prosperity. Real factors and supply side stimuli are important for the economic takeoff of the now mature economies but less important for the now developing world. Why? Because the economic incentive and opportunity set faced by developing economies is far different from that of OECD in its heyday of development. Securing high profits could *only* be achieved by invention and innovation that lowered unit costs. There were no rich neighbors living alongside the now mature economies in their heyday of development. Hence, this inquiry places technological progress, invention, productivity, real factors and supply side stimuli on the backstage of East Asia's economic take-off and development as they are long-term in nature. The weakness of growth theory in a developing economy context is the lack of appreciation of the multi-origin of profits, of economic take-off and the financial dimension of economic growth. So what short-term forces of growth should then appear on the front stage?

12-4 Extensions of Growth and Development Theory

An attempt is made to both collect and amalgamate the above extensions to growth theory in a formal Western Shuttle Model (WSM). Demand-side growth is represented by the rocket whereas supply-side growth by the shuttle. The Solow model is preserved in terms of the importance of the accumulation of factors of production as per fuel for the rocket boosters. Jones and Manuelli (1991) make a contribution in terms of the MPK not being cursed by diminishing returns, in this WSM by exports exploding the MPK and so delaying diminishing returns setting in. This is the rocket engine of super-profits and the power of investment in the export sector stimulating allocative and technical efficiency. Pack and Page (1994) stress the importance of technical efficiency, imitation and being well inside the production possibility frontier. Parente and Prescott (1994) also stress the importance of tapping the pool of world knowledge. Hence, the WSM describes the transition phase of growth to the international steady state as being a function of accumulation, allocative and technical efficiency – serving as *fuels* of transitional growth. The twin engines of transitional growth are super- profits and hard currency from exports and FDI. A hump shaped trajectory of profits occurs until the shuttle disconnects from the rocket. During this rocket flight path, it is profitability rather than productivity that drives economic growth – even though the latter is growing in potency. Upon maturity (the steady state), the shuttle undertakes its own propulsion and flight path based on productivity, and not profits from exports. In fact, the only engine of propulsion in this international steady state is technology driven productivity growth – as per the Romer model (1990). Why? Cost and income levels converge to one and so monopolistic profits from exports approach normality.

The WSM makes a contribution to growth theory in the following manner. Firstly, the inherent nature of catch-up growth (convergence) is demand-side in origin, at least in terms of initial economic take-off. After take-off, the complexion of catch-up growth becomes more supply-side in nature as the developing nation moves away from simple manufactured goods and up the product ladder.

Secondly, a set of relative international prices not only acts as a spur to allocative efficiency but also to growth. Given the law of one price, a sizeable wedge is driven between world prices (in $US) and domestic costs (in local currency) as well as relatively low wage rates creating super profits. Exports cause such profits to be realized.

Thirdly, international competitiveness via a low real exchange rate is crucial for the achievement of economic growth. A Hecksher-Ohlin trade model is married to a Solow type model in an attempt to inject relative prices (profits) back into a traditional growth model. There may be the law of one price but there is not the law of one profit. Exports bias the MPK upward in this setting.

Fourthly, while the Solow model predicts an explosive MPK from a low K/L ratio base, it fails to explain why an open economy MPK is far more explosive than a closed economy MPK. This present research points to the value of the MPK (MRP) as divorced from the physical MPK as being the major reason why export biased economies gain greater potency from investment.

Fifthly, the productivity debate 'that is not' is revealed, as being more akin to a profitability debate in that developing economies have access to monopoly profits via natural competitiveness and so the low level of the real exchange rate. Along the flight path, profitability from exporting diminishes and is eventually subsumed by productivity as economic maturity is reached.

12-5 Where Are We Now?

Upon reflection, the extensions to existing growth theory come from the trade, finance, development and industrial organization literature. The strength of this study lies not in its econometric sophistication nor in its 'newness' but in its eclectic approach to achieving a formal synthesis, from various economic disciplines, of East Asian growth and development. Moreover, it has challenged the way in which economists view the East Asian miracle, especially from the timely illumination of East Asia's recent demise. Common forces were at work. Some old dogmas have died, as have old paradigms. Reformed, or perhaps new, paradigms are required in order to clarify our understanding of how the global village interacts and evolves. The ascent and demise of East Asia has provided the closest analogy possible, in modern history, for academic inquirers of all disciplines to examine, in a laboratory-type setting, the mechanics of economic development.

ENDNOTES

Chapter 1

1. This book has agressively pushed the exogeneity of East Asia's rapid growth experience, particularly from the 1950's to the 1970's. However, as incomes converged closer to developed country levels, the role of domestic investment and consumption played a more significant role in East Asia's growth process.
2. Even when the West experienced recessions the economic growth rate in East Asia was still positive and often around 5%.
3. The oil of this tradeoff may not have been the traditional productivity view but an exogenous trade (profitability) force that raised income growth far faster than labour growth.
4. This is not to conclude that labour productivity was efficiency driven.
5. Conventional economic theory claims that current account deficits that are privately driven are optimal and so require no government invention.
6. Such projects were no doubt undetaken because social returns were considered to be greater than private returns.

Chapter 2

1. There is a caveat to this statement. In some ways Great Britain acted as a large market of attraction for the rest of the world in the 18th century. Its industrial revolution generated vast amounts of wealth, that caused other nations to want to exchange their goods for the most advanced technology laden goods. However, as Bairoch (1993) points out the disparities in national incomes in the 18th century were far less than in the 20th century.
2. It should be noted that US income as a percentage of world income was around 40% in 1970 and still a hefty 26% in 1996. (World Bank Data)

3. Madison (1995) assembled long time-frame data that confirms this point.
4. The high level of US productivity is confirmed by Helliwell and Chung (1992) and Hooper (1992). However, high rates of productivity growth appear to found in EA – from a low base in the 1950's.
5. Rogoff (1996) claims that deviations from relative PPP occur and take as much as 8 years to converge.
6. This is a Krugman (1994) view of the EA growth experience.
7. This rocket deceleration caused by over-investment in the non-export sector is discussed in Chapter 6. Such deceleration was also caused by a loss of international competitiveness in mid-1990's.
8. Parente and Prescott (1994) emphasize a model drawing on the stock of world knowledge. Some nations in EA have been more successful than others in exploiting this technology gap, in part by dismantling or minimizing barriers to adoption.
9. Warr (1994) articulates this distinction.

Chapter 3

1. This concept represents a violation of absolute PPP as the nominal exchange rate has not moved sufficiently to offset the vast differences in the levels of prices between EA and the OECD.
2. Lucas (1988) calls for a common framework between development and growth theory.
3. An approach built on by Cass (1965) and Koopmans (1965).
4. Solow (1959) and Phelps (1962) considered technology embedded in new capital equipment. Therefore vintage capital has a greater potential to explain why investment has some transitional 'growth' properties. It also explains why De Long and Summers (1992) finding that equipment investment is important in cross-sectional growth evidence.
5. Wolff (1987) found a strong relationship between technological progress and the *speed* of investment.
6. The origins of this approach are found in Arrow (1962), a scale effect learning by doing effect.

7. Sheehan (1998) notes the technical difficulty of incorporating increasing returns into a competitive general equilibrium framework.
8. Aghion and Howitt (1992) emphasize a different approach, that of creative destruction, as being a stimulus to innovation.
9. Harberger (1996) points out that TFP growth represents an index of cost reduction. What also should recognized is that the relative *level* of unit costs between countries should be related to the *contribution* of TFP to the growth rate.
10. It should be noted, however, that this study employed trade not exports as a shift factor.
11. Barro and Xavier Sali Martin (1995, p.87) question the empirical validity of the international dynamics of the Solow model.
12. Pack (1994) and Solow (1994) question the 'newness' of new growth theory.

Chapter 4

1. The debate over whether the export supply curve is 'perfectly' elastic or subject to major rightward shifts in an EA context may be misplaced. No one questions that a massive export supply response has taken place, but the key question is *why* it was so massive when developed countries could not mount a similar kind of export response. The resolution of this dilemma rests in that fact that the rightward shift in the export supply curve was a function of the *distance between* the EA domestic demand curve and the foreign (US) demand curve. The greater the distance, the greater the supply-side response – and no such response would have been forthcoming without such a lucrative demand-side opportunity.
2. If the law of one price holds for tradable goods – worldwide – and given such a huge difference in manufacturing wage rates between EA and the OECD then this 'law' would dictate that huge profit differentials are realizable for EA producers.
3. Large export profits have provided a challenge both the EA policy maker and the econometrician alike. The policy maker is ever aware of feedback pains in the form of rising domestic income distorting pro-growth choices of sweat and sacrifice.

Suppressing inflation rates and encouraging savings rates have always been challenges. For the econometrican there is the test of exogeneity – that is, exports driving income and not the other way around. See Chapter Two, pages 69-71.

4. What also needs to be noted when testing export growth into the US market is that it is the *wealth and not just the income* of the US that is important in attracting foreign manufactured goods. 5. Such a huge stock of wealth acts as a permanent magnet of attraction.

Chapter 5:

1. The concept of MRP is analogous to the MEI_x. That is, so long as the marginal productivity of capital from exporting rests above the domestic (non-export sector) marginal productivity of capital, then rational EA producers are attracted more to the foreign than domestic market. However, according to the WSM, this 'productivity differential' is better explained as a profitability differential.

2. By marrying a Solow growth model to a Heckscher-Ohlin trade model, the essential driving force of EA economic growth is captured, that of low unit costs playing a key role in driving exports. Given vast differences in the level of unit costs between EA and the OECD, the dichotomy in the MPK's between export and non-export sectors is exposed.

3 A perusal of estimates of TFP growth and contribution to economic growth from Chapter 2 reveals a fairly clear pattern of low cost producers whose exports display higher TFP estimates than even the OECD or other non-exporting nations. On the path to maturity profitability eventually becomes productivity. In transition there is a mixture of both, but closer convergence to US income levels reduces the profitability element of TFP.

4. A criticism of this approach is to argue that even though wage differentials are large, there have been and still are large offsetting differences in productivity *levels* between the OECD and EA. But this implies that the US manufacturing worker, for example, is 33 times more efficient than the Chinese manufacturing worker given that the Chinese wage rate is 1/33

rd that of the US rate. This argument is difficult to accept in the production of labor intensive goods. Nor is the argument that the capital stock, technology and human capital of the US is so superior to that of China that the huge advantage in pure labor costs is offset by such non-wage superiority.

Chapter 6

1. Several South American counries are prime examples of generating hyperinflation from the excessive printing of money.
2. The opposing view is that huge trade profits and large capital inflows caused the advancement of financial maturity.
3. This direction of causation issue is particularly challenging. Despite a strong correlation between money and growth, for some economists, proves very little.
4. Over commitment.as well as under commitment has its costs in terms of not being able to deliver 'promised' stability.
5. Obviously the US does not need large amounts of foreign exchange reserves, as the $US is the reserve currency.
7. GDP is measured in $ and so may be driven by both profitability and productivity in the transition phase of growth.

Chapter 7

1. See Canterbery (1994) for further discussion of the casino mentality and how so- called investors actually undertake highly speculative asset purchases in the hope of making quick profits.
2. In some ways Krugman is right in that diminishing returns to accumulation will eventually hurt East Asia's growth momentum, but the kind of diminishing returns discussed in this study relate to the exhaustion of first-stage labor intensive exports. It is here that greater price competition is emerging from the developing world in general. Hence, international competitiveness rather than accumulation of factors per se is more relevant in an EA crisis context.
3. East Asia absorbed most of the world's capital flows to the developing world in the 1990's. Some financial experts claim that OECD banks 'lined up' to lend EA funds in recent years.

4. The East Asian crisis is quite distinct from the Mexican or Chilean crises in that private rather than public debt was the key problem and current accounts deficits were not consumption good dominated.

5. It should not come as a surprise that the East Asian Nations with sizable foreign exchange reserves were not hit as hard by this crisis. Taiwan and Hong Kong in particular have exceptionally high foreign exchange reserves by world standards.

6. Neo-Classical economists have long argued that foreign borrowing by domestic investors is undertaken after a cold business calculus is performed. The expected rate of return is compared to the cost of capital (foreign interest rate). Only profitable investments will be undertaken. Likewise, consumers indulge in intertemporal choice – borrowing now and paying back later – according their rate of time preference. Such decisions result in optimal foreign borrowings and optimal current account deficits. Rational economic agents make it so.

7. With the economic downturn in Europe and with Japan languishing in recession, there was a *push effect* in terms of capital searching for higher rates of return than in those recessed environments. And EA did both offer and yield higher rates of return in the early 1990's.

8. The sheer volume of capital inflows probably would have been 'too much' for any developing region in the world. There is the concept of 'social capability' and 'absorptive capacity' that needs to be considered – financial fragility is a matter of degree – under such enormous weight.

9. The work of Minsky (1986) is relevant here in that output and employment severely contracts under asset price deflation. Businesses are forced to sell any asset or good in order to stay afloat and so avoid bankruptcy. Such a 'fire sale' of asset prices in a confined time frame only accentuates to the fall in asset prices and so revenue proceeds from such sales.

10. Indonesia was accused of printing money in order to keep afloat its financial sector suffering under large foreign debt obligations. Although the costs in terms of inflation and currency weakness were well known, the alternative of a total financial sector collapse and civil disorder appeared more expensive.

11. Thailand enjoyed a strong flow of FDI from Japan in the mid 1980's to early 1990's partly as a result of a strong Yen and a stable Baht. A change in Japan's fortunes curbed this flow. Given Thailand's economic takeoff, more short-term investors were willing to purchase Thai assets.

12. The irony with this situation is that Thai authorities were caught between a rock and a hard place, in that raising interest rates to halt the soar in real estate prices would have entailed a greater differential between domestic and foreign interest rates. Such a move may have stimulated more capital flows, adding further liquidity to the system and pressuring asset prices higher.

13. There has been much heat in international financial circles about opening up of the capital accounts of developing nations. This is just part of the overall openness debate. However, the crisis and the destabilizing nature of 'hot money' has delayed any proposal by the IMF to push for more capital account openness.

14 Foreign exchange traders not only keep a close watch on economic fundamentals such as inflation rates, current account deficits, budget deficits and so forth but also on financial fundamentals such as rates of return, asset prices, leverage ratios, price-earnings ratios and short-term debt deadlines. Hence, liquidity rather than long-term solvency is of particular interest to opportunistic foreign exchange traders.

15. There is no doubt that the close relationship between business and government created an air of false security in terms of safety and bailout help. Moreover, foreign government help may not be far off in the minds of some EA investors as many foreign mutli-national firms themselves would be lobbying their own foreign governments for assistance.

16. Krugman's emphasis on private and corporate balance sheets and the inflow of capital in 'blowing up' the entire economy and its exit as causing balance sheet destruction is an excellent 'pump model' that fits the experience. Large capital flows are a self-fulfilling cause of wealth creation in a developing economy – at least for a time.

17. Unfortunately, the constraints or conditions in early months were draconian and caused the real sector to take a hard hit in the form of negative growth.

Chapter 8

1. In a normally functioning economy it is the financial sector that 'intermediates' between borrower and lender, bearing much of the risk of default. The real economy benefits from such a function. However, when the financial 'disintermediates' it is restricting the flow of credit, acting as a drag on the flow of wealth creation and economic activity. Why does the financial sector indulge in this type of behavior? The answer lies in risk aversion, large shares of non-performing loans, shareholder aggression and the urgent need to repair its own damaged balance sheets.

2. Unfortunately, this view does not incorporate permanent damage done to corporate balance sheets and future economic capacity.

3. Low interest rate strategies worked in the US during the savings and loans debacle and also when the FED made the economic system liquid after the stock market crash of 1987. However, the key distinction between the US experience and the EA episode is that the $US was never going to enter into a free-fall or foreign creditors demand payment 'now.'

4. George Stiglitz (1999) takes this view that the IMF has stayed too close to US business interests (a Washington Consensus) and formed 'strategies' that are no doubt favorable to the recovery of debt for such vested interests.

5. The secret to East Asia's recovery rests in the asset market. To the extent that asset prices recover, lending flows shall resume, financial sector health shall be restored and real activity and profits will rise. Capital flows should respond. Even strong export growth from a lower real exchange rate will be tested to overwhelm such domestic balance sheet destruction.

Chapter 9

1. Stiglitz (1999) and others note the importance of adverse wealth effects in restricting *flows* of activity and so point to the ineffectiveness of the Neo classical model in generating wise policy prescriptions for EA.

2. Perhaps this 'convoy approach' reflects Japanese culture – all for one and one for all.
3. When the MEI is below r there is an obvious reluctance and pessimism on behalf of investors to invest. This fear of a capital loss was ever present in Japan – and justifiably so, as Japan's stock market generated many 'false dawns.'
4. Rational bank behavior, amidst severely damaged balance sheets, can involve a loss of lending confidence and the desire 'to serve' the interests of bank shareholders before those of potential borrowers. Lending flows suffer from the supply side not the demand side, in that borrowers do not wish to borrow or lack a viable set of investment opportunities. This is not only a stalemate but a self fulfilling prophesy.
5. From hindsight a big bang approach to fiscal policy was required, not a tentative, piecemeal, one step forward and one step back approach. An aggregate demand side problem required an aggregate demand solution- enough to reverse expectations.
6. Japan failed to arrest the decline of asset prices long after they had crashed. The longer asset prices remained depressed the greater would be the destruction in balance sheets of the financial sector. A rise in non-performing loans may appear to be Japan's nemesis, but in fact this suffocating disease is but a reflection of asset price deflation that spreads uncertainty and pessimism throughout the whole economy.
7. The current account deficit for the US in 1999 is an estimated 3.4% of GDP, close to the recent high of 3.6% reached in 1987.
8. A more direct approach to raising asset values was required, rather than the indirect approach of partial assistance to a crippled financial sector. Although self-correcting forces are dependable under 'normal circumstances,' the policy question is how long to wait? Given such horrific balance sheet destruction and the damage done to the real economy, there is a case for government intervention.

Chapter 10

1. To the extent that large volumes of funds search developing countries for high rates of return, and given the destruction of the

'sudden reversal' or exit of such funds, there may be a need for EA governments to filter out the hotter-type of capital flows and rank them as low priority attractions.

2. The problem with this approach is that it seeks to preserve the old "Asian Development Model" of close ties between business and government and so risks of moral hazard. In the light of what has happened in EA, a rekindling of this approach is not likely given the stance of the IMF.

3. For many years the 'apparent success' of the Asian interventionist type model was an embarrassment to Washington that preached the virtues of free trade and openness. This crisis turned the tables.

4. A major reason why EA's economic cruise speed was higher than that of the OECD for many years was the semi-exogeneity of export-led growth that bestowed super-profits on the corporate sector. Inflationary threats were subdued given the abundance of cheap labor.

5. In a sense the cross-real exchange between EA nations should matter in terms of respective export responsiveness. However, given that the US and European markets are relatively large and the low *level* of EA's real exchange rate – all EA nations should witness an export-led recovery. However, the constraint of trade credit has and may restrict the full export response in the short-term.

6. Many Asian leaders distrust the motives of the West in the quest for more openness and the 'suspicious way' in which the crisis broke. The end result was that assets were sold to foreigners at 'fire sale' prices.

7. This figure was quoted by K.S.Jomo (1998), p10.

8. However, isolationism and an inward looking trade bloc may be self-defeating in the long run as 'hard currency' may not accumulate.

9. The key for an East Asian recovery rests in the finance sector and the re-capitalization of this sector. Lending flows will not be restored until such capitalization ratios meet Western standards.

Chapter 11

1   Even the strong link between FDI and exports and the pivotal role played by trade credit there is no doubt that exports will respond once stability is restored.

1. Artificially altering comparative advantage in this model, via exchange rate falls, only complicates the investment decision as productivity driven unit costs are a safer long-un guide to competitiveness than volatile exchange rate changes.

2. The acid test for this claim will be when a tight monetary policy is implemented in the US that involves credit contrcation.

3. According the Asian Development Bank (2000) there are signs that developed economies are converging on a similar business cycle.

BIBLIOGRAPHY

Aghion, P., and Howitt, P., (1992), A Model of Growth Through Creative Destruction, *Econometrica*, 60, 323-351

Alles, L., Chang, R., and Koundiya, R.,(1998), *Debt Financing by Industrial Firms in the Pacific Basin: An Empirical Study*, Institute for Research into International Competitiveness, Discussion Paper Series, 97:07.

Amsden, A., (1990), *Asia's Next Giant*, Oxford University Press, Oxford.

Arndt, H. (1989), *Industrial Policy in East Asia*, National Center for Development Studies, The Australian National University, Canberra.

Arnt, H., W., (1993), *Competitiveness*, Center for Economic Policy Research, No. 290, April.

Arrow, K. J., (1962), The Economic Interpretation of Learning By Doing, *Review of Economic Studies*, 29, 155-73.

Aschauer, D.A., (1989), Is Public Expenditure Productive? *Journal of Monetary Economics*, 23,177-200.

Asian Development Bank (2000), *Asian Economic Outlook 2000*, website.

Athukorala, P., and Reidal, J.,(1991), The Small Country Assumption: A Reassessment with Evidence from Korea, *Developing Economies*.

Azariadis, C., and Drazen, A., (1990), Thresholds in Economic Development, *in Quarterly Journal of Economics*,105, 501-26.

Bahmani-Oskooee M., and Alse, J., (1991), Export Growth and Economic Growth: An Application of Cointegration and Error Correction Modeling, *Journal of Developing Areas*, 27, 535-42.

Baily, M., (1990), *Comments: Competition, Increasing Returns, and the Solow Productivity Residual*, in Growth/ Productivity/Unemployment, MIT Press, Cambridge, Mass.

Baily, M., and Schultz, C., (1990) The Productivity of Capital in a Period of Slower Growth, *Brookings Papers on Economic Activity*, Brookings Institution, Washington.

Balassa, B., (1978), Exports and Economic Growth: Further Evidence, *Journal of Development Economics*, 5, 181-9.

Balassa, B., (1988), The Lessons of East Asian Development: *An Overview*, Economic Development and Cultural Change, 16, 273-91.

Bairoch,P., (1993), Economics and World History, Harvester Wheatsheaf, New York.

Barro, R., (1991), Economic Growth in a Cross Section of Countries, *Quarterly Journal of Economics*, 2, 407- 443.

Barro, R., and Xavier Sala-i-Martin (1990), Convergence, *Journal of Political Economy,*100, 223-25

Barro, R. J., Economic Growth and Convergence, Occasional Papers, Number 46, *International Center for Economic Growth*, San Francisco, 1994.

Barro,R.J., and Lee,J., (1993), International Comparaisons of Educational Attainment,NBER Working Paper No 4349, April.

Baumol, W.J., (1986), Productivity Growth, Convergence and Welfare: What the Long Run Data Show, *American Economic Review*, 76, 1072-85.

Bloch, H., and Kenyon, P.,(1998), The Meaning and Measurement of International Competitiveness. *Mimeograph*, Curtin University of Technology, August.

Boskin, M., and Lau, L., (1990) Post War Economic Growth in the Group of Five Countries: A New Analysis, *NBER, Working Paper No. 3521*, *National Bureau of Economic Research*, Cambridge, Mass.

Brulhart, M., and Thorpe, M., (1999), East Asia Export Growth, Intra-Industry Trade and Adjustment in Ian Kerr, editor, The Asian Pacific Journal of Economic and Business, Curtin University of Technology, Dec., Vol 3, 34-47.

Busche, D., Kravis I., and Lipsey R., (1986), Prices, Activity, and Machinery Exports: An Analysis Based on New Price Data, *Review of Economics and Statistics*, 68, 248-55.

Canterbery, E. R., (1991), An Evolutionary Model of Technical Change with Markup Pricing in William Milburg, editor, *The Megacorp and Macrodynamics*, M.E. Sharpe:Armont, New York, 87-100.

Canterbery, E. R., (1993), Reaganomics, Saving and the Casino Effect, in James Gapinski, *The Economics of Saving*, Kluwer Academic Publishers, Boston, 153-75.

Canterbery, E., R., (1994), A General Theory of International Trade and Domestic Employment Adjustments, in Michael Landeck, editor, *International Trade, Regional and Global Issues*, Macmillan, London, 147-163.

Canterbery, E. R., (1999), Irrational Exuberance and Rational Speculative Bubbles, *Journal of International Trade,* 13, 1-33.

Canterbery, E.R., (2000), *Wall Street Capitalism*, World Scientific Publishing Company, Covent Garden, London.

Cass, D., (1965), Optimum Growth in an Aggregative Model of Capital Accumulation, *Review of Economic Studies*, 32, 233-40.

Chenery, H., (1961), Comparative Advantage and Development Policy, *American Economic Review,* 51,18-51.

Chen, E., (1979), *Hypergrowth in Asian Economies: A Comparative Survey of Hong Kong, Japan, Korea, Singapore and Taiwan*, Macmillan, London.

Chen, B., Hsu, M. and Chen J., (1999), Technology Adoption and Technical Efficiency in Taiwan: Foreign Investment Led versus Export Performance Promoted, in *Economic Efficiency and Productivity Growth in the Asia Pacific Region*, Edward Elgar Publishers, Cheltenham, UK.

Collins, S.M. and Bosworth, B.P., (1996), Economic Growth in East Asia: Accumulation versus Assimilation, *Brookings Papers on Economic Activity*, 2,135-203.

Chow, P.C., (1987), Causality Between Export growth and Industrial
Performance: Empirical Evidence from the NIC's, Journal of Development
Economics,26, 55-63

Chowdrey, K., (1998), The Relationship Between Trade and Growth:
International Evidence, in Satya Paul, editor, *Trade and Growth*, Allen and
Unwin, St. Leonards, NSW.

Clark, G.L., and Kim,W.B., (1995), *Introduction*, in *Asian NIE's and the Global
Economy: Industrial Restructuring and Corporate Strategy in the 1990's*,
eds. G.L. Clark and W.B.Kim, John Hopkins University Press, Baltimore, 3
-21

Corsetti, G., Pesenti, P., and Roubini, N., (1998), *What Caused the Asian
Currency and Financial Crisis*? available at nroubini@stern.nyu.edu.

D'Andrea Tyson, L., (1995) ,Managed Trade: Making the Best of Second Best,
in *International Economics and International Economic Policy*, edited by
Philip King, McGraw-Hill, New York, 129-158.

DeLong, J., and Summers, L., (1991), Equipment Investment and Economic
Growth, *Quarterly Journal of Economics*, 106, 445-502.

De Long, J., and Summers, L., (1992), Equipment Investment and Economic
Growth: How Strong is the Nexus? *Brookings Papers on Economic
Activity*, 2,157-99.

Department of Foreign Affairs and Trade, (1992*), Australia and North East Asia
in the 1990's: Accelerating Change*, Australian Government Printing
Service, Canberra.

Dessus, S., (1999), Total Factor Productivity and Outward Orientation in
Taiwan: What is the Nature of the Relationship?, in *Economic Efficiency
and Productivity Growth in the Asia Pacific Region*, Edward Elgar
Publishers, Cheltenham, UK.

Diamond, D., and Dybvig, P., (1983), Bank Runs, Liquidity, and Deposit
Insurance, *Journal of Political Economy*, 91, 401-419.

Dollar, D., (1991) Outward Countries Really Do Grow More Rapidly: Evidence
from 95 LDC's, 1976 -1985 , *Economic Development and Cultural
Change*, 48, 523 - 543.

Dowling, M., and Summers, P., (1999), TFP Estimates for East Asia, *Australian Economic Review*, Institute of Applied Economic and Social Research, Melbourne.

Dowrick, S., (1990), Why Did The Productivity of Australian Labor Grow Slower in the 1980's? *in Center for Economic Policy Research, Discussion Paper* No. 232, Canberra.

Dowrick, S., and T., Nguyen, (1989) *OECD* Comparative Economic Growth 1950-85: Catch Up and Convergence, *American Economic Review*, 79, 1010-1030.

Dowrick, S., (1992), Technological Catch-up and Diverging Incomes: Patterns of Economic Growth *1960-88*, *Economic Journal*, 102, 600-610.

Dowrick, S., (1993), Estimating the Impact of Government Consumption on Growth: Growth Accounting and Optimizing Models, Conference Paper, *National Bureau of Economic Research.*

Dowrick, S., and Quiggin, J., (1997), True Measures of GDP and Convergence, *American Economic Review*, 87, 41-64.

Drysdale, P., and Huang, Y., (1995), Technological Catch-up and Economic Growth: Medium-Term Trends, *OECD Economic Studies*, 22, 111-29.

Easterly, W. and Rebelo, S. (1993), Fiscal Policy and Economic Growth: An Empirical Investigation, *Paper presented at Conference on How Do National Policies Affect Long-Run Growth?*, World Bank, 8-9 February.

Edwards, S., (1988), *Exchange Rate Misalignment in Developing Countries,* Baltimore, John Hopkins University Press, Baltimore.

Edwards, S., (1992), Trade Orientation, Distortions and Growth in Developing Countries, *Journal of Development Economics*, 39, 31-57.

Esfahani H. S, (1991), Exports, Imports and Economic in Semi - Industrialized Countries, *Journal of Development Economics,* 35 , 93 -116.

Falvey, R., and Kim, C. D., (1992), Timing and Sequencing Issues in Trade Liberalization, *Economic Journal*, 102, 908-924.

Feder,G., (1983), On Exports and Economic Growth, *Journal of Economic Development*, 12, 59-73.

Flood, R., and Garber, P. M., (1984), Collapsing Exchange Rate Regimes: Some Linear Examples, *Journal of International Economics*, 17,1-17.

Forsyth, P., (1990), Competitiveness, Microeconomic Reform and the Current Account Deficit? *Centre for Economic Policy Studies*, Australian National University, No. 228.

Fournier, G. M., and Martin, D.L., (1983), Does Government-Restricted Entry Produce Market?: New Evidence from the Market for Television Advertising Bell, *Journal of Economics*,14.

Friedman, M., (1968), The Role of Monetary Policy, *American Economic Review*, 58,1-17.

Fruest, T.,S., (1992), Lquidity, Loanable Funds, and Real Activity, Journal Of Monetary Economics, 1-26.

Fukushima, K., and Kwan, C., (1995), Foreign Direct Investment and Regional Restructuring in Asia, *Foreign Direct Investment in Asia*, Nomoura Research Institute.

Fujita, N, and James W, (1989), Export Promotion and the Heavy Industrialization of Korea, 1973 – 83, *Developing Economies*, 27, 236-250.

Gapinski, J., (1997a), Economic Growth in the Asian Pacific Region, *Asia Pacific Journal of Economics and Business*, 1, 68-91

Gapinski, J., (1997b), The Growth of Tigers, Elephants, and Other Metaphorical Creatures under Heterogeneous Capital, *Southern Economic Journal*, 64, 147-66.

Gapinski, J., (1998a), A Tiger's Tale of Two Cities, *Asia Pacific Journal of Economics and Business*, 2, 79-94.

Gapinski, J., (1998b), Developing ICOM: An Index of International Competitiveness, *Mimeograph*, Florida State University and Curtin University of Technology.

Galetovic, A., (1996), Specialisation, Intermediation and Growth, Journal of Monetary Economics, 38, 549-559

Gapinski, J., (1999), *Economic Growth in the Asia Pacific Region*, St. Martin's Press, New York.

Garnaut, R., (1990), *Australia and the Northeast Asian Ascendancy*, Australian Government Publishing Service, Canberra.

Gerschenkron, A.,(1962), *Economic Backwardness in Historical Perspective: A Book of Essays*, Harvard University Press, Cambridge, Mass.
Goldsmith, R.,W., (1969), Financial Structure and Development, New Haven, Conn: Yale University Press.

Gonclaves, R., and Richtering, J.,(1987), Intercountry Comparison of Export Performance and Output Growth, *Developing Economies*, 25, 3-18.

Grenville, S.,(1998), The Asian Crisis, *Reserve Bank of Australia Bulletin*, 9-19.

Grossman, G., (1982*)*, Import Competition from Developed and Developing Countries, *Review of Economics and Statistics*, 48, 212-222.

Grossman, G., and Helpman, E., (1991), Trade, Knowledge Spillovers and Growth, in *European Economic Review*, 35, 517-26.

Hall, R., (1988), The Relation Between Price and Marginal Cost in U.S. Industry, *Journal of Political Economy*, 96, 921-45.

Haggard, S., (1990), *Pathways from the Periphery*, Cornell University Press, New York.

Han S., and Weston A., (1993), A North American Free Trade Agreement and East Asian Developing Countries, *ASEAN Economic Bulletin*, 9,

Harberger, A., (1996), Reflections on Economic Growth in Asia and the Pacific, *Journal of Asian Economics*, 7,365-92

Hayakawa, H., and Maeda, E., (2000), Understanding Japan's Financial and Economic Debvelopments Since Autumn 1997, *Working Paper Series, Research and Statistics Department*, Bank of Japan.

Helliwell, J., and Chung, A, (1991), Macroeconomic Convergence: International Transmission of Growth and Technical Progress, *NBER Working Paper No. 3254*, Cambridge, Mass.

Hill H., (1990*)*, Foreign Investment and East Asian Economic Development, *Asia Pacific Economic Literature*, 4, 21-58.

Hooper, P., (1992), *Changes in US Competitiveness: A Relative Study*, Growth, Productivity and Competitiveness, editor E Boldin, McGraw-Hill, Singapore, 255-270.

Hughes, H., (1993), *Is there an East Asian Model?* Research School of Pacific Studies, Australian National University, Working Paper 93/4.

Hughes, H., (1995), Why Have East Asian Countries Led Economic Development? *Economic Record*, 71, 88-104.

Hsiao, C. 1987, Tests of Causality and Exogeneity between Exports and Economic Growth: The Case of the East Asian NIC's, *Journal of Development Economics*, 12, 143-59.

International Labor Office, *International Labor Statistics Yearbook*, various issues, Geneva.

International Monetary Fund, *Direction of Trade Statistics*, various issues, Washingtion.

International Monetary Fund, *International Financial Statistics*, various issues, Washingon.

Jomo, K.S., (1998), Introduction: Financial Governance, Liberalization and Crises in East Asia, *Tigers in Trouble*, Zed Books Ltd, London, 1-23.

Jones, L., and Manuelli, R., (1990), A Convex Model of Equilibrium Growth: Theory and Policy Implications, *Journal of Political Economy*, 98, 1008-38.

Jung, W., and Marshall, P., (1985), Exports, Growth and Causality in Developing Countries, *Journal of Development Economics*, 18, 1-12.

Kim, J., and Lau, L.,(1994), The Sources of Economic Growth of the East Asian Newly Industrialized Countries, *Journal of the Japanese and International Economies*, 8, 235-71.

King R., and Rebelo, S., (1990) Public Policy and Economic Growth: Developing Neoclassical Implications, *Journal of Political Economy*, 98, S127-149.

King, R., and Plosser, C.I., (1984), Money, Credit and Prices in a Real Business Cycle, A.E.R., 363-380

Knox-Lovell, C.A. and Tang, Y.P., An Alternative Tale of Two Cities, in *Economic Efficiency and Productivity Growth in the Asia Pacific Region*, Edward Elgar Publishers, Cheltenham, UK.

Koopmans, T.C. (1965), On the Concept of Optimal Economic Growth, in The *Econometric Approach to Development Planning*, North-Holland, Amsterdam, 229-87.

Kormendi R., and McGuire P.,(1985), Macroeconomic Determinants of Growth - Cross Country Evidence, *Journal of Monetary Economics*, 16,141-64.

Kregel, J.A., (1998), East Asia is not Mexico: The Difference Between Balance of Payments Crises and Debt Deflation, in *Tigers in Trouble*, Hong Kong University Press.

Krueger, A., (1989) Asian Trade and Growth Lessons, *in American Economic Review*, 80, 108-12.

Krueger, A., (1990) Lessons for Development from the Experience of Asia in *American Economic Review*, 80, 108-12.

Krugman, P., (1987), Is Free Trade Passe? *Journal of Economic Perspectives*,1, 131-41.

Krugman, P.,(1991), The Move Toward Free Trade Zones, in *International Economics and International Economic Policy*, edited by Philip King, McGraw- Hill, New York.

Krugman, P., (1994), The Myth of Asia's Miracle, *Foreign Affairs*, 73, 62-78.

Krugman, P., (1999), *Balance Sheet, The Transfer Problem, and Financial Crises*, available at nroubini@stern.nyu.edu.

Kubo, Y., (1989), A Model of Dual Industrial Development in a Semi Industrial Economy, *Developing Economies*, 27, 331-349.

Kydland, F.E., and Prescott, E.C., (1982) Time to Build and Aggregate Fluctuations, *Econometrica*, 50,1345-70.

Levine, R., and Renelt, D., (1992), A Sensitivity Analysis of Cross Country Growth Regressions, *American Economic Review*, 82, 942-63.

Lewis, W.A., (1954), *Economic Development with Unlimited Supplies of Labor* Manchester School of Economics and Social Studies, 22, 139-91.

Liang, C., and Jorgenson,D., Productivity Growth in Taiwan's Manfacturing Industry, 1961-1993, in *Economic Efficiency and Productivity Growth in the Asia Pacific Region*, Edward Elgar Publishers, Cheltenham, UK.

Lau, S., and Sin, C., (1993), Distinguishing Between the Neoclassical and Romers Increasing Returns Growth Models- A Stochastic Integration Test, mimeograph, Australian National University, Canberra, October.

Long, J., and Plosser, C., Real Business Cycles, *Journal of Political Economy*, 91, 39-69.

Lynde, C., and Richmond, J., (1993), Public Capital and Total Factor Productivity, *International Economic Review*, 34, 401-14.

Lucas, R., (1988*)* On the Mechanics of Economic Development, *Journal of Monetary Economics*, 22, 3-42.

Lucas, R., (1989) Why Doesn't Capital Flow from Rich to Poor Countries? *American Economic Review*, 80, 92-98.

Lucas, R., (1993), In Making a Miracle, in *Econometrica*, 61, 251-72.

Madison, A., (1987), Growth and Slowdown in Advanced Capitalist Economies: Techniques of Quantitative Assessment, *Journal of Economic Literature*, 25, 649-98.

Mankiw, N., Romer, and Weil, D., (1992) A Contribution to the Empirics of Economic Growth, *Quarterly Journal of Economics*, 107, 407-37.

Manzur, M., (1996), International Competitiveness: Do We Have a Good Measure? *Discussion Paper Series 96.10*, Institute for Research into International Competitiveness, Curtin University of Technology.

Marquez, J., and Mcneilly C., (1988), The Income and Price Elasticities for Exports of Developing Countries, *Review of Economics and Statistics*, 70, 306-14.

Marquis,M.,(1996), *Monetary Theory and Policy*, West Publishing Company, Minneapolis/St Paul.

Meltzer, A.H., (1995), Monetary, Credit and (Other) Transmission Processes: A Monetarist Perspective, *Journal of Economic Perspectives*, 9, 49-72.

McKinnon, R., (1973), *Money and Capital in Economic Development*, Washington, Brookings Institute.

Michaely, M., (1977), Exports and Growth: An Empirical Evidence, *Journal of Development Economics*, 4, 49-53.

Montes, M.F., (1998), *The Currency Crisis in South East Asia*, Singapore: Institute of South East Asian Studies (ISEAS).

Minsky, H., (1986), *Stabilizing an Unstable Economy*, New Haven: Yale University Press.

Muscatelli, V.A., Srinavasan, T.G., Vines, D., (1992), Demand and Supply Factors in the Determination of the NIE Exports: Simultaneous Error Correction Model for Hong Kong, *Economic Journal*, 1467-1477

Mussa, M., (1993), Making the Practical Case for Free Trade AEA Papers and Proceedings, *American Economic Review*, 83, 372 -76.

Nakagawa, S., and Oshima, K., (2000), Does a Decrease in the Real Interest Rate Actually Stimulate Personal Consumption?, *Working Paper Series, Research and Statistics Department,* Bank of Japan.

Nishimuzu, N., and Robinson, S., (1984), Trade Policies and Productivity Changes in Semi - Industrialized Countries, *Journal of Development Economics*,16, 177-206.

Nurske, R., (1967), *Patterns of Capital Formation in Underdeveloped Countries and Patterns of Trade and Development*, New York, Oxford University Press, New York.

Ohno, K, and Imaoka, H, (1987), The Experience of Dual Industrial Growth: Korea and Taiwan in *Developing Economies* , 25, 311-323.

Oneill, H., and Ross, W., (1991), Exchange Rate and Income Effects on S. Korean Exports: The US Case *Journal of Economic Development*, 22, 87 - 111.

Organization of Economic Development, *OECD Economic Outlook*, various issues, Paris.

Obstfeld, M.,(1994), The Logic of Currency Crises, *Cashiers Economiques et Monetaires* (Bank de France, Paris), 2, 369-450

Parente,S.,and Prescott, E., (1994), Barriers to Technology Adoption and Development, *Journal of Political Economy*, 102, 298-321.

Pack, H., (1994), Endogenous Growth Theory: Intellectual Appeal and Empirical Shortcomings, *Journal of Economic Perspectives*, 8, 55-72.

Pack, H., and Page J. M., (1994), *Accumulation, Exports, and Growth in the High-Performing Asian Economies*, Carnegie-Rochester Conference series on Public Policy, 40, 199-236.

Paul, S., and Chowdhury, K., (1995), Export-Led Growth Hypothesis: Some Empircal Evidence, *Applied Economic Letters*, 22, 177-9.

Park, Y. C., (1989), The Little Dragons and Structural Changes in Pacific Asia, *The World Economy*, 12, 125-61.

Perkins D., (1994), Completing China's Move to the Market, *Journal Economic of Perspectives*, 8, 23-46.

Petri, P., (1995), The Interdependence of Trade and Investment in the Pacific, in *Corporate Links and Foreign Direct Investment in Asia and the Pacific*, edited by Chen, K., and Drysdale, 29-55.

Plosser (1989), Understanding Real Business Cycles, *Journal of Economic Perspectives*, No 3, 51-77.

Porter, M., (1990), *The Competitive Advantage of Nations*, Free Press, New York.

Prebisch, R., (1964), *Towards a New International Policy for Development*, the United Nations, New York.

Posner, M.V., (1961), *International Trade and Technical Change*, Oxford Economic Papers, 323-341.

Pritchett, L.,(1997), Divergence, Big Time, *Journal of Economic Perspectives*, 11, 3-18.

Radelet, S., Sachs, J., and Jong-Wha Lee, (1997), Economic Growth in Asia, HIID Development Discussion Paper No. 609.

Radelet, S., and Sachs, J., (1998) *The Onset of the East Asian Currency Crisis*, HIID website:www.hiid.harvard.edu.

Radelet, S., (1998), "The East Asian Financial Crisis: Diagnosis, Remedies, Prospects,"available at nroubini@stern.nyu.edu.

Rebelo, S., (1991), Long Run Policy Analysis and Long Run Growth, in *Journal of Political Economy*, 99, 500-521.

Reidal, J, (1984), Trade as an Engine of Growth in Developing Countries, Revisited, *Economic Journal*, 78, 34-45.

Reidal, J., (1988) The Demand for LDC Exports of Manufactures: Estimates from Hong Kong, *Economic Journal*, 98, 138-148.

Reidal, J, (1989), Economic Development in East Asia: Doing What Comes Naturally? in *Achieving Industrialization in East Asia*, edited by Hughes, H, Cambridge University Press, New York.

Revenga, A.,(1992), Exporting Jobs? The Impact of Import Competition on Employment and Wages in US Manufacturing, *Quarterly Journal of Economics,* 107, 255 - 84.

Roggoff, (1996), The Purchasing Power Parity Puzzle, *Journal of Economic Literature*, 36, 647-668.

Romer, P., (1990), Endogenous Technological Change, *Journal of Political Economy* 98, S 71 - S 102.

Sachs, J., (1997), Secretive Workings of the IMF Call for a Reassessment, New Straits Times, 23 December.

Salvatore, D., (1993), *International Economics*, MacMillan Publishing Company, New York.

Sarel, M., (1996), Growth in East Asia: What We Can and Cannot Infer from It, *Economic Issues 1*, International Monetary Fund, Washington.

Sergerstrom, P., (1991), Innovation, Imitation, and Economic Growth, *Journal of Political Economy*, 99, 808-27.

Shaw, E., Financial Deepening in Economic Development, New York, Oxford University Press, 1973.

Sheehan, P., (1992), *Economic Theory and Economic Strategy. New Growth Models*, Australian 21st Conference of Economists, July.

Sheehan, P., (1998), The New Growth Models: Recent Theoretical Developments, *Trade and Growth*, editor S.Paul, Allen and Unwin, Sydney.

Singer, H., (1950), The Distribution of Gains Between Investing and Borrowing Countries, *American Economic Review*, 32, 21-39.

Solow, R., (1957), Technical Change and the Aggregate Production Function, *Review of Economic Statistics*, 39, 312-20.

Stiglitz, J., (1999), Beggar-Thyself versus Beggar-Thy-Neighbor Policies: The dangers of Intellectual Incoherence in Addressing the Global Financial Crisis, *Southern Economic Journal*, 66, 2-37

Stern, N, (1991), The Determinants of Growth, *Economic Journal*, 101, 123-33.

Summers,L.,(1990), What is the Social Return to Capital Investment, in *Growth/Productivity/Unemployment*, MIT Press, Cambridge, Mass.

Summers, R., and Heston, A., (1993), Penn World Tables 5.5, available on diskette from NBER, Cambridge, Mass.

Swee, G.K, and Low, L., (1996), Beyond 'Miracles' and Total Factor Productivity: The Singapore Experience, *ASEAN Economic Bulletin*, 13, 113.

Thurow, L., (1992), *Head to Head*, Warner Books, New York.

Thurow, L., (1996), *The Future of Capitalism*, W. Morrow and Co., New York.

Tobin, J., (1978), A Proposal for International Monetary Reform, *Eastern Economic Journal*, 4, 13-25.

Townsend, R. M., (1983), Financial Structure and Economic Activity, *American Economic Review.*, 73, Dec., 895-911

Urata S., (1993), Changing Patterns of Direct Investment and the Implications for Trade and Development. Chapter 8 in Bergstein C and Noland M (eds), *Pacific Dynamism and the International Economic System*, Longman, N.Y.

United Nations Development Report, (1994), *Human Development Report, The Human Development Index Revisited*, Chapter 5, Oxford University Press, London.

Wade, R, (1989), The Role of Government in Overcoming Market Failure: Taiwan, Republic of Korea and Japan in *Achieving Industrialization in East Asia*, edited by Hughes, H., Cambridge University Press, New York.

Warr P.G., (1994), Comparative and Competitive Advantage, *Asia - Pacific Economic Literature,* 8, 46-55.

Western, D.L., (1996), *The East Asian Miracle: A View From the South*, San Casa Publishers, Perth, Australia.

Wolff, E.N., Capital Formation and Productivity Convergence over the Long Term, *American Economic Review,* 81, 565-79.

World Bank, (1991), *World Development Report 1991: The Challenge of Development*, Oxford University Press, London.

World Bank, (1993) ,The East Asian Miracle, *A World Bank Policy Research Report*, Oxford University Press, London.

World Bank, *World Tables*, various issues, Washington.

Yamazawa, I., (1990), *Economic Development and International Trade: The Japanese Model*, Resources Systems Institute, Honolulu, Hawaii.

Young, A., (1995), Tyranny of Numbers: Confronting the Statistical Realities of the East Asian Growth Experience, *Quarterly Journal of Economics*, 110, 641-80.

Wu, Y., (1999), Productivity and Efficiency in China' Regional Economies, in *Economic Efficiency and Productivity Growth in the Asia Pacific Region*, Edward Elgar Publishers, Cheltenham, UK.